Approaches to Teaching
the Works of Louise Erdrich

D1127857

Approaches to Teaching
World Literature

Joseph Gibaldi, series editor

For a complete listing of titles,

see the last pages of this book.

Approaches to Teaching the Works of Louise Erdrich

Edited by

Greg Sarris,
Connie A. Jacobs,
and
James R. Giles

The Modern Language Association of America
New York   2004

© 2004 by The Modern Language Association of America
All rights reserved
Printed in the United States of America

For information about obtaining permission to reprint material from MLA book
publications, send your request by mail (see address below), e-mail
(permissions@mla.org), or fax (646-458-0030).

Library of Congress Cataloging-in-Publication Data

Approaches to teaching the works of Louise Erdrich / edited by Greg Sarris,
Connie A. Jacobs, and James R. Giles.
p. cm.—(Approaches to teaching world literature ; 83)
Includes bibliographical references and index.
ISBN 0-87352-914-6 (alk. paper)—ISBN 0-87352-915-4 (pbk. : alk. paper)
1. Erdrich, Louise—Study and teaching. 2. Women and literature—United
States—Study and teaching. 3. Indians in literature—Study and teaching. I.
Sarris, Greg. II. Jacobs, Connie A., 1944– III. Giles, James Richard, 1937–
IV. Series.
PS3555.R42Z55 2004
813'.54—dc22   2004017319
ISSN 1059-1133

Cover illustration of the paperback edition: *Bear Clan*, a painting by Joe Geshick.
Owned by the artist.

Published by The Modern Language Association of America
26 Broadway, New York, NY 10004-1789
www.mla.org

*To A. LaVonne Ruoff, Kenneth Lincoln, and
Louis Owens, whose early critical work in
Native American literary studies helped shape
the discipline. Your groundwork made
this volume possible.*

CONTENTS

Preface to the Series   xi

Preface to the Volume   1
    Greg Sarris

Introduction   5
    Connie A. Jacobs

PART ONE: MATERIALS *Connie A. Jacobs*

Primary Works
    Novels   11
    Poetry   15
Other Works   16
Recommended Student Readings   17
The Instructor's Library   17
    Books on Erdrich   18
    Critical Studies   18
    Cultural Studies   20
Audiovisual Materials   20

PART TWO: APPROACHES

History and Culture
A History of the Turtle Mountain Band of Chippewa Indians   23
    Connie A. Jacobs
Of Bears and Birds: The Concept of History in Erdrich's
    Autobiographical Writings   32
    David T. McNab
Beneath Creaking Oaks: Spirits and Animals in *Tracks*   42
    Susan Scarberry-García
Sisters, Lovers, Magdalens, and Martyrs: Ojibwe Two-Sisters Stories
    in *Love Medicine*   51
    Karah Stokes
Tracing the Trickster: Nanapush, Ojibwe Oral Tradition, and *Tracks*   58
    G. Thomas Couser
Tracking Fleur: The Ojibwe Roots of Erdrich's Novels   66
    Amelia V. Katanski

Erdrich's Fictional World

Family as Character in Erdrich's Novels   77
  Gay Barton
Does Power Travel in the Bloodlines? A Genealogical Red Herring   83
  Nancy L. Chick
"Patterns and Waves Generation to Generation": *The Antelope Wife*   88
  Alanna Kathleen Brown

Pedagogical Strategies

An Indigenous Approach to Teaching Erdrich's Works   95
  Gwen Griffin and P. Jane Hafen
Sites of Unification: Teaching Erdrich's Poetry   102
  Dean Rader
"And Here Is Where Events Loop Around and Tangle": Tribal
  Perspectives in *Love Medicine*   114
  Paul Lumsden
Tracking the Memories of the Heart: Teaching *Tales of Burning Love*   118
  Debra K. S. Barker
Academic Conversation: Computers, Libraries, the Classroom, and
  The Bingo Palace   130
  Sharon Hoover
Gender and Christianity: Strategic Questions for Teaching *The Last
  Report on the Miracles at Little No Horse*   140
  Peter G. Beidler

Critical and Theoretical Perspectives

Collaboration in the Works of Erdrich and Michael Dorris:
  A Study in the Process of Writing   147
  Tom Matchie
Doubling the Last Survivor: *Tracks* and American Narratives of Lost
  Wilderness   158
  John McWilliams
Identity Indexes in *Love Medicine* and "Jacklight"   170
  James Ruppert
Reading *The Beet Queen* from a Feminist Perspective   175
  Vanessa Holford Diana
Gender as a Drag in *The Beet Queen*   183
  Kari J. Winter
A Postcolonial Reading of *Tracks*   191
  Dee Horne
"This Ain't Real Estate": A Bakhtinian Approach to
  The Bingo Palace   201
  Patrick E. Houlihan

Appendixes
   A. Genealogical Charts   211
      Nancy L. Chick
   B. Maps   223
      Connie A. Jacobs
   C. Important Dates in the History of the Turtle Mountain Band of
      Chippewa Indians   227
      Connie A. Jacobs
   D. Study Guides to Eight Erdrich Novels   230
      Peter G. Beidler

Notes on Contributors   239

Survey Participants   243

Works Cited   245

Index   259

PREFACE TO THE SERIES

In *The Art of Teaching*, Gilbert Highet wrote, "Bad teaching wastes a great deal of effort, and spoils many lives which might have been full of energy and happiness." All too many teachers have failed in their work, Highet argued, simply "because they have not thought about it." We hope that the Approaches to Teaching World Literature series, sponsored by the Modern Language Association's Publications Committee, will not only improve the craft—as well as the art—of teaching but also encourage serious and continuing discussion of the aims and methods of teaching literature.

The principal objective of the series is to collect within each volume different points of view on teaching a specific literary work, a literary tradition, or a writer widely taught at the undergraduate level. The preparation of each volume begins with a wide-ranging survey of instructors, thus enabling us to include in the volume the philosophies and approaches, thoughts and methods of scores of experienced teachers. The result is a sourcebook of material, information, and ideas on teaching the subject of the volume to undergraduates.

The series is intended to serve nonspecialists as well as specialists, inexperienced as well as experienced teachers, graduate students who wish to learn effective ways of teaching as well as senior professors who wish to compare their own approaches with the approaches of colleagues in other schools. Of course, no volume in the series can ever substitute for erudition, intelligence, creativity, and sensitivity in teaching. We hope merely that each book will point readers in useful directions; at most each will offer only a first step in the long journey to successful teaching.

Joseph Gibaldi
Series Editor

PREFACE TO THE VOLUME

My Auntie Anita. Big. Broad. We don't say fat: we say powerful. "Let me explain things in plain English," she says, then chuckles. "But English ain't my first language."

She wears stretch pants, the customary sateen blouse, full-bodied of course and usually a deep purple, maybe an apple green. She pushes back her close-cropped gray hair with one hand; with the other she points to the chair opposite her, where she wants you to sit at the kitchen table.

You sit. What else can you do? She's forthright. She's powerful.

"You don't know what that is, do you?" she asks, pointing now to the Tupperware bowl of oatmeal-colored acorn mush.

She talks about the mush, its importance to the Coast Miwok and Pomo Indians. If there will be a ceremony—if we are to sing or dance—she'll talk about that too. With the ease and skill of an experienced docent, she introduces you to the culture and the community you find yourself in. After some talk about the food and the ceremonies, she'll tell you who's related to whom. It's her way of saying, Welcome. It's her way of saying, Be comfortable. If you spend the night, stay a few days, you'll learn more. Family stuff. For example, why the ninety-five-year-old woman sitting next to you with the bandana tied tightly over her head won't take off her sunglasses, why she won't acknowledge the teenager with the shaved head standing in the doorway. She's not blind, not that.

Louise Erdrich burst onto the literary scene in 1984 with *Jacklight*, a highly praised collection of poetry, and a novel, *Love Medicine*, for which she won the National Book Critics Circle Award. In these works and in successive collections of poetry and fiction, she situates the reader in the center of "family stuff" without an introduction, no auntie to introduce the reader to the world of her interrelated Ojibwe families on and around an imaginary North Dakota reservation. Instead, the reader experiences long and entangled personal histories acted out, for better or worse, as if the reader were suddenly in the middle of the action. In the kitchen, pies get smashed in a family brawl. A Vietnam vet drowns himself in a rain-swollen river. An orphan finally bonds with his father on a drive to the Canadian border. Back in the kitchen, a woman forgives her husband's infidelity. In fact, it is this immediacy as well as the notable absence of one central protagonist or overriding point of view in any of Erdrich's works that distinguishes her from her two prominent predecessors, N. Scott Momaday and Leslie Marmon Silko, in what Kenneth Lincoln has called this body of literature the Native American Renaissance. Both Momaday and Silko utilized a central character, specifically a male on a journey, who guided the reader through the character's world, albeit not always easily. Still, the reader had a unifying point of view and, ultimately, a conclusion regarding events and characters in those worlds. Erdrich's central character, or protagonist, if we can call it that, is the community, where, again, none of the conflicting narrative voices and associated points of view is privileged one over the other. Some critics call this a tribal point of view. Regardless of what we might want to call it (Faulkner most certainly could be accused of the same practice), the fact remains that the readers of Louise Erdrich might find themselves in the middle of a family argument or caught between two versions of the same story and feel lost or at least wanting to know more. Who is related to whom? What might such relationships mean? And not just about the complex interrelationships of the characters but also about the Ojibwe culture and history, which is often alluded to and always the backdrop for characters' action. It would be as if you only heard the old woman at my auntie's table croak, "Son of a bitch," and then listened as the young man with the shaved head explained why he sold the basket she'd made for him. Yes, you'd get a sense of interpersonal conflict, even a sense of tribal culture and history. But with Auntie's introduction, you get a broader picture of the world these two persons share, a broader context for understanding the issues, a larger view for their story.

That's what the essays in this book can do: provide a bigger picture, a powerful aunt's introduction to Erdrich's magnificent fictional world. They can help teachers and students understand not just the rich and multiple cultures and histories that intersect in Erdrich's fictional world but also Erdrich as a writer, influenced herself by multiple traditions, both cultural and literary.

No one essay should be read as definitive, the last word on a given text, a framing device for any of the novels or poetry. Just as Erdrich's characters argue with and contradict one another, so do some of the essayists. While some writers, discussing Erdrich's third novel, *Tracks*, link her use of the bear to the Ojibwe clan totem, John McWilliams sees Erdrich using the bear as a way of also rewriting Faulkner's famous bear in "Go Down, Moses." Nancy L. Chick downplays the importance of blood ties regarding Erdrich's characters and their relationships with one another, stating that "a genealogical chart becomes irrelevant and even misleading. . . . It is finally a narrative chart of who passes on stories to whom that is far more significant."

So while the essayists provide an introduction to the world of Erdrich's fiction and poetry, the introduction is itself composed of a community of often conflicting voices and associated points of view. G. Thomas Couser, speaking of *Tracks*, warns against the "danger of glossing the novel's Ojibwe features too readily or easily. Students should be encouraged to look *at* as well as *through* the cultural codes required to understand the plot." Erdrich's readers should look at the various cultural influences that compose her writings and her art and then look further in as many directions as possible. Together, the essayists create a dialogue that helps open the writings of Louise Erdrich in meaningful ways, but it is a dialogue that, extended to teachers and students, should ultimately be joined by them.

My Auntie Anita's description of our Coast Miwok and Pomo culture is subjective: obviously, she is one reader of the ongoing tradition. If the old woman with the sunglasses would talk, she might vary the information, as would the young man with the shaved head. Different stories. Different people.

And if you ask me, I could tell you about Auntie Anita. A few things, anyway. "I only know so much," she often says, and I don't know exactly how to take her. She sets me thinking. How far do you go with a woman who is going to explain the world to you in plain English, after she laughs and says, "But English ain't my first language"?

Greg Sarris

INTRODUCTION

The novels and poetry of Louise Erdrich are now routinely taught in a variety of college classrooms nationally and internationally, reflecting a larger phenomenon borne out of the activism of people of color in the 1960s and the emergence of their voices into the academy. Educated Native writers were among those minority writers whose work challenged the existing literary canon. N. Scott Momaday's 1968 Pulitzer Prize–winning *House Made of Dawn* set the stage for what is now referred to as the Native American Renaissance, and novels and poetry by James Welch, Leslie Marmon Silko, Gerald Vizenor soon followed in the 1970s. After Erdrich published *Love Medicine*, in 1984, and won the National Book Critics Circle Award, she quickly became one of the most popular Native writers. Her work began to appear regularly in a variety of anthologies: freshman composition, creative writing, ethnic literatures, Native American literature, poetry collections, short story collections, and women's literature. Erdrich's works have entered the academy; teaching them, however, presents special challenges, especially to non-Native students who lack knowledge of Native culture and traditions in general and Ojibwe history specifically. Add to this Erdrich's interlocking novels with huge casts of characters from generations of families and her incorporation of traditional cultural elements and figures, and teachers often find themselves in unfamiliar and uncomfortable territory. As is done with all volumes in the Approaches series, the editors sent a survey to teachers who have been using Erdrich in a variety of classrooms and asked them for information: what works they most regularly teach, what background references they recommend, and what materials they use most in teaching Erdrich. The survey, along with discussions with colleagues, became the basis for this book.

The first part, "Materials," provides readings that can help acquaint teachers with Native traditions, history, customs, and culture and establish a context for teaching Erdrich. These readings, as well as critical materials on Erdrich's novels and poetry and cultural materials on the Ojibwe, are discussed in the section "The Instructor's Library." Allan Chavkin and Nancy Chavkin assembled a series of interviews given by Erdrich and her former husband, Michael Dorris, in the 1980s, and, along with some audiovisuals, they provide teachers and students with Erdrich's comments and discussions of her work. For teachers who have not read all the novels, we offer an overview of each work and explain how the works fit together into one continuous story of Erdrich's Ojibwe and German ancestors.

Part 2 of the book, "Approaches," is made up of essays that address the areas in which teachers requested help. Contributors provide background information and pedagogical and critical approaches to Erdrich's novels and poetry. Knowing the world from which Erdrich writes is fundamental to understanding her work, and the first section, "History and Culture," contains information on Erdrich's tribe, the Turtle Mountain Chippewa of North Dakota, and its distinctive cultural elements. Connie A. Jacobs provides an overview of tribal history for the past 150 years. David T. McNab looks at how Erdrich's clans foreground her autobiographical works. A fascinating but often confusing aspect of Erdrich's writing is the way in which she incorporates traditional Ojibwe animals, stories, and figures, especially the trickster Nanabozho. Essays by McNab, Susan Scarberry-García, Karah Stokes, G. Thomas Couser, and Amelia V. Katanski help teachers identify the abundance of cultural references in Erdrich's works.

The next section, "Erdrich's Fictional World," is designed to help students and teachers alike sort through Erdrich's large cast of characters, with their complicated family ties and personal and clan relationships. Although *Love Medicine* is the first book she published, chronologically *Tracks* anchors the novels. Here Erdrich introduces readers to the main families who appear throughout the North Dakota novels: Pillagers, Nanapushes, Kashpaws, Morrisseys, Lamartines, Lazarres, and Puyats. Stories of the major characters Fleur Pillager, Nanapush, Nector and Eli Kashpaw, Lulu Lamartine, June Morrissey, and Pauline Puyat are in *Tracks, The Beet Queen, Love Medicine, The Bingo Palace*, and *The Last Report on the Miracles at Little No Horse*; and essays by Gay Barton and Nancy L. Chick provide a valuable roadmap through Erdrich's often bewildering array of characters. Her sixth novel, *The Antelope Wife*, takes place in Minnesota and introduces readers to three other major families and their descendants: Shawanos, Roys, and Whiteheart Beads. Alanna Kathleen Brown's essay serves as a guide through this fictional world as it describes how patterns and stories continue down through the generations.

The third section, "Pedagogical Strategies," presents specific teaching strategies. Gwen Griffin and P. Jane Hafen suggest how non-Native teachers can present Erdrich's work in a way that reflects a Native perspective, and Paul Lumsden, Debra K. S. Barker, and Peter G. Beidler offer their experiences and suggestions for teaching three of the novels: *Love Medicine, Tales of Burning Love*, and *The Last Report on the Miracles at Little No Horse*. Erdrich's poetry, while often anthologized, is frequently so difficult that students find it inaccessible. Dean Rader shares his love of teaching her poetry and provides analysis, cultural references, and teaching strategies for the best-known poems. Sharon Hoover provides teachers with a computer-based approach to *The Bingo Palace* that replicates the communal voice of the novel and practices the Native approach to Erdrich's work advocated by Griffin and Hafen.

The final section, "Critical and Theoretical Perspectives," provides information from readers who have read widely about Erdrich's world, studied its culture and history, and can situate her novels and poetry within larger critical and theoretical frameworks. The essays are designed to help teachers deepen a discussion of Erdrich's work through application of contemporary critical theory. John McWilliams contextualizes *Tracks* within the American literary tradition of the lost wilderness, while James Ruppert analyzes the dual identities of Erdrich's characters, who are members of a tribal nation as well as citizens of the United States. Ruppert argues that the very nature of this dual identity forces Erdrich's readers to examine closely the differing worldviews and values her Native characters hold. Tom Matchie takes a close look at the unique collaborative writing relationship Erdrich and Dorris shared on their first four novels. This collaboration raises interesting and provocative questions about the roles of gender and sexuality in the novels, and Kari J. Winter and Vanessa Holford Diana look at *The Beet Queen* from differing feminist perspectives. Contemporary American Indian writers live and write in a postcolonial world, and Dee Horne analyzes *Tracks* through the lens of postcolonial theory. Finally, since Erdrich draws on traditional materials in her writing, one of the distinctive narrative features of her novels is the communal voice. Mikhail Bakhtin calls this a "polyphony," a perspective Patrick E. Houlihan applies to a reading of *The Bingo Palace*.

We have provided several appendixes with materials for quick references: genealogical charts showing family relationships in Erdrich's novels, maps, important dates in the history of the Turtle Mountain Chippewa, and study guides to eight of Erdrich's novels. The volume closes with notes on contributors, a list of survey participants, a works-cited list, and an index of names.

A point of clarification is needed on the various names for Erdrich's tribal people. In traditional materials and early anthropological reports, the following names are the ones most commonly found to refer to the tribe: Ojibwa, Ojibway, Ojibwe, and Chippewa. The anthropologists named the people the Chippewa, which is the name used on the treaties with the United States government. According to the tribal member Glenn Welker, Ojibway with its various spellings is a term in popular use among the people (2). Anishinaabeg (singular is Anishinaabe) is the word the people use to refer to themselves. Gerald Vizenor in *The People Named the Chippewa* explains that the term Anishinaabeg is a phonetic transcription from the oral tradition (13). Amelia V. Katanski in her article discusses the birch bark scrolls the singers used in the Midéwiwin ceremony, and Ojibwe refers to those who make the scrolls. In this book, we use the term Ojibwe everywhere, except for quoted matter, which uses various spellings.

We are grateful for all the help we have received from survey participants, contributors, MLA editors, readers, and colleagues who have been supportive of this project. We hope the essays in this volume will help teachers and students deepen their appreciation of Erdrich's novels and poetry and enrich their understanding of the fictional world Erdrich creates, the characters who inhabit that world, her poetic language, her use of traditional materials, and the theme of the power of love that inspires all of her work.

Connie A. Jacobs

Part One

MATERIALS

Primary Works

Novels

Erdrich scholars refer to her North Dakota novels—*Love Medicine, Tracks, The Bingo Palace, The Last Report on the Miracles at Little No Horse*, and *Four Souls*—as the reservation or the Matchimanito novels. Together they relate one long story of her people from the late nineteenth century to contemporary times. The novels were not written chronologically, and to read them in chronological order as opposed to the creative order engenders a very different experience for readers. Reading the novels in chronological order is like looking at a family album; readers follow tribal and governmental policies and their consequences through time and celebrate births, marriages, and deaths of members of a large tribal family. To read the novels in the order in which Erdrich wrote them is to participate in the creative process of an author as she continues to expand and enlarge her story that no one novel could contain.

Erdrich's first novel, *Love Medicine* (1984), was a national bestseller that garnered several prestigious awards: the National Book Critics Circle Award, the Sue Kaufman Prize, and the Virginia McCormick Scull Award. In 1985, Erdrich received the American Book Award from the Before Columbus Foundation. The stories in *Love Medicine* are told by six narrators—Albertine Johnson, Marie Lazarre Kashpaw, Nector Kashpaw, Lyman Morrissey, Lipsha Morrissey, and Lulu Nanapush Morrissey Lamartine—who relate family, tribal, and personal events from 1934 to the present. In a nonlinear narrative style, Erdrich tells stories of reservation families: the Kashpaws, hereditary tribal leaders; the Lamartines, a mixed-blood family; the Lazarres, a mixed-blood family who have become the scourge of the reservation; and the Morrisseys, a once-prosperous Métis (mixed-blood) family who, all but Bernadette, lose their land, their prosperity, and their pride. A popular novel, *Love Medicine* is the one teachers most frequently use in their classrooms. Stories from *Love Medicine* like "Saint Marie," "Lulu's Boys," "Scales," and "The Red Convertible" regularly appear in anthologies of women's literature, American literature, and Native American literature. In 1993, Erdrich revised *Love Medicine* and added four more chapters. By this time, she had published two other novels in the series, and the added chapters explain and adjust the stories.

The Beet Queen (1986) takes place in Argus, a fictional small rural community near a reservation. The novel recounts the lives of immigrant families—the Adares, Jameses, Kozkas, and Pfefs—who settled the area and the physical and emotional toll the land extracts from its inhabitants. Erdrich's focus on the German immigrants caused Leslie Marmon Silko to acerbically denounce the book in her review "Here's an Odd Artifact for the Fairy-Tale

Shelf" for not being an Indian novel. Nevertheless, *The Beet Queen* is important as a novel about Erdrich herself. Given Erdrich's Ojibwe, Métis, and German ancestry, this novel is significant in her series for the way in which the land figures prominently as a character, the reservation and town people connect and are connected to each other, and Argus becomes a place where mixed-bloods settle and uneasily live between two worlds. Instructors do not often teach this work, more frequently choosing to teach one of the reservation novels.

Tracks (1988) chronologically anchors the reservation novels and lays the foundation for the events that unfold in the following novels. The alternating narrators—Nanapush, a combination of a traditional grandfather and the Ojibwe trickster figure, Nanabozho, and Pauline Puyat, a delusional, fanatical, aspiring Christian martyr-saint—describe events involving individuals and the tribe from 1912 to 1924. *Tracks* is very popular among students and teachers alike because of the two contrasting narrators, the use of traditional storytelling, the amount of tribal history recounted, and the character Fleur Pillager, the powerful medicine woman.

The Bingo Palace (1994) is the story of Lipsha Morrissey's journey to know himself and to come into his rightful powers as, with some help from the dead and encouragement from community and family members, he slowly transforms himself from comic fool to heir to the powerful Pillager medicine. His story is juxtaposed to the story of the tribal faction headed by Lyman Lamartine, who schemes to erect a bingo palace on sacred Pillager land. The novel is amusing because of the character of Lipsha, who is both humorous and likable, while at the same time serious as Erdrich addresses the complicated and controversial issue of Indian gaming. Teachers report that they are more likely to teach *Tracks* or *Love Medicine* than *The Bingo Palace*.

Tales of Burning Love (1996) is a less successful novel artistically. The reservation is far in the background, as it is in *The Beet Queen* and *The Master Butchers Singing Club*, and the major characters are mixed-blood and Anglos living in Argus and Fargo. The main character is Jack Mauser, who is raised by his paternal German relatives and who has little contact with his maternal Ojibwe family. Jack's life through his five marriages connects to several characters from previous novels: Lyman Lamartine, Dot Adare, and Pauline Puyat, now Sister Leopolda, who is over one hundred years old. The themes of love and storytelling, which anchor all the novels, are important forces in this one, as Debra K. S. Barker discusses in her essay in this volume. *Tales of Burning Love* allows Erdrich's readers to hear familiar stories told from different viewpoints and to follow the lives of characters who are well known to them. This novel is most often used in women's literature courses.

The Antelope Wife (1998) is notable in several respects. It is the story of urban Ojibwe: the Roys, Shawanos, and Whiteheart Beads, who live and work in Minneapolis. They have formed their own urban community and regard the traditional reservation as the place to which one retreats in times of desperation or sorrow. These first-, second-, and third-generation urban Indians navigate with varying degrees of success within the large, predominantly Anglo city. Although there are no major characters who carry over from the North Dakota novels and there is a different home reservation,[1] the themes are familiar: the importance of community; the presence of the mythic still extant in the lives of contemporary urban Natives; tricksters; the importance of storytelling; the power of love, which propels otherwise reasonable people into unreasonable actions; the power of the old stories and traditions to affect the contemporary urban Indian; and the unfolding of the lives of three families whose shared histories, blood, and stories bind the community.

In 2001, *The Last Report on the Miracles at Little No Horse*, a companion novel to *Tracks*, came out. The story begins in 1910 with Agnes DeWitt assuming the identity of Father Damien Modeste. "He" serves the Ojibwe people for over eighty years on the now-named Little No Horse reservation and is befriended by Nanapush, who knows Damien's true sexual identity. In this novel, familiar characters abound: Fleur, Sister Leopolda, Marie, Nector, Lulu, Margaret, and Father Jude Miller. Father Damien's letters to Rome for nearly a century frame the story, as does Father Jude's determination to promote Sister Leopolda to sainthood.

There are many surprises in this novel as readers learn key pieces of information about major characters from other novels in the series: Nanapush's parents, his death, and his relationship to Kashpaw; the identity of the Anglo-looking boy Fleur brings back to the reservation in *The Bingo Palace*; and the identities of the original Kashpaw's four wives and of Jack Mauser's mother. Sister Leopolda is finally exposed as a malicious fanatic, Marie Kashpaw learns the identity of her biological mother, and a mysterious black dog makes a Faustian pact with Father Damien. Readers of Erdrich's reservation novels will welcome the additional stories about familiar characters, but the novel would be difficult to teach as a stand-alone work, as Peter G. Beidler discusses in his essay on *The Last Report*, in this volume.

Dedicating *The Master Butchers Singing Club* (2003) to her father, Erdrich returns to the townspeople of Argus and to her German ancestors. The cover of the book features Erdrich's paternal grandfather, Ludwig Erdrich, at age seventeen wearing a butcher's apron. From this picture and stories of her paternal grandparents, Erdrich creates a fictionalized story of Fidelis Waldvogel, a German sniper in World War I, who comes to America, establishes a butcher shop in Argus, starts a singing club, and with his wife, Eva, raises their four boys. His butcher shop is rival to Pete Kozka's shop from *The Beet Queen*, but Kozka is one of the few characters Erdrich integrates from previous North Dakota novels. There is Cyprian Lazarre, but his connection to the reservation Lazarres is unknown.

What is familiar are the odd topics from *The Beet Queen* that Erdrich details in *The Master Butchers Singing Club*: circus life, embalming, and butchering. Other familiar themes also appear: flying, World War II German prisoners in Minnesota prison camps, and the interspersing of non-English words and phrases throughout the novel. However, these words and phrases are German, not Ojibwe as in previous novels.

New to this story is a singing club Fidelis begins in order to replace his group of singing butchers back in Germany. The club (whose only butchers are Fidelis and Pete Kozka) brings together an assortment of the men townfolk: sheriff, bank loan officer, bank clerk, doctor, bootlegger, and town drunk.

Resembling the linear narration of *The Beet Queen*, this novel begins with the end of World War I and continues into the 1950s, with a brief flashback to the 1890 massacre at Wounded Knee. While the Métis characters Cyprian Lazarre and Step-and-a-Half play important supporting roles, the story revolves not so much around Fidelis as around Delphine Watzka, a poor Polish girl with a lovable but alcoholic father and an unknown mother. It is Delphine's story that drives the narration and pulls all other stories into her own. *The Master Butchers Singing Club* is a stand-alone novel, although reading it alongside *The Beet Queen* expands and enlarges the story of German immigrants, like the Erdrichs, coming to North Dakota and forging a life alongside the Ojibwe and Métis from the nearby reservation.

Four Souls (2004), the second companion book to *Tracks*, begins where *Tracks* ends. Fleur follows the trees logged off her land into Minneapolis, where an architect intends to use them in building John James Mauser's mansion. Vowing revenge for the cutting of her trees, Fleur carries out her plan by working in the Mauser household as a laundress; healing Mauser, who suffers from either nerve gas damage received in the war or venereal disease; and then marrying him. They have a child, John James Mauser, Jr. He turns out to be the strange white boy with the Pillager hands in *The Bingo Palace* who is with Fleur when she returns to the reservation. This boy becomes the father of Jack Mauser from *Tales of Burning Love*. *Four Souls* is the story of Fleur in Minneapolis, her marriage, her child, and the cost of her revenge. It takes a healing ceremony by Margaret to restore Fleur back into right relationship with her spirit helpers and to purify her from the ravages of alcohol and her vengeance. In this novel, readers will find a picture of Fleur that is different from the powerful Pillager medicine woman in the other reservation novels. This Fleur is more vulnerable, more careless, and more human. While *Four Souls* is primarily her story, Nanapush is also an important character. Readers see his foolish trickster characteristics more than in other reservation novels and gain additional insights into his relationship with Margaret.

The story is told by alternating narrators, following the pattern in *Tracks*. Nanapush continues to relate Fleur's story to her daughter, Lulu, in hopes of softening Lulu's heart toward her mother. The second main narrator has characteristics of Pauline Puyat, the other *Tracks*'s narrator. Polly Elizabeth Gheen is a romantic, arrogant, self-righteous young woman who tells the stories of what happens in the Mauser mansion. She runs the household, both when Mauser was married to her "artistic" and very rich sister, Placide, and when Mauser annuls that marriage and weds Fleur. Once Polly Elizabeth finds a husband and disappears from the story, Margaret and Nanapush end the novel with alternating stories of Fleur's healing.

Tracks, Four Souls, and *The Last Report on the Miracles at Little No Horse* belong together. The latter two novels enlarge and enrich the story Erdrich begins in *Tracks* and exemplify what readers have come to expect with Erdrich's novels: there are stories within stories, there is no one "correct" version of a story, and storytelling is how we learn about one another and about ourselves.

Poetry

Erdrich began her writing career as a poet and has written three books of poetry: *Jacklight* (1984), *Baptism of Desire* (1989), and *Original Fire: Selected and New Poems* (2003). *Jacklight* has been a critical success, and selections from this volume often appear in anthologies of women's literature, American literature, poetry, and Native American literature. The most frequently anthologized pieces include stories about Potchikoo, a traditional Ojibwe trickster figure, and the poems "Jacklight," "A Love Medicine," "Family Reunion," "Indian Boarding School: The Runaways," "Walking in the Breakdown Lane," "Captivity," "The Butcher's Wife," the Mary Kroger poems in "The Butcher's Wife" section, and the well-known "Dear John Wayne."

Teachers and students often find the poetry in *Baptism of Desire* difficult to understand because of the references to Catholic rituals and the emphasis on redemption, prayer, and personal revelations. However, the Potchikoo stories in this volume as well as in *Jacklight* remain popular. *Original Fire* includes well-known poems from Erdrich's two other poetry books as well as new works. The Potchikoo stories from both the earlier volumes are included together, while most of the new poems are found in section 5, "Original Fire." The new poems are linked by the themes of endurance, strength, and healing, as beautifully expressed in "Grief":

> Sometimes you have to take your own hand
> as though you were the lost child
> and bring yourself stumbling
> home over twisted ice.

Erdrich's lyrical language, rich imagery, and use of traditional Ojibwe culture are hallmarks of both her poetry and her prose. Therefore teachers often use her poetry to introduce students to Erdrich's themes and style. Dean Rader's essay in this volume serves as a helpful guide through Erdrich's poetry.

Other Works

Erdrich's collaboration with her husband, Michael Dorris, is a complex topic (see Tom Matchie's essay in this volume). In interviews, Erdrich and Dorris claimed to function as each other's editors as well as collaborators, helpmates, and coauthors. However, only two pieces carry both authors' names. In 1991, HarperCollins published Erdrich and Dorris's book *The Crown of Columbus*, the story of Professors Vivian Twostar and Roger Williams, whose search for a lost diary of Christopher Columbus reads like a script for a grade-B movie. The publishers advanced the couple $1.5 million and heavily promoted the work, which was published during the Columbus quincentenary. The book was not a commercial or literary success. Less well known is *Route 2*, also published in 1991, a short account of a 1985 family trip across the United States, visiting reservation relatives and sightseeing.

To date, Erdrich has only two works of nonfiction. *The Blue Jay's Dance: A Birth Year* (1995) is a record of one year in the author's life. While the autobiographical essays, recipes, and reflections on mothering and motherhood provide an engaging glimpse into Erdrich's world, teachers report they rarely use this book in their classrooms.

Books and Islands in Ojibwe Country, published by the National Geographic Society in 2003, belongs to the travel writing genre. It describes both the author's physical journey back to the islands in Lake of the Woods that were inhabited by the traditional Ojibwe and a spiritual journey that connects Erdrich to her ancestors. The term *books* in the title refers to the actual volumes she carries on her journey, the painted rocks and islands that tell the story of the people who have lived there, and the visit she makes to the special collection of rare books housed in the Ernest Oberholzer residence on one of the islands. This book, along with *The Birchbark House*, reflects Erdrich's growing interest in tracing her Ojibwe heritage.

Erdrich's first children's book, *Grandmother's Pigeon* (1996), tells the story of a magical grandmother and her passenger pigeons. In 1999, Erdrich's story for young adults, *The Birchbark House*, came out. The story of Omakayas, Little Frog, provides readers with a wealth of information on the lives of traditional Ojibwe and is highly recommended for teachers wishing to better contextualize Erdrich's novels within her tribal history.

Erdrich's third children's book, *The Range Eternal* (2002), is for younger readers. It tells the story of an old stove whose fire keeps the cold and the winter monster, windigo, at bay on blistery chilly days; provides the heat to cook the family's food; and is the heart of the home. In an afterword Erdrich explains that her mother told her the story of this stove, from her childhood on the Turtle Mountain Reservation in North Dakota. Erdrich's book is a tribute to this Range Eternal, which filled the home of her grandparents with warmth and good memories.

Recommended Student Readings

Most teachers responding to our survey indicate that their students are predominantly Anglo from diverse socioeconomic backgrounds with little knowledge of Native people beyond Hollywood images. Therefore teachers find it necessary to put on reserve traditional myths, tales, and stories as well as readings in Native American critical perspectives and language. These readings help provide a context from which students can better appreciate Erdrich's work.

Students from minority groups often feel an affinity with Erdrich's work, and although the background materials enrich their reading, they are not as critical to ground the students. Native students tend to respond enthusiastically to Erdrich and are delighted to find her work in English courses.

Readings recommended particularly for students are Paula Gunn Allen's *The Sacred Hoop: Recovering the Feminine in American Indian Traditions*; Nora Barry and Mary Prescott's "The Triumph of the Brave: *Love Medicine's* Holistic Vision"; William Bevis's "Native American Novels: Homing In"; Dee Brown's *Bury My Heart at Wounded Knee*; Louise Flavin's "Louise Erdrich's *Love Medicine*: Loving over Time and Distance"; P. Jane Hafen's "Sacramental Language: Ritual in the Poetry of Louise Erdrich"; N. Scott Momaday's "Man Made of Words"; Louis Owens's *Other Destinies: Understanding the American Indian Novel*; Nancy Peterson's "History, Postmodernism, and Louise Erdrich's *Tracks*"; Paul Radin's *The Trickster: A Study in American Indian Mythology*; Catherine Rainwater's "Reading between Worlds: Narrativity in the Fiction of Louise Erdrich"; and Leslie Marmon Silko's "Language and Literature from a Pueblo Perspective."

The Instructor's Library

We asked respondents, many of whom are Erdrich scholars, to recommend reference and background works on Erdrich, Ojibwe life, and Native American literature and culture to aid teachers with minimal background in Native

American studies. The following lists reflect their recommendations as well as suggestions from colleagues and the editors. Many of these critical and cultural essays would be equally useful for students.

Books on Erdrich

It wasn't until the end of the twentieth century that book-length studies on Erdrich started to appear, a most fortuitous development for teachers new to Erdrich. There is a book on Erdrich's novels, a reader's guide, a collection of essays, a casebook, as well as a collection of the many interviews Dorris and Erdrich gave during the 1980s. To date, Connie A. Jacobs's *The Novels of Louise Erdrich: Stories of Her People* is the only book focusing on Erdrich's fictional world. This study positions Erdrich as a tribal storyteller in contemporary times by contextualizing her work within the history and culture of her Turtle Mountain Band of Chippewa Indians. Peter G. Beidler and Gay Barton's *A Reader's Guide to the Novels of Louise Erdrich* is a welcomed map through Erdrich's complicated fictional world. Erdrich herself reportedly finds the book useful to help her keep track of her cast of characters. This book provides a geographical, genealogical, and chronological guide to the novels as well as a dictionary of characters. Two collections of essays are also useful. Allan Chavkin's *The Chippewa Landscape of Louise Erdrich* brings together some of the best essays to date in the field. The afterword by A. LaVonne Ruoff and selected bibliography make this a valuable reference work. Teachers using *Love Medicine* in their class should refer to Hertha D. Sweet Wong's casebook on the novel. In 1994, Allan Chavkin and Nancy Feyl Chavkin collected some of the best interviews from Erdrich and Dorris, and their *Conversations with Louise Erdrich and Michael Dorris* provides students and teachers with insights into the writers' creative, collaborative, and personal worlds.

Critical Studies

There is a wealth of critical material that relates directly or indirectly to Erdrich. In the category of general critical works, recommended works include Mikhail Bakhtin's *The Dialogic Imagination*; Trinh Minh-ha's *Woman, Native, Other*; and Edward Said's *The World, the Text, and the Critic*.

Books on Native American studies include Paula Gunn Allen's *Studies in American Indian Literature: Critical Essays and Course Designs*; Joseph Bruchac's *Survival This Way: Interviews with American Indian Poets*; Laura Coltelli's *Winged Words: American Indian Writers Speak*; Elizabeth Cook-Lynn's *"Why I Can't Read Wallace Stegner" and Other Essays: A Tribal Voice*; Arnold

Krupat's *The Voice in the Margin: Native American Literatures and the Canon*; Kenneth Lincoln's *Indi'n Humor: Bicultural Play in Native America* and *Native American Renaissance*; Peter Nabokov's *Native American Testimony: A Chronicle of Indian-White Relations from Prophecy to Present, 1492– 1992*; John Purdy and James Ruppert's *Nothing but the Truth: An Anthology of Native American Literature*; Patricia Riley's *Growing Up Native American: An Anthology*; A. LaVonne Ruoff's *American Indian Literatures: An Introduction, Bibliographic Review, and Selected Bibliography*; James Ruppert's *Mediation in Contemporary Native American Fiction*; Greg Sarris's *Keeping Slug Woman Alive: A Holistic Approach to American Indian Texts*; Jeanne Rosier Smith's *Writing Tricksters: Mythic Gambols in American Ethnic Literature*; Brian Swann and Arnold Krupat's *I Tell You Now: Autobiographical Essays by Native American Writers*; Alan Velie's *American Indian Literature*; Gerald Vizenor's *Narrative Chance: Postmodern Discourse on Native American Indian Literatures*; Robert Warrior's *Tribal Secrets: Recovering American Indian Intellectual Traditions*; Jack Weatherford's *Native Roots: How the Indians Enriched America*; Andrew Wiget's *Handbook of Native American Literature*; and Craig Womack's *Red on Red: Native American Literary Separatism*.

Recommended articles on Erdrich and her fiction include Peter G. Beidler's "Louise Erdrich"; Kathleen Brogan's "Haunted by History: Louise Erdrich's *Tracks*"; Susan Perez Castillo's "The Construction of Gender and Ethnicity in the Texts of Leslie Silko and Louise Erdrich" and "Postmodernism, Native American Literature, and the Real: The Silko-Erdrich Controversy"; Joni Clarke's "Why Bears Are Good to Think and Theory Doesn't Have to Be Murder: Transformation and Oral Tradition in Louise Erdrich's *Tracks*"; Sidner Larson's "The Fragmentation of a Tribal People in Louise Erdrich's *Tracks*"; Kristan Sarve-Gorham's "Games of Chance: Gambling and Land Tenure in *Tracks*, *Love Medicine*, and *The Bingo Palace*"; Lydia Schultz's "Fragments and Ojibwe Stories: Narrative Strategies in Louise Erdrich's *Love Medicine*"; Jennifer Sergi's "Storytelling: Tradition and Preservation in Louise Erdrich's *Tracks*"; Leslie Marmon Silko's "Here's an Odd Artifact for the Fairy-Tale Shelf"; and James Stripes's "The Problem(s) of (Ojibwe) History in the Fiction of Louise Erdrich: Voices and Contexts."

For critical works on Erdrich, students and teachers are advised to check past issues of the *American Indian Culture and Research Journal*, *American Indian Quarterly*, *Wicazo Sa Review*, and *SAIL* (*Studies in American Indian Literatures*) for critical work on Erdrich. Of particular note is the winter 1985 *SAIL* issue (9.1), devoted solely to *Love Medicine*; *SAIL*'s two-part special issue on Erdrich, winter 1991 (3.4) and spring 1992 (4.1); and the student guide to *Love Medicine* in *American Indian Culture and Research Journal* 1992 (16.4).

Cultural Studies

The following works provide important cultural background: Victor Barnouw's *Wisconsin Chippewa Myths and Tales and Their Relation to Chippewa Life*; Victoria Brehm's "The Metamorphosis of an Ojibway Manidou"; Gregory Camp's "Working Out Their Salvation: The Allotment of Land in Severalty and the Turtle Mountain Chippewa Band, 1897–1920"; Basil Johnston's *Ojibway Ceremonies* and *Ojibway Heritage*; Ruth Landes's *Ojibwa Religion and the Midéwinin* and *The Ojibwa Woman*; *Saint Ann's Centennial: One Hundred Years of Faith, 1885–1985*; Mary Jane Schneider's *North Dakota's Indian Heritage*; Christopher Vecsey's *Traditional Ojibwa Religion and Its Historical Changes*; and Gerald Vizenor's *The Everlasting Sky: New Voices from the People Named the Chippewa*.

Audiovisual Materials

There are several good audiovisual resources that help introduce students to Erdrich. Erdrich spoke on *New Letters on the Air: Contemporary Writers on Radio*, and the tape is available from the University of Missouri, Kansas City. Interviews with Erdrich and Michael Dorris on two videos, one with Paul Bailey, in the Roland Collection, and the other with Bill Moyers, provide good background material on the author.

NOTE

[1]While there are no major characters found in both the reservation novels and *The Antelope Wife*, there is a startling minor connection revealed in *The Last Report on the Miracles at Little No Horse*. Sister Leopolda has a half brother, Shesheeb, whom Erdrich describes in *The Antelope Wife* as "the court-convicted windigo, bear-walker, bad holy dream-man" (935). Shesheeb is one of the Roy ancestors.

Part Two

APPROACHES

A History of the Turtle Mountain Band of Chippewa Indians

Connie A. Jacobs

There is not a separate group of people called Indian; there are Indians.[1] There is not one tribe of Native Americans; there are tribes. Henry Dobyns estimates that by AD 1500 there were between seven million and fifteen million people living in what constitutes the present-day United States (190), and the ancestors of these original Americans today account for "more than 400 different languages and distinct cultures" (Bruchac, "Four Directions" 4). These distinctions, foundational for Native studies, are unfortunately often lost on undergraduates in their first encounter with works written by Native American authors. One of the first tasks of teachers of Native American literature, then, is to deconstruct the monolithic image students have of Native people and to enlarge student knowledge of the variety of traditions, customs, and lifestyles among Native people.

Literature helps open these cultural doors, but if students are to appreciate the context out of which a work is written, they need to learn about the specific tribe. For readers of Louise Erdrich, an enrolled member of the Turtle Mountain Band of Chippewa Indians of northern North Dakota, knowledge of her tribe's history is of major importance, since Erdrich is a contemporary Native storyteller, who, through her novels and poetry, relates her tribal history from the last half of the nineteenth century to the end of the twentieth century. To participate as listener and reader in this storytelling session necessitates an understanding of the events that shaped the lives of Erdrich's people.

The Historical Ojibwe

The story begins a long time ago when the Algonkian people, living in the East long before Columbus "discovered" America, were driven out by the more powerful Iroquois. The Algonkians migrated to the Great Lakes region around AD 1200, where they gradually split into groups: Ottawa, Cree, Potawatomi, Menomini, and Ojibwe. According to Stanley Murray, sometime around 1600 the Ojibwe group began moving westward and split again into groups occupying areas around Lake Superior. He writes, "Those to the south of the lake now commonly are known as the Chippewa, and those on the north side came to be known as the Northern Ojibwe" (15), a distinction of importance when relating the history of the Turtle Mountain Band of Chippewas. The Northern Ojibwe eventually moved into the Saskatchewan and Rainy Lakes regions, where they intermixed with their Cree kin, while Chippewa bands began moving into northern Wisconsin and northern Minnesota.

The first Europeans to come upon the various Algonkian tribes were the French fur traders, who in the late 1600s encountered the people occupying the area around Sault Sainte Marie and the Upper Peninsula of Michigan. The ensuing French influence from the missionaries and fur trading posts plays an important part in the economy, culture, religion, and language of the Northern Ojibwe and Chippewa people.

These early French trappers encouraged the Northern Ojibwe and Chippewa, who were hunters and gatherers before contact, to bring them fur-bearing-animal pelts for trade, primarily beaver pelts. However, by early 1802, the depletion of game forced some of the people to again move further west. Whereas most of the Chippewa remained in Minnesota (after they had driven out the Lakota) and Wisconsin,[2] around 1820 small groups of Chippewa from Leech Lake and Red Lake along with Northern Ojibwe moved into the Red River Valley of eastern North Dakota, where, at Pembina, the Northwest Fur Company of Montreal, the XY Company, and the Hudson Bay Company had established a trading center (Murray 15). The presence of a major post in the region ensured a secure trading partner, and soon the Ojibwe and Chippewa joined their Cree relatives to hunt a new and plentiful fur-bearing animal, the buffalo.

This newly formed North Dakota group, who spent part of their year in the Turtle Mountains of north-central North Dakota, came to be known by many names: Bungi, Plains Ojibwe, Saulteaux, Chippewa-Cree, Plains Cree, Little Shell Band, and Turtle Mountain or Pembina Band of Chippewas. From their assorted backgrounds emerges a distinctive people complete with their own language and culture. However, the Ojibwe ancestors carried many traditions and practices across the plains and prairies that continued as cultural foundations for the tribe. It is out of these traditions and tribal history that Erdrich builds her stories of the Turtle Mountain Chippewa people.

Traditional Woodland Culture in Erdrich's Novels

Of prime importance was the Midéwiwin, or Grand Medicine Society, performed in the spring and fall, which according to legend the Great Bear brought to the people. The Midéwiwin ceremony, Basil Johnston explains, commemorated the gift of healing through ceremony and celebrated the lives of medicine men and women who led upright lives in conferring their gift of medicine (*Ojibway Heritage* 83). All Midés (members of the Midéwiwin) learned hunting-song and curing ceremonies, and the role of the Midé doctors was to cure the sick and aid the people.[3] In *Tracks*, it is Nanapush's knowledge of this traditional medicine that allows Eli to kill a moose during a time of starvation, and it is Nanapush's song that brings Eli safely home. Likewise, the other powerful practitioner of traditional medicine is Fleur Pillager, who, throughout the North Dakota novels, uses traditional healing knowledge. Although in the twentieth century Christianity replaced the Midéwiwin as the primary religion, through Nanapush and Fleur Erdrich asserts the power of the old ways to cure and to provide for the people.

The members of the traditional Midéwiwin additionally had the ability to turn their gift of healing into malevolent forms; fear ran rampant among the people that these powerful doctors might direct their medicine to destructive ends and witchcraft. That powerful medicine persons could and would misappropriate their healing knowledge promoted terror and a strong belief in the possibility and even the probability of such witchcraft. A sorcerer could secretly place certain herbs in a victim's food or use various entities from the victim's body—hair, nail parings, and even excrement—to fix his or her evil spell on someone (Landes, *Ojibwa Religion* 60). However fearsome these spells were, there loomed an even more frightening possibility that Christopher Vecsey describes:

> Particularly fearsome to the Ojibwas were witches who posed as bears, either by wearing the skins of bears or by metamorphosing into bears. The bear-walkers owed their powers to their personal manitou, the bear, and traveled in disguise at night, causing disease among their victims.
> (*Ojibwa Religion* 148)

Erdrich suggests that Fleur can transform herself into a bear, leave the tracks of the bear, and assume the spirit of the bear, thus planting the suspicion that Fleur may, indeed, use her powers for darker purposes, as Pauline Puyat, later Sister Leopolda, avers.

Other ancient Woodland traditions that persist in the reservation novels include the Underwater Manitou, the culture hero Nanabozho, visions and hunting, the clan system, and the importance of the family. The great Underwater Manitou evolved from a people who feared and honored the spirit who controlled the large bodies of water that served as both a food source and a highway. When the Ojibwe-Chippewa migrated from the Great Lakes into the hills and lakes of the Turtle Mountain region, they brought with them stories of the Underground Manitou, and in *Tracks*, Erdrich relates that "Misshepeshu had appeared because of the Old Man's [Fleur's father] connection" (175). Misshepeshu, one of the most powerful and important of the manitous, consequently becomes one of Fleur's spirit helpers, and she derives much of her power from his guardianship.

Nanabozho is a culture hero, for it is he whom the manitous sent into the world to teach the Ojibwe and to give them the gift of hunting and healing. According to Johnston, Nanabozho serves as the intermediary between the spirits and the people and has the power to change himself at will to perform his tasks (159–60). Erdrich transforms this traditional hero-trickster in *Tracks* into grandfather Nanapush. Nanabozho has been identified as the Great Rabbit or the White Hare (Coleman, Frogner, and Eich 56–57) that Erdrich manifests in another trickster figure, the culture hero Gerry Nanapush, whom she describes as a rabbit (*Love Medicine* 209).

One of the most important experiences in the life of the male Ojibwe was fasting for a dream or vision at the time of puberty in order to evoke a spirit that would appear as an animal. Life was difficult, and the presence of a spirit guardian helped a person to survive and to understand his life's purpose (Johnston, *Ojibway Heritage* 120). This spirit then served the person as the source of power throughout his life. In *The Bingo Palace* Lipsha Morrissey, heir of the Pillager magic, seeks a vision to impress his girlfriend, Shawnee Ray, with his practice of traditional ways. However, his vision is anything but ordinary. The bear, wolf, and marten are Pillager totem animals, but they do not come to Lipsha. Instead, a spirit skunk, possibly Fleur Pillager, appears to him and admonishes him not to allow Lyman to requisition the sacred Pillager land to build a bingo palace. To show her annoyance with Lipsha's flippant attitude about the vision quest, the skunk douses him with her powerful scent, a comic scene but also one that suggests Lipsha's obvious lack of seriousness as he practices traditional ceremonies.

The Woodland Ojibwe organized themselves into patrilineal exogamous clans that originated when, according to legend, the Great Spirit ordered the crane to fly down from the sky and to find a suitable place for the people to live. When the crane saw the Great Lakes, she settled down at Sault Sainte Marie and called out for help. The bear, catfish, loon, moose, and marten answered and came to live with the people (Bleeker 31–32). Vecsey points out that these special animals became the totem animals for individual families, their personal family mark, and served to identify a person in the society and to regulate whom he or she could or could not marry (*Ojibwa Religion* 78). The bear clan's members were medicine people and fighters, and in the novels, the bear is the clan totem for Fleur, the powerful medicine woman, and for Gerry Nanapush, the fighter for justice.

The family served as the most important unit in the Woodland economy, primarily because the people seasonally broke off from the main group into family bands to hunt and to gather maple syrup and rice. "Tribal families were the basic political and economic units in the woods and the first source of personal identities" (Vizenor, *People* 13). Hereditary leaders from the large families assumed leadership roles and made the important decisions for their relatives. The Bureau of Indian Affairs (BIA) disrupted this traditional leadership pattern by establishing councils and elected officials, favoring those individuals who would acquiesce to government proposals and policies. The Kashpaws, Nector and Lyman, reflect this pattern by serving first their own interests and the interests of the BIA, often at the expense of traditional tribal values and unity. What family leadership remained into the twentieth century was not in the hands of the men who, according to Vizenor, seem to have lost their pride, but rather in the hands of the women and grandparents who keep alive traditional cultural values (*Everlasting Sky* 58).

The grandparents (the term is used as a sign of respect and does not always denote a blood relative) were the ones designated by tribal custom to name a child and to instruct the child in traditional values and beliefs. Throughout a child's life, grandparents continued to play a vital and respected function; and the children were expected to honor and assist grandparents, who would care for the child if the need arose. Grandparents in Erdrich's Indian novels are the strongest and most enduring family tie, and the devoted mothers, Marie and Lulu, become in their later years the grandmothers who hold their families together and fight to maintain and restore cultural values on the reservation.

Many cultural patterns and traditions from the Woodlands survived with the Ojibwe who migrated to North Dakota. The structure of their society and their worldview was transported into the new homeland with relatively little modification: however, with the introduction of the Métis into the Plains Ojibwe (full-blooded Woodland Ojibwe, Saskatchewan Cree, and Northern Ojibwe from southern Canada), a cultural blending forever transformed the identity of the Turtle Mountain Chippewa, Erdrich's tribal people.

The Métis

Around the 1800s, the full-bloods joined forces with the Métis. David Delorme explains what resulted:

> The intermixture of Caucasoid and Mongoloid blended to produce a physical type that drew from both races, but did not approximate either

of its progenitors: divergent societies clashed and compromised to create
a disparate culture—new language, religion, social order, and economy.
(124)

In this case, it was the fur traders, particularly the French but also the English
and the Scots, who, encouraged by their trading companies, married Indian
women. These unions provided stability in the new country for the Europeans
and produced a distinct group of people, the Métis, or mixed-bloods. Patrick
Gourneau (Erdrich's maternal grandfather) points out, "The 'Mechifs' [Métis]
are descendants of traders, le voyageurs, the canoe paddlers of the fur trade
period and wagonmen, the Red River Cart drivers of the same period" (9).
The trappers most commonly married Cree and Northern Ojibwe women,
and the English and French surnames immediately marked the offspring as
different from the full-bloods.

Close association with the fur companies provided the Métis with a natural
entry into the economy, and Murray relates that the Métis were encouraged
by the merged Northwest and Hudson Bay companies to become full-time
hunters (16). They aptly adapted to this role, and when they depleted the
supply of smaller fur-bearing animals, they turned to hunting larger game, the
buffalo. Murray describes how, around the beginning of the 1800s, "the buffalo hunt created a cultural and political unity among the Métis" (18). By
1850, the Métis had become the dominant group in the region, numbering
more than five thousand (16). Because the Métis proved to be such successful
hunters, the Cree, Northern Ojibwe, and Chippewas soon joined them, and
the various groups became further blended. This combined group, which
hunted all the way from Minnesota to Montana, made a successful transition
from one way of life, traditional woodland hunting and gathering, to another,
hunting buffalo herds on the Plains.

The Métis became an integral part of the Turtle Mountain community, and
Murray reports that by 1870, they were the dominant people of the group
inhabiting Pembina and the Turtle Mountain region (19). Delorme estimates
that the total number of Métis in the United States and Canada at this time
was around thirty-three thousand (125). The mixed-bloods developed cultural
traditions distinctive from those of the full-bloods, notably the jigs, reels, fiddle
playing, log cabins, and Roman Catholic religion. What the two groups did
share was a language. According to James Howard, "Cree was a sort of *lingua
franca* in the Northern Plains during the latter half of the 19th century, and
was spoken by the Assiniboine, Blackfoot, and Dakota as well as Plains-Ojibwe
and Métis" (7). Cree emerged as the language of trade, while the group united
through hunting developed their own pidgin dialect, Michif. Delorme explains
the language as a mixture of French, Cree, and Chippewa, with roots stretching back to an "obsolete French of the type still to be heard in Normandy"
(126).

The Turtle Mountain Reservation

The first treaty for the Turtle Mountain group occurred in 1863 when the group ceded the Red River Valley, but as long as the area remained free from European settlers and the buffalo herds continued to supply trade, clothing, hides, and meat, the loss of this land did not significantly alter the tribe's way of life. In less than two decades, however, the Black Hills' gold rush brought hordes of settlers onto the Plains, and the extermination of the great buffalo herds was nearly complete. The Turtle Mountain band, recognizing the need for an established and permanent land base, began negotiations with the United States government.[4] However, among the full-bloods (Chippewa from Minnesota, Northern Ojibwe from the Rainy Lake area, and Ojibwe-Cree) and the Métis (the Canadian mixed-bloods and the mixed-bloods who considered themselves United States citizens), there was not a unified community.[5] By 1885, tension among the various groups threatened the life of the tribe.

At the time of negotiations for a common reservation, problems among the various factions became exacerbated for several reasons: long after the Canadian–United States border was established in 1818, the Métis continued to move back and forth across the forty-ninth parallel (Murray 14); the Métis outnumbered the full-bloods; and the mixed-bloods (in the novels, the Lazarres, Morrisseys, and Puyats) wished to accept land in severalty. Chief Little Shell (Es-ssence), who had negotiated earlier treaties, was now living in the Milk River country in Montana, but he returned to North Dakota to fight for a common reservation area, and in 1882 President Chester Arthur "designated a twenty-four-by-thirty-two-mile tract in Rolette County as a reservation for the Chippewa" (Murray 23). Cyrus Beede, the agent the government sent to make recommendations and to fix the reserve site, found himself negotiating with two different groups: the thousand or so Métis, who wanted individual tracts, and the approximately three hundred full-bloods, who continued to push for a common area. Subsequent government agents "found" that many of the people on the tribal rolls were Canadian mixed-bloods who agents felt had no claim to North Dakota lands, and this misinterpretation resulted in hundreds of tribal members being stricken from the rolls. Their removal gave the government an excuse to again reduce the land base, and in 1884, "the original twenty-two township reserve was reduced to two townships" (Murray 23). As a result, the best land remained available to Anglo settlers.

The government continued to erode the land base of the Turtle Mountain people. The McCumber Agreement of 1892 "divested the Turtle Mountain Indians of their rights and title of almost 10,000,000 acres for the consideration of $1,000,000. This 'ten cent treaty' was amended and approved by Congress on April 21, 1904" (Delorme 133). The tribe still claimed these lands when the government summarily opened them for European settlement. The reservation was reduced to 275 quarter sections that needed to be divided among 326 families (Murray 32). The result was a dispersal of the people to lands off the reserve, with some people settling on public domain lands near the reservation, in the Trenton and Walhalla communities in North Dakota and on Graham's Island, a peninsula of Devil's Lake (Murray 32). Because the Dawes Act of 1887 gave women and children rights to land, some tribal members were allocated property as far away as Montana on the Rocky Boy Reservation. The beginning of the twentieth century found the fortunes of the Turtle Mountain people very bleak: the best farmland in the hands of the European settlers, the dispersal of the tribe, the encroachment of government-supported lumber companies, the depletion of buffalo herds, the assault of disastrous flu and smallpox epidemics, a national depression between 1893 and 1896, and questionable property taxes levied on the people of the band receiving land off the small reservation area. The 1910 census found 229 full-bloods and 2,546 mixed-bloods (only 569 of whom had received allotments) (Camp, "Working Out" 30) living on one of the smallest reservations in the United States. In *Tracks*, which opens in 1912, Erdrich describes the condition of her tribe, now removed by the United States government from most of the lands it had been occupying in North Dakota and living in blighted circumstances on a small reservation in the Turtle Mountain region.

The Current Turtle Mountain Tribe

There were some favorable developments in the twentieth century. Based on the Wheeler-Howard Indian Reorganization Act of 1934, 33,435 acres near the reservation were purchased for tribal use (M. J. Schneider 131), and in 1979, the Indian Claims Commission awarded the tribe $52,527,338 as compensation for the unfair seizure of tribal lands under the "ten cent agreement" (Delorme 133). In 1994, each tribal member was awarded an additional $3,000 (Bruce). Belcourt remains the administrative center for the tribe, and the town contains many businesses owned by tribal members; there are a tribally owned shopping mall and junior college; Saint Ann's Catholic Church, where most of the people worship; and as of the late 1980s, a bingo hall. In January 2000, Doreen Bruce, director of the Turtle Mountain Heritage Center, reported 28,021 people on the census rolls, most of them enrolled as mixed-bloods, and 15,000 tribal members living on or near the reservation.

Since the 1800s, the Turtle Mountain Band of Chippewa Indians has struggled for recognition, rights, and a unified tribal identity, while barely surviving crippling epidemic diseases and governmental policies. As teachers of literature, we can help students interpret Erdrich's literary voice and her portrayal of one tribe of Indian people who, despite overwhelming odds, have endured and are thriving in the twenty-first century.

NOTES

[1] I use the terms *Indian, Native,* and *Native American* interchangeably throughout this essay since there is no single designation Native people agree on.

[2] Today there are seven Ojibwe reservations in Minnesota: Bois Forte, Fond du Lac, Grand Portage, Leech Lake, Mille Lacs, Red Lake, and White Earth (Molin 398). There are six Ojibwe reservations in Wisconsin: Bad River, Lac Courte Oreilles, Lac du Flambeau, Red Cliff, St. Croix, and Sokaogon (Baker and Eckert 404).

[3] For detailed information on the Midéwiwin, see Landes, *Ojibwa Religion*; Dewdney; and Vecsey, *Ojibway Religion*.

[4] Gourneau relates, "The Ojibway began to enter into treaties with United States as early as 1815, and by the time the Treaty making period between the Indians and the United States ended they were record breaking treaty makers, having been involved in a total number of 42. The Potowatomis, an ally, shared this record with them" (8).

[5] Gourneau offers important information on full-bloods and the Métis: "The term 'full-blood' can be applied sociologically and does not imply that the group is made up entirely of people of pure Indian descent. It merely means that these individuals prefer and adhere to the Indian way of life instead of the Métis, or 'half-breed' way of life. . . . This 'full-blood' group definitely forms a distinct minority of the Turtle Mountain Band. The minority percentage of Band population could be as small as a fraction of one percent by today's statistics" (9).

Of Bears and Birds: The Concept of History in Erdrich's Autobiographical Writings

David T. McNab

Alberto Manguel has observed that "a society can exist—many do exist—without writing, but no society can exist without reading" and that even "in societies that set down a record of their passing, reading precedes writing; the would-be writer must be able to recognize and decipher the social system of signs before setting them down on the page" (2). Similarly, to understand Aboriginal histories and oral traditions, one must learn how to read the names and the clans and become informed about their cultures. In this respect, Louise Erdrich's stories are like a cultural intersection. In *The Antelope Wife*, Klaus Shawano, the Ojibwe trader, observes that his "stories have stories. My beadwork is made by relatives and friends whose tales branch off in an ever more complicated set of barriers" (27). This "set of barriers" encompasses Erdrich's concept of history, which has come down from the Creator to her as an Ojibwe (meaning literally "whence lowered the male of the species")/ Cree person. In this essay, following Manguel's paradigm, I describe a pre-colonial approach to understanding the writings of Louise Erdrich, especially her concept of family histories.

Erdrich's idea of history is circular. It has the meaning of "duration that cannot be expressed because it has no limits, time"; it is "the sum of all possible solar cycles." It "gives life, destroys and recreates without end the reality in which men [and women] move and think" (McNab, *Circles* 1). This idea of history begins with the sun. Each day the sun rises, travels its course, and then sets in the West. It is in this way that history exists for Aboriginal people. The sun is also represented by the metaphor and the shape of the drum. The sound of the drum is the heartbeat of Mother Earth as we walk her each day, through the seasons of our lives. The circular idea of history is both simple and complex; it is far more complicated than the linear notions of time and history in European-based knowledge systems, in the theoretical perspectives that they have engendered and the colonialism that has resulted.

The notion of circles of time is common to all indigenous peoples, including the Ojibwe (see Johnston, *Manitous*). In the mid-nineteenth century, in his writings, George Copway (Kahgegagahbowh) described the concept:

> [The] Ojebwas, as well as many others, acknowledged that there was but one Great Spirit, who made the world; they gave him the name of good or benevolent; *kesha* is benevolent, *monedoo* is spirit; Ke-sha-mon-e-doo. They supposed he lived in the heavens; but the most of the time he was in the *Sun*. They said it was from him they received all that was

good through life, and that he seldom needs the offering of his Red children, for he was seldom angry.   (81)

The sun, the sustainer of life, is also a metaphor for time (Bainbridge).

The bead is a representation of circles of time, of one and many (McNab, *Circles* 1–3; Williams), an Aboriginal metaphor for family history. Each bead is like an event that binds Aboriginal family histories together. Gerald Hausman has described the purpose of the bead:

> [T]he bead, like the basket, is round; and, like the old tribal culture, a single part of many other parts. The string of beads, the blazon of beads told a story in which the single bead was a necessary link to all the others. . . . One and many; the meaning of the tribe. Together there is strength, unity. The tribal man or woman was as strong as the tribe from which he/she came. And the tribe, naturally, got its strength from the single bead, the pearl, the individual man or woman.   (8–9)

This metaphor finds its way, with similar meanings, into Erdrich's fiction. *The Antelope Wife*, for example, opens with the joining of families across time in historical context with blue beads representing both the conjoining of time and intuition (1, 5).[1]

Although all of Erdrich's autobiographical writings are based on her own and her family's history, this essay focuses on her concept of history in those writings. Erdrich is from the Turtle Mountain Reservation in North Dakota, just south of the border between Canada and the United States. Her fictional world is filled with harmony, balance, and order as well as with brilliant light and vivid colors.[2] It is inhabited by unpredictable two-leggeds who desperately, almost crazily, strive for balance and better relationships with one another, with the four-leggeds, and with the places from which they have originally come and to which they always return as their home. Such is the place created by Erdrich in all her writings.

Erdrich was born in 1954, in Little Falls, Minnesota. She is a Chippewa-Cree-Métis person[3] of the bird and bear clans (also known among them as Anishinaabe and by anthropologists and linguists as Ojibwe) on her mother's side and of German-Jewish-Catholic descent on her father's side (*Books* 80). The Ojibwe Nation has resided since time immemorial in Indian territories, or "birchbark country," which includes places along the Great Lakes and connecting waterways of northeastern North America now as far west as North Dakota and Manitoba (McNab, Hodgins, and Standen). The Cree Nation is the neighbor of the Ojibwe, and it trades and intermarries with them. The Cree Nation—both of the Plains and the Swampy Cree—and also the Métis Nation continue to reside in northern Ontario and Quebec and the Prairie provinces in Canada[4] as well as in the northwestern states of the United States, especially the Dakotas and Montana. The indigenous knowledge that informs Erdrich's writings comes from these places and the families who reside there (McNab, "Gathering Gum").

Knowledge of the clans and the clan system is important, for without that knowledge one cannot know who Erdrich's characters—her literary animals—are and where they are going, much less interpret them. Not all nations have the same clans. Each of the clans has different responsibilities—political, social, cultural, philosophical, and spiritual—though these categories do not do justice to the character of the duties (Benton-Banai 74–78).[5] But Erdrich's literary characters are not one-dimensional. Each clan is like an extended spiritual family that cuts across nations. Erdrich has two significant clans on her mother's side. On her Ojibwe side Erdrich is a Be-nays, which is a bird of the great blue heron clan,[6] as indicated repeatedly in her autobiography of a birth year, *The Blue Jay's Dance* (36). In the Ojibwe clan system, the birds are spiritual leaders (Benton-Banai 74–78). On her Cree side, Erdrich is a member of the Bear Clan (*Books* 80). Members of the Bear Clan are the protectors and the healers, and they suffer a great deal in their life journey. Leonard Peltier, of Wounded Knee fame, is also a bear from the Turtle Mountain Reservation[7] and may be the model for her trickster character Gerry Nanapush in her stories.

Spiritual messages through storytelling, warnings, and healing are dominant themes in all her works. Her writings are filled with indigenous knowledge of places—the higher elevations of the mind—as well as the gift of *ah-mun'-ni-soo-win*, or intuition, which includes *nee-goni-wa'bun-gi-gay-win*, the ability to see into the future. This ability is made even more potent because Erdrich has the female spirit of the bear within her, giving her the gift of prophecies.

Erdrich is a spiritual leader. She tells stories—indeed her life story is one of testing, of trial and stress—to find her sense of self, her place, and her spirituality. In *The Blue Jay's Dance*, Erdrich provides a composite of her experiences from her diary of the birth of her children in the early 1990s. Seasonal in structure, it begins in the winter—the time for telling stories, after the first snow has fallen—and ends in the fall. Her prose is lyrical and haunting, as, for example, in the chapter "The Chickadee's Tongue":

> Today a chickadee hits the window with a small surprising thunk. I walk outside, pluck it off the warming earth. The bird is stunned, blinking, undamaged. I stand motionless with the bird in my hand, examining it carefully, but not a feather seems to have snapped or ruffled. . . . I have always wanted to catch a chickadee and look at its tongue, but now that I've got one, my hands seem as big and clumsy as paws. I don't dare try to open its beak. Regaining its wits, the bird seems to trust me—it vibrates, its breath spins, its heart ticks too fast to apprehend, but it doesn't leave the palm of my hand. I wouldn't close my fingers on it for

anything, and it knows. It looks up at me, alert and needle-sharp, but very calm, and I feel suddenly that I am an amazingly fortunate woman.
(82–83)

The clan relationships are clearly spelled out here. The birds are the spirit protectors of the bears, and the two clans are powerfully linked. As a bear, with hands "big and clumsy as paws," Erdrich cares for and heals the chickadee. Her place—Turtle Mountain—is powerful, a home of eagles and bears. It is border country between the Cree and the Ojibwe: "I've lived in many different places but feel most attached to the outdoor West and Great Plains, the sky, the mountains, the broad reaches" (Chavkin and Chavkin 227). It is a place that infuses her writings.

Erdrich understands that her writing is spiritual, acknowledging in an interview, "Life is religious, I think, and that includes writing." She goes on to list the "common themes and preoccupations" in her work: "Abandonment and return. Pleasure and denial. Failure. Absurdity. The inability to get a sound night's sleep"(Chavkin and Chavkin 228). Winter, which begins *The Blue Jay's Dance*, is the time for spiritual renewal among the Cree and Ojibwe. It is here that one encounters the spiritual component of the Ojibwe concept of time. Erdrich explains:

The world tips away when we look into our children's faces. The days flood by. Time with children runs through our fingers like water as we lift our hands, try to hold, to capture, to fix moments in a lens, a magic circle of images and words. We snap photos, videotape, memorialize while we experience a fast-forward in which there is no replay of even a single instant.   (*Dance* 4)

The Aboriginal concept of history is both specific to a place and infinite—circular, not linear (*Dance* 82–84). This circular notion is unfamiliar to non-Aboriginal people and perhaps helps explain the difficulties that readers have with Erdrich's lack of linear chronology in her narratives. Her characters are bound not by this concept of time but rather by the indigenous knowledge residing in their special or sacred places. Erdrich's concept of time as a bird and a bear enables her to foretell events through intuition and prophecy.[8]

For Erdrich, time is connected to the female body, and it involves an understanding of narrative about oneself as events take place. The "problem of narrative" is "more than just embarrassment about a physical process"; it is the cycle of birth and rebirth within the circle of life:

We're taught to suppress its importance over time, to devalue and belittle an experience in which we are bound up in the circular drama of human fate, in a state of heightened awareness and receptivity, at a crux where we intuit connections and, for a moment, unlock time's hold like a brace, even step from our bodies.

It is a narrative of a child, its birth and its own story. The act of giving birth "often becomes both paradigm and parable." The woman's body in this way "becomes a touchstone, a predictor":

> A mother or a father, in describing their labor, relates the personality of the child to some piece of the event, makes the story into a frame, an introduction, a prelude to the child's life, molds the labor into the story that is no longer a woman's story or a man's story, but the story of a child.   (*Dance* 44–45)

It is from her concept of time as circular[9] that she begins to understand that her home is spiritual and that it is where her spirit is born and where she is from and where she is going. She cannot share her husband's life. In the section "Finches and the Grand Sky," Erdrich observes:

> I picture the female goldfinch settling herself into a nest the color of her husband and suddenly I think—*that's what I've done, moving to this, my husband's farm*. All around me, kind trees and slabs of rocky land, violet and archaic gold shadows that Maxfield Parrish painted into his *Saturday Evening Post* covers. This is a beautiful place but it is not where I belong. Over and over, in anguish, in hope, we utter the same lines in a long established argument "I'm homesick," I keep saying. "This is home," he keeps answering. Each of us is absolutely right.
> (87–88)

It is to the sky world of the prairies and the birds, of the power of Turtle Mountain and the rock medicine of the bears, that Erdrich knows that she must return.

Erdrich's *The Birchbark House* continues the chronicle of her family history begun in *The Blue Jay's Dance*. It is dedicated to her daughter, "Persia, whose song heals," and illustrated with her beautiful black and white drawings. Erdrich acknowledges and thanks her mother, Rita Gourneau Erdrich, and her sister Lise Erdrich, who researched their family life and found "ancestors on both sides who lived on Madeline Island during the time in which this book is set. One of them was Gatay Manomin, or Old Wild Rice" (*House* [1])

For the Ojibwe people these sacred places—frequently islands—are the source of their knowledge of themselves as a people, who they are and where they are going as persons and as a people with their own independent history. This notion of history encompasses the past but also the present and the future in the form of prophecy. So, in this way, Spirit and Madeline Islands are central to Ojibwe history and understanding of time. For example, according to Ojibwe oral traditions, Spirit Island is the sixth stopping place in Ojibwe history; it was here that the

> Sacred Shell rose up to the people from the sands of its shore. . . . It was near Spirit Island that the words of the prophets were fulfilled. Here the Ojibwe found "the food that grows on water." Here they found Ma-no-min (wild rice) [which has] always been regarded . . . as the sacred gift of their chosen ground. (Benton-Banai 101)

Madeline Island is the seventh, and final, stopping place in Midéwiwin history. It has been described as follows:

> One of the prophets of long ago had spoken of a turtle-shaped island that awaited them at the end of their journey. . . . The people sought out this island and placed tobacco on its shore. The Sacred Shell rose up out of the water and told the people this was the place they had been searching for. Here, the Waterdrum made its seventh and final stop on the migration. The Sacred Fire was carried there and it burned brightly. This island was called Mo-ning-wun-a-kawn-ing (the place that was dug, in a way in which the golden woodpecker makes its house by digging into the Standing People) by the Ojibway. (Benton-Banai 102)

In these places Erdrich begins her exposition of Ojibwe history in *The Birchbark House*.

The story of *The Birchbark House* in history, and its heroine is Omakayas, or Little Frog in Ojibwe.[10] The structure of the narrative is based on the seasons and the daily passage of the sun, the notion of time as events take place. It begins in the winter of 1840 when Ojibwe voyageurs on their way home stop on Spirit Island and find Omakayas alone. Seven years later, the story begins again when it is Neebin (summer), which is followed by Dagwaging (fall), Biboon (winter), and Zeegwun (spring). Omakayas, born on Spirit Island (at the west end of present-day Lake Superior near Duluth), is rescued by Old Tallow, an Ojibwe medicine woman. That Omakayas is the last person left alive among her people after a smallpox epidemic makes her a transformer in history, a person imbued with medicine power from birth who is able to transform events as they take place. As a Cree of the Bear Clan, Omakayas is adopted by the Ojibwe. She becomes the healer (since she had the smallpox as a baby, she cannot get it again) and saves the Ojibwe from this dreaded disease seven years later on Madeline Island (*House* 2). The power of Spirit and Madeline Islands gives the story its theme of self-discovery and its healing powers. From the beginning, the birds protect Omakayas, for the birds are the spirit protectors of the bears in the clan system.[11] This is the first scene in this novel: "Birds were singing. Dozens of tiny white-throated sparrows. The trilling, rippling sweetness of their songs contrasted strangely with the silent horror below" (2). Birds are also singing to Omakayas in the last, much happier, scene.

The character of Old Tallow is also a transformer in this story. The metaphors for this power are lightning, tallow, lard, speck.[12] Old Tallow is an Ojibwe of the Bear Clan, as evidenced by "the bear claw that swung on a silver hoop from Old Tallow's ear lobe" (30) as well as by Erdrich's illustration and description of her and her dog and wolf companions, her friends on her life's journey (*House* 19–32). Her role as a bear is to help Omakayas discover who she is and in this fashion to heal her. It is Old Tallow who sends the female bear spirit to Omakayas on Omakayas's return to the birchbark house. Here is part of the description of Omakayas's encounter with her brothers, the bear boys, and their mother:

> For long moments, the bear tested her with every sense, staring down with her weak eyes, listening, and most of all smelling her. . . . The bear smelled all. . . . Omakayas couldn't help but smell her back. Bears eat anything and this one had just eaten something ancient and foul. Hiyn! Omakayas took shallow breaths. Perhaps it was to take her mind off the scent of dead things on the bear's breath that she accidentally closed the scissors shearing off a tiny clip of bear fur, and then to cover her horror at this mistake, started to talk. . . . "Nokomis," she said to the bear, calling her grandmother. "I didn't mean any harm? I was only playing with your children. Gaween onjidah. Please forgive me."
>
> (*House* 30–31)

And then the mother bear recognized that Omakayas was also a bear, having the spirit of the bear: "But having totalled up all of the smells and sifted them for information, the bear seemed to have decided that Omakayas was no threat" (*House* 32). This event transformed Omakayas. She became a woman and a healer, saving her adopted family in the winter and thereby transforming their family history into a story of survival. Time and history are thus interconnected when events from the spirit world take place.

From this encounter with the female bear, Omakayas discovers more and more about herself. She finds out that her spirit protector is Andeg, the crow, whom she saves while protecting the family's field of corn. Her adopted grandmother helps her understand that the spirits of the plants and herbs can tell her how they heal the sick or help those in pain. She helps heal her adopted family from the smallpox that came to destroy them during a cruel winter.

The female bear spirit also comes to Omakayas in the maple-sugaring time when she is feeling low and weak-spirited after giving so much of herself to little Neewo and feeling his death so deeply. She needs to be healed herself.

She meets her bear brothers in the woods and offers tobacco to them as a gift. She asks them if they will give her their bear medicine—not for herself but "to save my family" (*House* 202). After the bears leave, she hears the voices of the spirits of the plants talking to her and telling her of their medicines. In this way she discovers that she is a healer. Her Nokomis told her that the bears

> dig for medicine and are a different kind of people from us. They don't use fire, but they laugh. They hold their children. They eat the same things we do and treat themselves with medicine from certain plants. They are known as healers. Those in the bear clan are often good at healing others.   (*House* 207)

Omakayas becomes a medicine woman and helps heal her brother when he accidentally scalds himself during the maple-sugaring time. In so doing, she gives back to the Ojibwe their gift from the Creator of their seventh sense— the sense of humor (*House* 212–15). One aspect of the renewal of one's spirit is to become detached from oneself and to tell stories that are filled with humor. Seeing oneself anew also aids in the healing process. And so the story comes full circle when Omakayas visits Old Tallow, who tells Omakayas who she is and where she is going:

> "You were sent here so you could save the others," she said. "Because you'd had the sickness, you were strong enough to nurse them through it. They did a good thing when they took you in, and you saved them for their good act. Now the circle that began when I found you is complete."   (*House* 235)

Erdrich uses the metaphor of the circle to denote time and Aboriginal history. It is at this point that Omakayas remembers being on Spirit Island and how the birds had saved her by their songs.

So it is the continuity provided by Aboriginal storytellers, like Erdrich, through their songs that will enable Aboriginal people to continue on their spirit journeys and to survive as Omakayas did. On a sunny, spring morning Omakayas discovered herself in the voices of the tiny sparrows:

> She heard Neewo. She heard her little brother as though he still existed in the world. She heard him tell her to cheer up and live. *I'm all right,* his voice was saying, *I'm in a peaceful place. You can depend on me. I'm always here to help you, my sister.* Omakayas tucked her hands behind her head, lay back, closed her eyes, and smiled as the song of the white-throated sparrow sank again and again through the air like a shining needle, and sewed up her broken heart.   (*House* 239)

Now reunited with her younger brother, who is in the spirit world, she has been healed spiritually, and her brother is one of her spirit protectors. She rediscovers who she is and what has happened to her family on Spirit Island. There the story ends; then the seasonal circles of time and life are renewed, and the story begins again. Omakayas can now continue on her own journey of healing herself and others.

Teaching the autobiographical writings of Erdrich is a process of discovery of both one's self and the spiritual world of the Cree and the Ojibwe. These works tell us her life story in the natural and spiritual world and help us understand more clearly our own journeys and those in Erdrich's fictional world (*Tales*). In the end, they enable us to be transformed and healed by directly connecting her and us through our shared pasts as human beings—our families and the histories of those families. Erdrich thus fulfills the responsibilities of her clans—telling stories as a bird and through them healing others as a bear and ultimately healing herself and her family.[13] From research into her family history, Erdrich discovered the name of Omakayas and has given it power and has empowered herself in the healing.

Erdrich's world is one that is, in her stories, filled with messages from the Creator of love and of healing through the telling of stories through which one sees, as in a mirror, oneself. The stories heal both the storyteller and the listener. The process of storytelling includes private experiences and public performances. In themselves the stories are rich in ancient traditions and are powerful in their telling. Erdrich has a heart to remember by, and her stories come straight as an arrow from the Creator. Chi Meegwetch, Louise.

NOTES

[1]For another example, in music, see Robbie Robertson's CD sound track to *The Native Americans*, which contains the reflective phrase "The bead in the story belt" from the song "Twisted Hair."

[2]Colors in Erdrich's work are important signifiers of time and history, highlighting persons and their connections with events. The colors also correspond to the clans of the characters. The Bear Clan's color is red and the Bird Clan's is blue, for example. The combination of red and blue is extremely powerful in terms of time, as in the case of Blue Prairie Woman in *The Antelope Wife* (8).

[3]On the family's clans, see Heid Ellen Erdrich (her sister), *Fishing for Myth*.

[4]Canada as a place name comes from an Iroquoian word, *Kanata*, which means a series of small villages located along the lakes and rivers.

[5]For example, the Ojibwe cranes are the political leaders; the fish, including turtles, are the philosophers and intellectuals; and the deer are the gentle people—the poets and artists. The clans tell us who Erdrich is in circles of time. Some Aboriginal people, if they are adopted, have two clans. The specific information about Erdrich also came to me from my trip on 6 September 1999 to Manitoulin Island, which is the fourth stopping place in Ojibwe history.

[6]My trip to Manitoulin Island.

[7]On Peltier's sufferings, see Erdrich, "Time." It was appropriate for Erdrich, a member of the Ojibwe bird clan, to write this article to protect Peltier, since the birds are the protectors of the bears and since she herself was a bear on the Cree side of her family.

[8]In *The Blue Jay's Dance*, there is the foretelling of the suicide of Michael Dorris, then her husband. She writes, "There was also, in this house's short life, a suicide. I don't know much about him except that he was young, lived alone, rode a motorcycle to work. I don't know where in the house he was when he shot himself. I do not want to know, except I do know. There is only one place. It is here, where I sit, before the window, looking out into the dark shapes of trees. Perhaps it is odd to contemplate a subject as grim as suicide while anticipating a child so new she'll wear a navel tassel and smell of nothing but her purest self, but beginnings suggest endings and I can't help thinking about the continuum, the span, the afters, and the befores" (8).

[9]In *The Blue Jay's Dance*, she writes, "For my thirtieth birthday, I was given a watch by a dear one who assumed with cheerful lovingness that, since I had never worn a watch, I would now like to start. I smiled and appreciated, but deep down I felt uneasy. Wear a watch? Early on in adult life I tried to wear a watch, but I didn't like the feel of time ticking itself away on my wrist, as if in a mortal race with my own pulse. I tried to tell time by the length of light, but I was always late. I resorted to keeping the watch in my pocket, where it was easy to forget. Even now, I only wear a watch to travel and keep appointments with friends" (83).

[10]The name Omakayas, Erdrich notes, is on a Turtle Mountain census, and one brings honor to the name when one speaks it out loud: "This book and those that will follow are an attempt to retrace my own family's history" (i). The book that followed *The Birchbark House* was Erdrich's novel *The Last Report on the Miracles at Little No Horse*. The history of her father's side of the family is in the novel *The Master Butchers Singing Club*.

[11]On the back of the dust jacket of this book is a photograph of Erdrich with Mab, the "raised crow," on her head. On the front is Erdrich's drawing of Omakayas with Andeg (the Ojibwe name for crow), her raised crow, on her left shoulder. Both Erdrich and Omakayas are bears and both have birds as spirit protectors.

[12]The transformer in history is signified by various elements of the natural world. *Tallow*, for example, is defined as "any of the various greases or greasy substances obtained from plants, minerals, *etc.*" See also McNab, "Perfect Disguise." In Buffy Sainte-Marie's CD *Up Where We Belong* a transformer would be, for example, "Starwalker."

[13]The bears are prominently displayed in Erdrich's bookstore, Birchbark Books and Native Arts, in Minneapolis (my visit to the bookstore, 10 and 13 April 2002).

Beneath Creaking Oaks:
Spirits and Animals in *Tracks*

Susan Scarberry-García

Perhaps the darkest of Louise Erdrich's early novels, *Tracks* opens breathtakingly, deep in the Ojibwe woods near the medicine line, the borderlands shared by Canada and the United States. This novel is stunningly lean in its central tale of starvation and decline in the early years of the twentieth century, yet strangely full of dense life-giving imagery that emanates from the animal essence of the human characters. Fleur Pillager and Pauline Puyat, for instance, are wolf and crane, respectively, and conduct their lives consistently with their embedded animal natures. Whereas it is relatively easy to teach about the human relationships of the characters, it is more difficult to help students probe the animal traits of the Ojibwe survivors of the great sicknesses of the early 1900s. This essay intends to provide helpful suggestions for a deep reading of the text *Tracks* through teaching the concepts of the interchange of animal and human persons and the signs and symbols that characterize Ojibwe "tracks" of identity. It is hoped that students can learn to identify traditional animal roles in Ojibwe culture, thus appreciating Erdrich's use of markers of ethnic identity in telling a fictional story grounded in the historic reality of the southern Ojibwe Nation.

The novel's title, *Tracks*, orients readers toward the impressions left behind as human beings and animals pass beneath the oaks of the North Dakota forest. Early on in chapter 2, Pauline describes Fleur's hunting powers and clearly indicates that Fleur physically transforms from human being to bear and back again into her human body: "we followed the tracks of her bare feet and saw where they changed, where the claws sprang out, the pad broadened and pressed into the dirt. By night we heard her chuffing cough, the bear cough" (12). Although she is a narrator prone to exaggeration, we trust Pauline here to convey the fearful, collective observation of the community, which Nanapush corroborates. When we meet this haunting description of Fleur as bear, we already know her as wolf. "She was wild as a filthy wolf, a big bony girl whose sudden bursts of strength and snarling cries terrified the listening Pukwan" (3). Even though Erdrich uses similes, likening her characters to native animals, there can be no doubt that this device indicates the centrality of the animal nature of the characters, so sustained are the animalistic descriptions and so consistent are they with traditional Ojibwe worldview. Thus convincingly explaining the multiple animal natures within each character is a task that a critical reading of *Tracks* demands.

If students wonder why Erdrich embeds multiple animal presences into her characters' personalities, the technique can be explained as essential to the development of her story because Ojibwe are descended patrilineally from totem animal ancestors who are the progenitors and keepers of their clan and Ojibwe express themselves ritually and interpersonally through both these hereditary clan affiliations and animal associations gained from life experiences. Those who have a central identity through their clan names, obligations, and restrictions may add on other identities as they mature and acquire life experiences.

To further complicate these identity issues, it should be understood that human beings may take on an animal form to accomplish certain tasks and then return to their human form to carry on in that bodily shape. In some cultures, such as the Navajo, this activity may be associated with darkness and witchcraft, but in Ojibwe culture much shape-shifting is seen as positive. (For example, see the character Gerry Nanapush in *Love Medicine*, who becomes heroic through his transformative powers of magical flight.) Additionally, some Native cultures view human hunters as another manifestation of their prey, the game. This interrelatedness of hunter and the hunted is revealed in Keresan Pueblo culture through the winter dance figure of Caiyai'k'a, who is at once dressed as hunter holding bow and arrows and wearing dangling mountain lion and fox tails. In this image, the hunter becomes mountain lion, himself a hunter of deer. This figure is also the father of the hunters who controls the game. A similar manifestation of the intimate reciprocal life-giving relationship between hunter and game is revealed in *Tracks* in the scenes where Fleur is butchering the deer Eli had been tracking and where Eli becomes moose man as he binds the steaming meat of moose to his body to carry the carcass home to Nanapush. Eli *is* moose. The spiritual connection between hunter and game holds. Spirit power is transferred to the hunter.

To assist students in coming to the realization that in *Tracks* Erdrich identifies characters with animals as a means to recognize specialized knowledge within the tribe and to reflect the diverse inner beings of characters, teachers may wish to ask students to research aspects of the origin/creation story of the Ojibwe, which has found its way into print in sources by George Copway (Kahgegagahbowh), Frances Densmore (*Customs, Music I, Music II*), A. Irving Hallowell, Basil Johnston (*Heritage, Ceremonies*), Ruth Landes, Thomas W. Overholt and J. Baird Callicott, Christopher Vecsey (*Ojibwa Religion*), Gerald Vizenor (*Anishinabe, People, Touchwood*) and William Warren. The complete Copway material, *The Traditional History and Characteristic Sketches of the Ojibway Nation*, originally published in 1850, is difficult to obtain, but other older texts, such as Densmore's *Chippewa Customs*, originally a report for the Bureau of American Ethnology in 1929, has been reprinted as recently as 1979 by the Minnesota Historical Society Press and should be available in most university libraries. These ethnographic sources yield authentic documentation of Ojibwe cultural elements in a historic context that is essential for developing a careful interpretation of meaningful events in *Tracks*. Vecsey's work, *Traditional Ojibwa Religion and Its Historical Changes,* is particularly good in analyzing episodes in the mythic stories, such as the trickster–culture hero Nanabozho's battles with underwater manitous, or spirits.

In the Ojibwe universe there is a sky world, an earth world, and a water world. The earth was created with the assistance of Muskrat during an earth-diving event and is presided over by Kitche Manitou, the Creator or Great Spirit. The Midéwiwin, known as the Grand Medicine Society, is the primary means human beings have of maintaining spiritual relationships with animals and manitous and of performing healing ritual within Ojibwe culture. During the ancient migrations of the Ojibwe, some of the branches of the tribe, associated with northern totem animals and clans, split off, whereas other extended family divisions moved west, associated with yet other clan animals. In a condensation of the Ojibwe origin story in *Ojibway Heritage,* Johnston tells us, "Without the animals the world would not have been; without the animals the world would not be intelligible," for animals have foreknowledge of events and provide their bodies to sustain the people. Voicing the interdependence of all life, Johnston continues, "More and more the Anishinabeg relied upon the animals. . . . Men and women understood the utterances of the animals; the animals understood man" (49, 50). A primary reason the Ojibwe understand animals so well is that their spiritual and physical essences are intertwined with each other and have been so since the dawn of creation.

In a revealing statement in the prologue to *The People Named the Chippewa: Narrative Histories,* Vizenor, a culture member, writes, "Naanabozho, the compassionate woodland trickster, wanders in mythic time and transformational space between tribal experiences and dreams. The trickster is related to plants and animals and trees; he is a teacher and healer in various personalities who, as numerous stories reveal, explains the values of healing plants, wild rice, maple sugar, basswood and birch bark to woodland tribal people" (3–4). So, too, can students come to understand the numerous complexities of Erdrich's characters' animal selves in *Tracks* when these readers learn that Nanapush of the novel is a manifestation of Nanabozho, for Nanapush is another form of the name Nanabozho. Densmore makes this identification clear: "Winabojo is the same personage as Nanapush and Nanabojo" (*Customs* 97). As students come to accept a multiplicity of names for mythic persons, manitous, and characters in the novel, they can more readily come to accept the multiplicity of selves that the ongoing process of transformation in Ojibwe life reveals. Moreover, as Vizenor tells us in a rare book, *Anishinabe Nagamon: Songs of the People:*

> The *Anishinabe* seldom told stories about *Manabozho* in the summer for fear that the trickster would be present and listening in some living

form. It was safe to tell *Manabozho* tales in the winter when he is not likely to be around as a plant or small animal.   (131–32)

In this animated Ojibwe universe, human beings, animals, and manitou spirits all have multiple interchangeable identities that bind this fluid world together in kinship or, on occasion, in enmity. Awareness of these multiple identities is the primary means of fully knowing one's relationships and powers in the cosmic landscape.

Once students are knowledgeable about this multiplicity of selves in Ojibwe oral traditional stories, they are prepared to read *Tracks* with a greater awareness of the roles of Nanapush, Pauline, Fleur, Lulu, Margaret, and the others who live near Matchimanito Lake. It is extremely helpful to know that Densmore, following Warren, cites "the entire list of 21 clans given" as "the crane, catfish, loon, bear, marten, reindeer, wolf, merman, pike, lynx, eagle, moose, rattlesnake, black duck or cormorant, goose, sucker, sturgeon, whitefish, beaver, gull, and hawk" (*Customs* 10). The crane, bear, and wolf are among the progenitors of the major families of the tribe. All these totem clan animals appear in the novel as well as fifty or so more mammals, birds, fish, and insects. Therefore one of the students' initial tasks is to keep track of the clan, animal, and family identifications of the characters as a key to profoundly knowing who they are.

After discussing individual characters' clan and animal associations in the context of specific events in the novel, I comment on the nature of the cosmic drama that *Tracks* has been constructed to be in terms of the clash of worldviews of the dominant Christian society and the "old way" Ojibwe during a time of famine and unprecedented social change, including the tragic loss of life and habitat. Lastly, I suggest that students can expand their awareness of Ojibwe culture even further by studying the indigenous art forms that image these animals on drums or on birchbark scrolls, as discussed in Carrie A. Lyford's *The Crafts of the Ojibwa*. In this manner, by moving visually beyond the scope of the text, students can come to interrelate these Native art forms to realize that these are complementary expressions of an abiding spiritual reality. Students may also be referred to materials in the works-cited list in this volume, including recordings of Ojibwe healing songs from the Midéwiwin (Densmore, *Healing Songs*) and commentary on bear songs, for instance, in Densmore's *Chippewa Music*. *Tracks,* then, can be lovingly "encased" in an expanded experience of Ojibwe culture like the way that a baby looks out on the world from her secure wrappings on the cradleboard.

Ojibwe characters in *Tracks* possess animal characteristics that create a dimension of their identities. Fleur Pillager, the focus of much of the intense action, is both wolf and bear. Erdrich delivers rich visual descriptions of the young woman who nearly drowned three times, who nearly died of disease and starvation, who repeatedly fought rescue, but who managed to survive by her wits using her hunting and medicine skills. As many fine critics such as Peter G. Beidler, Robert Gish, John Purdy, Jim Ruppert, Greg Sarris, and Annette Van Dyke have observed, Fleur is a medicine woman; yet she can manipulate her talents to harm, as a witch would. Students can recognize Fleur as bear in the opening of the novel when Nanapush carves the "four crosshatched bears" and the marten clan markers for Fleur's family's graves (5). Fleur had lost her parents, a brother, and two sisters to disease, and since the Ojibwe are patrilineal, the marten marker must belong to Fleur's mother, who married in.

Also, Fleur's bear nature is firmly established when Nanapush, as narrator, mentions that later on, stunned by cold, sickness, and starvation, he and Fleur were "numb, stupid as bears in a winter den" (7). Fleur exhibits bear qualities for healing. Since bear's life cycle of hibernation is symbolic of illness, her return to life in the spring is symbolic of strong renewed wholeness (see my *Landmarks of Healing* for a chapter on bear power in Navajo, Pueblo, and Kiowa cultures [39–83]). She also exhibits the qualities of wolf. Her disarming smile is a wolf grin. She "bared her teeth in a wide smile" (223) that everyone in the community recognizes as menacing except Nanapush, her "uncle-father." Thus these composite traits are threatening, revealing her aggressive side, whereas her slinky damp clothing, "her hips fishlike, slippery, narrow" covered by "an old green dress" that "clung to her waist" reveals her fish nature and her intimate connection with Misshepeshu, the dangerous lake spirit man (18). Students can readily see that she is both prey (fish) and predator (bear), embodying a link to watery and earthly worlds.

During the scene when Fleur gives birth to Lulu, Nanapush observes that "it was as if the Manitous all through the woods spoke through Fleur, loose, arguing. I recognized them. Turtle's quavering scratch, the Eagle's high shriek, Loon's crazy bitterness, Otter, the howl of Wolf, Bear's low rasp" (59). This keen comment verifies the multiple animal identities within Fleur Pillager, who cries out in pain. Nanapush continues, "Perhaps the bear heard Fleur calling, and answered," for a drunk bear rushed into the cabin and reared up, causing Fleur to give birth in a burst of frightful power (59). Since "it left no trail . . . it could have been a spirit bear," according to the witness Nanapush (60). It seems likely, furthermore, that the bear imparted some sacred energy to the newborn Lulu, as occurred similarly in N. Scott Momaday's retelling of an ancient Kiowa story, "Walking Bear's Shield," about the remarkable event of a bear walking into a Black Hills camp, up to the tepee of Otters Going On, as she was about to give "birth to a male child" (Momaday, *Presence* 95). Students can be encouraged to spot correspondences such as these through being assigned cross-cultural readings of Native North American texts.

Margaret, too, is bear, as indicated by her name Old Rushes Bear, her common moniker in *Love Medicine*. In *Tracks* Nanapush describes his some-times lover Margaret as "a little woman, but so blinded by irritation that she'd take on anyone. She was thin on the top and plump as a turnip below, with a face like a round molasses cake" (47). Her bear physique is imagistically reinforced in her annoyed reaction to Nanapush's reading the newspaper. " 'Sah!' She swiped at the sheets with her hand, grazed the print, but never quite dared to flip it aside" (47). This bear gesture is sustained in a scene when, perturbed with Nanapush, Margaret assaults him: "Her claws gave my ears two fast furious jerks that set me whirling, sickened me so that I couldn't balance straight or even keep track of time" (51). Margaret is also "like a young snapping turtle" and "like a watersnake or shrewd young bird" (50, 118). But it is Margaret's bear self that truly defines her personality, just as Fleur's bear side, often antagonized by Margaret, becomes pronounced in the scene when Pauline fails as midwife during Fleur's second child's birth. Pauline recalls, "She [Fleur] clutched my arms and dug in her fingers, the talons of a heavy bear" (157). Shortly after the baby was born, Pauline recounts, "She reared over me, great and dark as a fixed tree," thus merging images of Fleur as omnivorous bear and overarching tree (157–58). By studying conflated images such as these, students can come to understand the enormous complexity and fluidity of the transformational process that governs Erdrich's characterization, consistent with Ojibwe oral tradition.

Students should be encouraged to identify as many appropriate animal traits as possible for all the major and minor characters in *Tracks*. In my reading of the novel, I have found at least one predominant animal associated with each character. Nanapush is conceivably a figure representing the composite creatures and plants of all creation. Resembling hawk—according to Pauline, "He had a hawk nose and wide high cheekbones, aged into knobs" (144)—Nanapush the medicine man is also imaginatively a transgendered individual, woman-like in his sensitivity to pregnancy and childbirth. Nanapush observes, "Many times in my life, as my children were born, I wondered what it was like to be a woman, able to invent a human from the extra materials of her own body. In the terrible times . . . I gave birth in loss. I was like a woman in my suffering . . ." (167). Nanabozho the trickster here appears to be a manifestation of Mother Earth. Other characters are clearly female or male presences associated with well-defined animals. Sophie is cow: "Sophie was out front, drinking from the windmill trough. She leaned over the water, sucking it like a heifer" (80). "She was brainless as a newborn calf" (81) when it came to resisting Pauline's retaliatory love medicine powder/power over Eli.

Of the traditional hunters in *Tracks*—Nanapush, Moses, Eli, and Fleur— Eli is both badger (46) and moose, as previously indicated. In one of the most arresting scenes in the novel, with old Nanapush at home, guiding the young hunter by spiritual telepathic thoughts, Eli is able to successfully hunt moose during desperate times of starvation. Nanapush, worried that he "might be forced to boil [his] moccasins" (101) for food (a historical occurrence among some Ojibwe and Pueblos around 1900), sings a song that sharpens Eli's thinking. From miles away Nanapush states confidently, "The moose appeared. I held it in my vision. . . . [M]y song directed it [the bullet] to fly true" (102–03). After offering the liver, dusted with tobacco, to the manitous, Eli butchered the moose and tied it with sinew around himself. "He pressed to himself a new body, red and steaming . . . a moose transformed into the mold of Eli" (103–04). Eli here as moose man acquires moose consciousness and thus superior knowlege of forest plants.

Moses Pillager, a reclusive hunter and Fleur's cousin, is wolf, buffalo, and lynx. Descended from the wolfish Pillagers, Moses "had defeated the sickness by turning half animal and living in a den," Nanapush tells us. He also appears in town on occasion "long arms swinging, head shaggy and low as a bison bull" (35, 37). But more significantly, Moses is essentially lynx and keeps a cat family. He takes his protective power from the lion or lake lynx, a form of Misshepeshu, Pauline and Nanapush tell us (11, 36). At one point late in the novel Nanapush comments about Eli Kashpaw, "His hair still hung long, held in a tail down his back." Moses appears nearby and Nanapush recognizes him. "I smelled the sharp, sour warmth of cats, and knew Moses had walked behind me and was hiding" (221). It seems that in this scene Moses's and Eli's identities virtually merge as lynx, although only Moses is apparently clan related. By the time readers encounter this scene, they should be easily able to identify this physical correspondence, sensing that lynx's trait of fortitude is a crucial element of Moses's character.

Pauline in *Tracks* is readily identifiable as crane and crow, two large birds who, white and black, rise to have an unusual perspective on the human community. As a character-narrator, Pauline is eccentric to the point of caricature, especially when she admits to wearing potato-sack underwear, like a medieval ascetic, to mimic Christ's sacrifice (143). Denying her Indian identity, Pauline declares: "I was an orphan and my parents had died in grace, and also, despite my deceptive features, I was not one speck of Indian but wholly white" (137). Because of her need to transcend her earthly circumstances, Pauline fancies herself crane. From the moment we meet Pauline as "a skinny big-nosed girl with staring eyes," we suspect she is a bird person, but it is not until we see her perched in a tree that this observation is confirmed (16). As an angel bird Pauline rises—"twirling dizzily, my wings raked the air"—into the tree in response to the death of Mary, another young girl (68). Since we also see Pauline as the scavenger crow—Nanapush says: "She was the crow of the reservation, she lived off our scraps, and she knew us best because the scraps told our story"(54)—students can enjoy the task of identifying her vacillating selves before and after she becomes a nun in a black crow-like habit. Searching for the devil, Pauline says that she tries to "crane [her] neck," and she is repulsed by "Margaret's unbearable crane stews," made of relatives from the crane clan (193, 196). Students can discuss to what extent Pauline uses her white and black crane and crow identities to mirror her wrestling with love of God and the devil.

Tracks is a striking cosmic drama depicting the clash of "old way" Ojibwe and Christian worldviews during the leanest years of the early twentieth century. Even Father Damien appears gaunt and hungry, and the animals likewise are thin and weak. Erdrich makes it clear in the narrative that it is the aftermath of the encounter between cultures that has devastated the Ojibwe homelands. The animals are the physical gauge of this tragic decline in the quality of life near the medicine line. Nanapush laments that he conducted the last buffalo hunt, and even Pauline, who generally twists reality, gets it right when she states, "It was clear that Indians were not protected by the thing in the lake or by the other Manitous who lived in trees, the bush, or spirits of animals that were hunted so scarce they became discouraged and did not mate." Pauline knows that Nanapush saw the buffalo lose their minds and "their spirits slip between the lightning sheets" (139, 140). At the beginning of the last chapter, Nanapush notes that the animals are disturbed, obviously upset, sensing that catastrophe is about to occur. And like men, "squirrels bounded through the leaves, fighting pitched battles over territory" (206). The trees are coming down.

For the time being, Misshepeshu is sheltered in the lake, concealing his "horns, fangs, claws, fins," his "body of a lion, a fat brown worm," compositely emblematic of dangerous unpredictable transformation (11). As in *House Made of Dawn,* Momaday's novel, where the priest Fray Nicolas loathes the young man Francisco for dancing in the Pueblo kiva, adorned with "horns & hides" (46), and for transforming into an animal dancer during hunting season, the Christian order that Father Damien represents in *Tracks* is so disrespectful of the spiritual animal nature of the Ojibwe that the church is implicitly in collusion with the federal government and the Turcot Company that is clear-cutting the forests. And as the loss of habitat spreads like a wildfire, the ecosystem deteriorates in Ojibwe land, leaving Nanapush witness to the destruction. Nanapush is tree, akin to Nanabozho, who is stump in the old stories.

Shuddering, Nanapush "heard the groan and crack, felt the ground tremble as each tree slammed earth," and he grieved for his people (9). Nanapush declares that his "family was taken" (127). He dreamed:

> I stood in a birch forest of tall straight trees. I was one among many in a shelter of strength and beauty. Suddenly, a loud report, thunder, and they toppled down like matchsticks, all flattened around me in an instant. I was the only one left standing. And now, as I weakened, I swayed and bent nearer to the earth. (127)

Nanapush's eulogy for his fallen family is similar to his laments for the loss of cranberry bushes and the disappearance of animals. Student readers can now see that Margaret and Nanapush really are beautiful "creaking oaks" embracing Lulu in the final scene of the novel, just as Fleur becomes lakeweed and Napoleon transforms into "roots, stalks like threads, thin white blooms and blue moss. He was a powerful vine, a scatter of glowing mushrooms" (215). Erdrich's land-flesh imagery reveals how the community survives in spite of everything. As Nanapush declares to Father Damien, "We Indians are like a forest. . . . The trees left standing get more sun, grow thick" (184).

As Lulu listens attentively to the story of her people, Nanapush tells her that "old-time Indians" are "long-thinking" (180). This emphasis on reaching deep into the past to better shape the future characterizes Fleur's thinking too as the Ojibwe attempt to retain their land base. Fleur's quest in the penultimate scene of *Tracks* may appear ambiguous, but when she departs, she is undoubtedly searching for lost animals along her way, a motif from the old oral traditional stories, according to Johnston (*Heritage* 56). Her departure after carefully tending a mature garden may be seen as an act of defiance and resistance to the recent changes that have so reduced the quality of Ojibwe life. As she ties her family's grave markers, the cedar *adjedatigwin*, on the side of her cart, she symbolically carries her bear and marten people with her as she disappears, leaving no trace or tracks in the strange new light of the open forest.

Sisters, Lovers, Magdalens, and Martyrs: Ojibwe Two-Sisters Stories in *Love Medicine*

Karah Stokes

> Translation's very existence challenges our
> understanding of what a literary text is. Further, by
> asserting that things worth knowing exist outside the
> home culture's boundaries, translation challenges society
> as a whole. Translated works are Trojan horses, carriers
> of secret invasion. They open the imagination to new
> images and beliefs, new modes of thought, new sounds.
> —Jane Hirshfield, *Nine Gates:*
> *Entering the Mind of Poetry*

Even though Louise Erdrich writes novels, a genre originating in Europe, and grew up off reservation speaking English, the stories she tells are informed and ordered by Ojibwe as well as Euro-American storytelling traditions. Since her novels contain elements that must be translated for readers unfamiliar with Ojibwe culture, translation is a useful metaphor for the experience of leading students to better understand Erdrich's work.

Although she attended college and graduate school in writing and literature, Erdrich insists that a prior influence on her is the practice of storytelling, because she grew up in a household where both Native and non-Native relatives told and still tell wonderful stories (Erdrich and Dorris, Interview [Wong] 38–39). This oral influence is demonstrated formally in the episodic form of the novels and the fact that, like traditional stories of the Ojibwe, the same characters evolve through many works (Schumacher 175–76). Sometimes what happens in one story will be contradicted in another; no definitive version exists. Events happen that could be termed supernatural, which Erdrich prefers to term "unpredictable" (Caldwell 67; Chavkin and Chavkin, 224, 221). Stories continue "nose to tail" (Jones 4); sometimes people who are assumed to be dead live again in another story (for example, Leopolda apparently dies in *Love Medicine* but appears as a centenarian in *Tales of Burning Love*). These formal features of oral narrative in Erdrich's work have been noted by Barbara Pittman, Catherine Rainwater ("Reading"), James Ruppert, and others.

In addition to formal features, Erdrich's work uses characters, plot patterns, and relationships from traditional Ojibwe culture and mythology.[1] I want to outline here the patterns in Erdrich's work that may be invisible to readers unfamiliar with Ojibwe mythology. Specifically, the relationship between Oshkikwe and Matchikwewis, a polar pair of sisters in a cycle of stories commonly told by Ojibwe women to other women, gives the reader a new perspective on the relationships between women that are central to all Erdrich's novels. The relationship between these sisters, like that between co-wives in a hunting culture like that of the Ojibwe,[2] has no real counterpart in European agrarian-commercial-technological culture; therefore these paradigms make available to modern readers new possibilities for relationships between women.

Like the "tricky Nanabozho" (*Love Medicine* 236), the culture hero of the Ojibwe about whom innumerable stories are told, Oshkikwe and Matchikwewis reappear in cycles of stories. In fact, some storytellers claim they are the trickster's daughters (Barnouw 93). Their names are descriptive: Oshkikwe means "young woman" (*oshki-* means "young," "new," or "unmarried" and *ikwe* means "woman"); *matchi* means "bad" (Baraga). Oshkikwe, the younger, demonstrates the traditional virtues of politeness, modesty, and common sense; Matchikwewis, the elder, is rude, greedy, and impulsive, especially in matters that concern sex. Both mythical sisters, however, are equally loved by the Ojibwe. I see a close correspondence between these sisters and Marie Kashpaw and Lulu Lamartine of *Love Medicine*.[3] This correspondence illuminates the relationships between Erdrich's female characters, which can puzzle readers.

The bond between Marie and Lulu in *Love Medicine* fails to fit twentieth-century American assumptions about unfaithful husbands, wronged wives, and "other women" made explicit to me by my students, who often are confused and irritated by the characters' relationship. For example, if the women are bound through Marie's marriage to Nector Kashpaw and Lulu's long-term affair with him during his life, why do they grow closer after his death? If Marie is merely a wronged wife so saintly and forgiving that she assists her late husband's mistress in recovering from a cataract operation (in the chapter "The Good Tears"), why does their relationship endure and strengthen, as it does later in *Love Medicine* when they begin unofficially to run the tribe and continues to do so in *The Bingo Palace*? Certainly, one of the qualities of excellent fiction is that it escapes cliché; however, understanding these women as bonded like the mythical sisters acknowledges in a satisfying way the centrality of their relationship. Knowing the Ojibwe stories of the two sisters makes the pattern of relationship between women in all Erdrich's novels emerge from its background.

Outlining Ojibwe stories to students clarifies the relationship between Lulu and Marie in *Love Medicine*, especially since no European story pattern comfortably describes these relationships. The most obvious European analogue lies in the "good" and "bad" sisters (or stepsisters) in the tale of Cinderella. Yet there is a significant incongruity: in both the popular German version and its ninth-century Chinese ancestor, the bad sister is not only punished at the end of the story but also, and more important in its contrast with the Ojibwe tale, separated from the good sister by being maimed, having her eyes pecked out, or being killed by flying stones (Opie and Opie 155, 158). Other European versions of the Cinderella story also feature separation. Even when the good sister forgives her tormentors, she is irrevocably removed from them by being elevated far above them socially: they are commanded by her new royal husband "to make obeisance to her as their queen" (Italian), or they become her subjects and she marries them off to lords of her court (French) (Opie and Opie 157). Oshkikwe and Matchikwewis, however, remain equals and allies throughout the Ojibwe story cycle. Not only are these sisters not separated, but, in contrast with European tales in which Cinderella is always completely good and her stepsisters always completely bad, they also trade roles through the story cycle. Matchikwewis, often the bad sister, sometimes demonstrates superior virtues; for example, she rescues Oshkikwe's child when her younger sister loses him through her inattention.

The women in *Love Medicine* correspond to the mythical sisters in age, Lulu being older than Marie, and their personalities exhibit each sister's identifying traits. Like the elder sister Matchikwewis, Lulu is sexually assertive and adventurous, initiating liaisons with men who are taboo by blood relationship or marriage to other women (*Love Medicine* 74–75, 283–85). Marie, like the younger Oshkikwe, is sexually modest. At fourteen, she is not completely clear about what physically happens during sex (65). As an adult, when her husband Nector has apparently left her for Lulu, Marie does not even return the gaze of his brother Eli, who has begun to spend time at her house in Nector's absence and whispers her name late one evening (94). While Lulu presents herself as a sexual creature, wearing low-cut dresses, spike heels, lipstick, and "passion-pink fingernails" even in the retirement home (305), Marie lets her hair grow gray and favors long baggy traditional clothing (303).

Marie's and Lulu's relationships with Nector, from their meeting onward, reflect Matchikwewis's and Oshkikwe's relationships with men in the traditional tales "Bebukowe the Hunchback" and "The Star Husband" (Barnouw 93–106). In "Bebukowe," Oshkikwe (Marie) and Matchikwewis (Lulu) discover the corpse of a hunchback. Oshkikwe has "a certain power" and thereby knows that the corpse is not really a hunchback but a young man who has been transformed into one by a hunchbacked sorcerer. Oshkikwe builds a sweat lodge, drags the body inside, and brings it to life by dropping her hair oil on the stones while Matchikwewis idly stands outside. She too has hair oil but is too lazy or stingy to offer it. The corpse comes to life and regains his original form, "handsome and straight" (Barnouw 95).

Nector's early phase of excessive drinking, which stops only when Marie dries him out, mirrors the hunchback's reversible deformity. Marie claims, and no voice in the novel disputes her assertion, "[Nector] is what he is [tribal chairman] because I made him" (*Love Medicine* 154). As a young man, Nector is a serious drinker—he alludes to this phase later when thinking about Lulu causes "the kind of low ache that used to signal a lengthy drunk" (128)—until

Marie, in her words, "drag[s] him back from the bootlegger's house" and "ration[s] him down, mixing his brandy with water, until he [comes] clean" (154). Even Lulu admits that "it took Marie to grow him up" (73), transforming him from a drunk to tribal chairman, "the handsome, distinguished man" whom Lulu loves (277) and whom others admire for his looks (73). The sisters' intentions for the young man in "Bebukowe" mirror Lulu's and Marie's intentions for Nector when they are young. When the young man is revealed to be handsome, Matchikwewis, referring to the custom of polygamy, says immediately, "He will be our husband." But Oshkikwe says modestly, "No, he will be our brother." The young man sees a lot of turkeys, kills them, and presents them to Oshkikwe. She is the one he wants to marry (Barnouw 95). Like Matchikwewis, Lulu has designs on Nector from the beginning. She declares, "I could have had him if I'd jumped. I don't jump for men, but I was thinking of maybe stepping high" for Nector (71). Like the younger sister, Marie does not pursue Nector. They first meet when he accosts her on her way down from the convent, hoping to recover property he assumes she has stolen from the nuns, and she matches him insult for insult, kneeing him in the stomach when he twists her arm behind her (63). In a few moments, however, this adversarial relationship with Marie almost magically transforms into a union that lasts throughout Nector's life. What begins as Nector's prevention of a theft by a "little girl" in an instant becomes a sexual encounter with "a full-grown woman" (65).[4] Reflecting the story of Bebukowe and his mythical turkeys, Nector presents Marie with the pair of wild geese he carries (66). He takes her hand and does not let her go, an act as permanent as that in the traditional tale. To the reader who knows the story, their union makes sense and gains mythic resonance.

Another myth of Oshkikwe and Matchikwewis, "The Star Husband," is mirrored in the personalities of Lulu and Marie. Although this tale is told by indigenous people over North America, the Ojibwe version stresses the differences between the sisters and their personalities (Barnouw 104).[5] Sleeping under the stars one night, the older, sexually forward sister says that a certain bright star resembles a young man, while a dimmer star represents an old man. She would like to sleep with the young one. The younger, demure sister says she has no preference; yet the young handsome man comes and sleeps with the modest sister, while the old man sleeps with the forward one. The star husbands then take the two sisters to their lodge in the sky (Barnouw 102). In this story Matchikwewis again resembles Lulu because of her sexually adventurous nature: Lulu seduces Nector, a married man, in her car (132–33), "winks" at Bev Lamartine "with her bold, gleaming blackberry eyes" (116). The young sister resembles Marie: like Oshkikwe, Marie is modest and does not demand the man she wants—Nector—yet still she gets him.

Even though this insistence on modesty and selflessness in traditional tales may seem to counter late-twentieth-century ideals of female autonomy and assertiveness, the balance between the two sisters actually legitimizes female strength. This legitimation is suggested by two features of the story cycle. First, like the ambiguous trickster Nanabozho, and unlike the sister pairs in non-Native tales, each sister exhibits both desirable and undesirable qualities and actions. Second, in most tales the sisters remain allies: unlike Cinderella's stepsisters, Matchikwewis is never mutilated or separated from her good sister Oshkikwe by a shift in status. Like the trickster, who commits taboo acts such as marrying his own daughters, the "bad" sister never leaves the field of the story, and the tale is not assumed to continue without her.

In the one available tale in which Matchikwewis is punished for violating a taboo, it is significant that she is not separated from her sister; to the contrary, the fates of the sisters are both parallel and linked by association with the landscape. At the end of the "Star Husband" variant collected by Victor Barnouw, Oshkikwe is told by a mouse that her sister wants to marry her. She runs away across a frozen lake and tells "a man chopping a hole in the ice" that "somebody was bothering her and chasing her" (103). The man instructs her to go between his legs, which she does, and runs on. When Matchikwewis tries to follow her sister between the man's legs, he pushes her through the ice hole, saying, "That's where you belong. What sort of world would it be if people did what you wanted to do—marry your sister?" (103–04).

The most salient feature of this tale is the linking of the sisters' fates. As the man berates her, the ice hole closes and Matchikwewis is caught under the ice, where she is assumed to remain. The tale ends thus: "Now on cold winter days, when you hear ice cracking and making noises, that's Matchikwewis. But when you see a beautiful sunset on a winter evening, that's Oshkikwe" (104). Certainly, as Barnouw comments, the overt meaning of the tale is a warning against incest (105).[6] Matchikwewis is punished by being frozen under the ice, but both sisters are united in an eternal symmetry of lake and sky.

A major link between Lulu and Marie is their relationship with Lipsha Morrissey, which reflects and refracts the Ojibwe tale called "Oshkikwe's Baby" (Barnouw 112–15).[7] Raised by Marie, Lipsha discovers when he reaches maturity that Marie is his great-aunt and Lulu his biological grandmother. In "Oshkikwe's Baby," the two women live together, apart from all other persons, and Matchikwewis "takes good care of" her younger sister. Oshkikwe finds a magic pipe and "because of the pipe" gives birth to both a miraculous boy and a puppy, which she nurses together with the baby. Matchikwewis has a dream that warns Oshkikwe not to let the child out of her sight for ten days; when the younger sister briefly disobeys this warning, baby and pup are stolen by a witch who tells the baby, who is already supernaturally grown to be a young man, that she is his real mother. Oshkikwe hunts down the young man and convinces him of the truth by showing him a piece broken off of his old cradleboard when he was kidnapped; he corroborates her story by surreptitiously viewing the scar his witch-mother received while kidnapping him. Oshkikwe returns with her son just as Matchikwewis is about to go in search of them both.

In many ways the relationship between the women Lipsha's grandmother and his great-aunt reflects this tale. With his healing "touch," his insight, and his "personality [that] seems to transform personal pain into wonder" (Erdrich, Interview [Chavkin and Chavkin] 223), he is the miraculous child of Erdrich's reservation novels. Marie brings up Lipsha from childhood, but both women contribute to his spiritual nurture. Although at first he is unaware of his bio-logical connection to her, Lipsha calls Marie "Grandma" and considers her to be his mother because she took him in and raised him from an infant (*Love Medicine* 39). When Lipsha reaches adulthood, Lulu reveals that she is his grandmother and provides him with the crucial information about his parent-age that shapes his identity; his investigation of his origins drives both *Love Medicine* and *The Bingo Palace*.

June, Lipsha's biological mother, acts the role of the witch who steals the miraculous child. When he is an infant, June throws him into a slough tied in a gunnysack weighted with rocks (*Bingo Palace* 50–51). When told this story by Zelda, who fished him out of the water, Lipsha insists, "No mother . . ." but cannot finish his statement (50). These words attest that June was no mother to him. As Matchikwewis does to her stolen nephew, Marie proves her relationship to Lipsha. Growing up in the Kashpaw household, Lipsha would not have had an old-fashioned cradleboard but would probably have seen the dresser drawer he slept in later holding the family's clothing (*Love Medicine* 126). In the tale, Matchikwewis proves her relationship to the young baby-man by producing a piece of flesh bitten by the pup off the witch's buttocks (Barnouw 114). He then makes up an excuse to check his witch-"mother" for scars. In a thematic parallel, Lipsha spends time in *Love Medi-cine* and *The Bingo Palace* contemplating evidence of June's emotional scars (*Love Medicine* 363–64; *Bingo Palace* 52–55, 257–58), and the reader is pro-vided with a view of these scars that Lipsha will never have, the formative scene of her rape as a child (*Bingo Palace* 57–60). Pondering these psychic scars, Lipsha reflects that June did not act as a mother to him and decides that Marie/Oshkikwe is his real mother (*Love Medicine* 334–35). In these novels, in which relationship is based on actions rather than biology, she is. And Lulu/Matchikwewis is the older relative who cares for them both.

Information about a culture is essential to understanding the literature that springs from it, whether or not a different language is involved. Supplying students with Ojibwe cultural information allows works such as *Love Medicine* to expand our idea of what a text can be, opening the imagination to new thoughts, ideas, characters, and plot possibilities. To thus expand our minds, we must educate ourselves and our students in unfamiliar plot patterns and characters in the Ojibwe storytelling tradition that informs Erdrich's work.

The new images and beliefs, new modes of thought that Jane Hirshfield refers to, then become available to be learned from.

NOTES

A longer version of this essay appeared as "What about the Sweetheart? The 'Different Shape' of Anishinabe Two Sisters in Louise Erdrich's *Love Medicine* and *Tales of Burning Love*" in *MELUS* 24.2 (1999). Used with permission.

[1]Helen Jaskowski ably illumines European, Ojibwe, and Christian mythological elements in *Love Medicine* but does not touch on the mythical sisters I discuss here. Kristan Sarve-Gorham discusses the mythical sisters in relation to Fleur Pillager and Pauline Puyat in *Tracks* ("Power Lines"). Sarve-Gorham refers to Matchikwewis and Oshkikwe as twins, emphasizing their equality. An important value of these myths is that even though the sisters are not twins, their relationship is equal and not hierarchical based on birth order.

[2]The Ojibwe tradition of multiple wives is mentioned by John Tanner and Frances Densmore (*Customs*) and is discussed in Ruth Landes (*Ojibwa Woman* 69–71). In the hunting culture, women's work was as necessary as men's to survival, as Tanner notes when his wife leaves him, and for a while he manages to do the work of both men and women, both hunting and preparing food. Eventually, however, exhaustion overtakes him. Landes relates examples of co-wives getting along harmoniously, while other observers mention jealousy between co-wives. Densmore remarks that "jealousy among the young girls was a marked feature of Chippewa life and often resulted in spirited fighting" between women (72).

[3]The two-sisters pattern can also be seen in the relationship between Dot Adare Nanapush Mauser and Eleanor Schlick Mauser in *Tales of Burning Love*. For a discussion of the pattern in this novel, see my article in *MELUS*.

[4]Their encounter is sexual but not sex: When Marie scoffs, "I've had better," Nector understands that "we haven't done anything yet. She just doesn't know what happens next" (65). Remarking on this passage, one of the few she altered in her 1994 revision of *Love Medicine*, Erdrich says, "I wanted to clarify [Nector's] act: wrong, but not technically a rape" (Interview [Chavkin and Chavkin] 234).

[5]Another version of this tale was told by David Red Bird in 1974 and appears as "The Foolish Girls" in Erdoes and Ortiz (158–60). Although Red Bird is identified as Ojibwe, the story differs significantly from that collected by Barnouw.

[6]Barnouw notes that in another tale Nanabozho is similarly pushed through the ice as punishment for attempting to marry his sister (105).

[7]In her introduction to the Erdrich story "American Horse" in *Spider Woman's Granddaughters*, Paula Gunn Allen notes similarities between "Oshkikwe's Baby" and "American Horse," which later became "Redford's Luck" and "Shawnee Dancing" in *The Bingo Palace*.

Tracing the Trickster: Nanapush, Ojibwe Oral Tradition, and *Tracks*

G. Thomas Couser

Despite its apparent popularity among general readers, Louise Erdrich's fiction presents a number of difficulties to undergraduates.[1] Not the least of these is the influence of Ojibwe[2] traditions on her fiction. In *Tracks*, both of the narrators, Nanapush and Pauline, assume knowledge of Ojibwe culture that will not be shared by most readers; well beyond discrete and annotatable allusions to phenomena like Misshepeshu, both narrators' stories include events whose causal processes defy secular Euro-American "common sense." Ultimately, one hopes, these very features of Erdrich's complex fictions will become sources of gratification to students, but getting students past initial confusion may require special preparation on the part of instructors.

This essay does not offer a reading of *Tracks*, nor does it constitute a primer in the Ojibwe lore crucial to a full understanding of the novel. Rather, it suggests an approach to *Tracks* that uses Nanapush's relation to the traditional trickster Nanabozho as a point of entry into *Tracks*'s strange, syncretic world. If, as Jeanne Rosier Smith has said, Erdrich has created a contemporary, postmodern trickster cycle,[3] then Nanapush, as the most literal and obvious personification of the trickster, can serve as a point of access not only to *Tracks* but also to the entire series of novels. (Of the novels, *Tracks* is first in conception and chronological order, though not in publication.) Focusing on Nanapush is particularly helpful, first, because he is an immensely appealing character, more accessible than the severe, self-torturing Pauline Puyat or the mysterious, fearsome Fleur Pillager, and, second, because (to appropriate Pauline's characterization of Fleur [139]) he can be seen as the "hinge" between some of the discrepant aspects of *Tracks*: its distinct cultural codes, the Ojibwe and the Catholic;[4] its invocation of the world of myth and its specific historical context; its reliance on traditional oral narratives and its undeniable postmodernism. In sum, if Erdrich writes a kind of magic realism, then Nanapush—as trickster—is a hinge between the magic and the realism, both of which make demands on readers.[5]

That Nanapush should offer access to seemingly opposed aspects of the novel should not be surprising; after all, as he reminds us, his namesake is Nanabozho (33),[6] the traditional trickster and the central figure of Ojibwe narrative, who combines aspects of the human, the superhuman, and the animal; the sacred and the profane; the clown and the revered culture hero. Indeed, it is the very nature of the trickster to combine or reconcile opposites:

> A protean shape-changer, he is the hero of the Ojibwa creation myth
> and the ceremonies of the Midewiwin (Grand Medicine Society), medi-

ating between human society and the realm of the manitous or spirits. Sometimes beneficent, sometimes malevolent, Nanabozho is both guardian and troublemaker, bringing both order and chaos, making rules and breaking them. Embodying the pleasure of humor as well as the humor of pleasure, Nanabozho is also a playful trickster, sometimes gentle and self-mocking, sometimes mean-spirited and cruel.   (Friedman 111)

Catherine Rainwater has argued that Erdrich's fiction invokes conflicting cultural codes in such a way as to frustrate narrativity—the process by which readers comprehend narration as paraphrasable plot ("Reading" 406); this aspect of her fiction produces an experience of marginality in readers, who "must pause 'between worlds' to discover the arbitrary structural principles of both" (422). For non-Ojibwe students, at least, part of the meaning of the novel—the content of the form—is the experience of being immersed in a world whose codes are at once unfamiliar—indeed, defamiliarizing—and yet not completely incomprehensible. To eliminate this salutary pause is not, in my view, a desirable pedagogical goal, since it would erase one of the distinctive literary qualities of the novel and diminish the value of reading it; thus there is a danger of glossing the novel's Ojibwe features too readily or easily. Students should be encouraged to look *at* as well as *through* the cultural codes required to understand the plot.

And yet we do not want students to remain arrested in this state of marginality; rather, we want to help them acculturate themselves to the world of the novel. Without help in dealing with the novel's complex cultural and literary codes, students may flounder. How much culture-specific knowledge instructors wish students to have varies with the context and the level of instruction. In most scenarios, conveying detailed knowledge of Ojibwe culture is not the goal of teaching the novel. But supplying students with some background will ease their access to the narrative; introduce them to distinctive Ojibwe traditions, beliefs, and customs; and disabuse them of any notion of a monolithic Native American culture. At a minimum, students may be provided ahead of time with information on basic Ojibwe beliefs regarding the existence of manitous, including the windigo and Misshepeshu; the nature of the soul; the afterworld; and burial customs.[7]

A way of getting students to work actively with this material (and to reflect on the novel's odd and unsettling ontology) is to ask them, as they read or in class, to list events that seem to defy common sense or the laws of nature. Any such list will quickly grow long, and there is no need to make a comprehensive catalog. The point is to draw attention to the extent to which the novel transcends simple realism and to try to identify and invoke the cultural codes that make sense of these events. Such an exercise should lead students to see how notions of what's real and what's not, what's alive and what's not, what's a person and what's not, are culturally constructed. It will enable them to see that the ontology of the novel is in part derived from a non-Western culture that does not take for granted the Euro-American distinction between waking and dream states (T. S. Smith 21).[8]

As a liminal figure, Nanapush offers entrée to this aspect of the novel. Space does not allow me to explore all the correspondences between Nanapush and Nanabozho. It must suffice to say that Erdrich draws closely and extensively on the traditional trickster cycle (more so than criticism to date seems to have recognized), even as she revises, modernizes, and extends the tradition. The best way to enable students to explore this complex phenomenon on their own is to have them read a version of the traditional Ojibwe trickster story before they read the novel. One short version can be found in Arthur P. Bourgeois, another in Theresa S. Smith (160–71), and a long, comprehensive one in Victor Barnouw (13–45). No single version of an oral tradition can be considered definitive or authoritative. Thus Christopher Vecsey's chapter "Nanabozho and the Creation Myth," in *Traditional Ojibwa Religion*, serves as a useful supplement. In addition to cataloguing many available versions, he lists what seem to be the eight primary episodes of the cycle:

A. the birth of Nanabozho
B. the theft of fire
C. Nanabozho and his brothers
D. Nanabozho and the wolves
E. the death of Nanabozho's hunting companion
F. the shooting of the underwater manitos by Nanabozho involving the stump episode
G. the killing of these manitos involving the toad woman episode
H. the deluge, earth divers, and re-creation of the earth. (89)

He then summarizes (89–91) and comments on the episodes (91–96). Perhaps the crucial aspects of Nanabozho to emphasize are his inherent ambiguity and self-contradictions—suggested already—and (the physical manifestation of this) his shape-shifting ability, for the Ojibwe belief in bodily transformation is one of the givens of the novel that may stymie students. Understanding the centrality of this characteristic to the trickster may help students accept the many ways in which the novel dissolves reassuring boundaries between what Richard Drinnon calls "our [Euro-American] cherished binary oppositions: time/matter, spirit/flesh, reason/passion, sacred/profane, animate/inanimate, subjective/objective, supernatural/natural" (112), and—I would add—male/female and living/dead.[9]

With firsthand knowledge of an earlier version of the Ojibwe trickster tale—and some cultural context in which to place it—students should be able to detect, decode, and interpret Erdrich's specific references to the cycle. (For example, the story of the flood that Nanapush tells to Pauline is a bawdy transformation of the Ojibwe version of the earth-diver creation story.) In addition, informed by their knowledge of Nanabozho, students should be able to track Nanapush's behavior as a trickster. They might be asked to compile a list of incidents in which his actions in some way allude to or reenact those of the traditional trickster—for example, his snaring of Clarence Morrissey (121–22).

One of his most obvious tricksterly characteristics is his pride in his sexual exploits, which are, at the time of the novel's events, mostly behind him. The sexual repartee between him and Margaret (48, 53) is at once funny—worth reading aloud in class—and a reminder that his sexual powers are in decline. This last point raises the question of what it means to historicize the trickster. On the one hand, placing a trickster figure in a postcontact era subjects him to restraints not found in traditional stories. Though traditional tricksters like Nanabozho are far from omnipotent—they are subject to bodily pain, defeat, and humiliation—they are immortal and indestructible. By comparison, the powers of historical tricksters are diminished—largely as a result of colonialism. It may seem, then, that historicizing the trickster entails acceding to the tragic emplotment of Indian history—the trajectory of a fall from a golden precontact age. On the other hand, placing a trickster figure in a postcontact era may be a way of affirming the reality and the value of the traditional trickster—indeed, of erasing the conceptual barrier between postcontact history and the setting of the traditional trickster stories in "an age before ours, in a time we might call with Vizenor 'mythic time' . . . a different sort of time, long past and inaccessible" (Velie 124). By making a central character and one of the novel's two narrators an avatar of, as well as an allusion to, Nanabozho, Erdrich weds the world of history (as known by Euro-American texts) to the world of Ojibwe myth (as known by traditional oral stories).

Examination of Erdrich's gesture in historicizing Nanabozho by reincarnating him in Nanapush is a useful way of getting at the subtle implicit politics of *Tracks*, which alludes quite specifically to the history of the Turtle Mountain Chippewa of North Dakota, a tribe often slighted in general histories of the Ojibwe (probably because it is the westernmost tribe, the only one whose reservation is located outside Wisconsin and Minnesota). As a historical trickster, Nanapush can serve as a hinge between the traditional tale and the novel's immediate historical context. Susan Stanford Friedman has pointed out that the years bracketing the action in *Tracks*, 1912 and 1924, are respectively the first year in which Indian land allotted under the Dawes, or General Allotment, Act of 1887 could be sold (after the expiration of a twenty-five-year period during which allotments were held in trust by the federal government) and the year in which American Indians were first granted citizenship (128n4).[10] Although these dates are suggestive, the history of the Turtle Mountain tribe does not correspond exactly to the more general picture suggested by Friedman. The policy of allotment, however, is crucial to the internal politics of the novel, especially the division of the tribe into factions differing on the disposition of tribal lands. According to Sidner Larson, Turtle Mountain land was not allotted until after the Indian Allotment Act of 1904, but laws passed soon afterward allowed fee simple deeds to be substituted for trust arrangements (1); thus for the Turtle Mountain tribe the twenty-five-year period during which ownership of allotted Indian land was supposedly guaranteed to remain with a tribe member was greatly foreshortened. The machinations among the various factions of the tribe—the holdouts and the sellouts—regarding taxes on allotments and leasing or selling of allotments to timber companies are a function of this legislation.

In any case, in *Tracks* (and the rest of the series), as in other modern-day trickster novels, the trickster confronts colonialism, with its aggressive methods of making American Indians into Indian Americans. In *Tracks* a good deal of Nanapush's libido goes not into sexual conquest but rather, by means of practical joking, into sexual aggression directed at Pauline; the bawdy story he tells her of the flood, which causes her to wet herself, is a variant of the Ojibwe creation myth (149–51). In this episode, then, Nanapush may seem to represent the trickster as cruel self-gratifier, flouter of rules and violator of decorum, rather than as beneficent culture hero and creator. His retelling of the creation story, however, can be seen as anticolonial aggression insofar as Nanapush may intuit that Pauline's self-mortification is part of her desperate and deliberate endeavor to redefine herself as a member of the dominant majority race and culture. In this context, the threatening flood that the trickster barely survives can be read as the engulfing forces of Euro-American culture, into which Pauline is all too ready to immerse herself. Nanapush's sexual provocation is a reality check; his tricking her into wetting herself is a way of puncturing her conceit that she can control her body, making it over into that of a Euro-American nun. (He does not simply retell an episode of the classic Ojibwe trickster story; he adapts it to contemporary circumstances and tribal needs—thus illustrating the proper use of oral traditions and enacting the role of trickster as protector and preserver of Native culture.)

Erdrich is far from alone in historicizing the trickster; as Alan R. Velie points out, other examples abound in modern Indian fiction. But in my experience of Native American novels, *Tracks* is unique in employing a trickster as a narrator. To do this (as Erdrich does it) is to make him not merely an avatar of the trickster but an agent in the perpetuation of oral traditions—and thus an exemplar of the power of oral narrative in Native culture.[11] Insofar as his retelling of an episode of the traditional trickster cycle is contained within a larger narrative addressed to his adoptive granddaughter and devised to educate her in Ojibwe ways—including tricksterly behavior (which she manifests in later novels)—then, as narrator as well as character, he enacts the traditional trickster's role—as culture hero (as savior of Fleur and adoptive parent to Lulu) and not just as clown. (Indeed, one could argue that his chapters, which are addressed to a young woman at a particularly difficult stage of her life,

are intended to take the place of the vision quest Lulu never has the opportunity to undertake: in recounting these chapters to her, Nanapush "appears
to her" and offers himself to her, again, as her guardian and spiritual guide.)

Thus, in addition to serving as a hinge between the novel's mythological
and historic modes—mixing precontact and postcontact elements—Nanapush
illustrates and literally voices the significance and power of orality in Ojibwe
culture.[12] Unique among the novels in the series, *Tracks* is narrated from two
points of view and entirely in the first person. Yet there is a significant difference between the two first-person narrations. A way to heighten understanding of Erdrich's meaning and her achievement here is to ask students to
describe the scenarios in which the chapters are narrated. Students should
notice that while Nanapush's chapters are addressed to a specific narratee
within the novel, Pauline's have no internal auditor. (Indeed, it is hard to
imagine any scenario in which Pauline could deliver these narratives to characters within the novel. They seem designed more to rationalize her own
behavior and to glorify herself by giving testimony of her martyrdom than to
affect another's values and behavior.) Thus, while there is no doubt about the
status and circumstances of Nanapush's narratives, it is not clear whether
Pauline's narratives are truly oral—that is, actually spoken.

As we have seen, Nanapush's chapters are traditional not only in content—
drawing heavily on stories of Nanabozho—but also in purpose: their
announced goal is to reintegrate Lulu into her immediate family and her tribal
context; to challenge her rejection of her mother, who seems to have betrayed
and abandoned her; and to counteract the acculturating effects of her time in
boarding school. Nanapush seeks to make of her a good Pillager and a good
Ojibwe, and to do so he tells her stories rooted in tribal tradition in a manner
faithful to tribal practices.[13] (Stories of Misshepeshu were traditionally told
only in winter, when the lakes were frozen and underwater monsters were
less of a threat.) Because *Tracks* concludes with Nanapush's account of Lulu's
reunion with her adoptive parents, himself and Margaret, one must of necessity look to the sequels for evidence of the success of his oral rhetoric on
Lulu's values and life. Whatever their eventual influence on Lulu, Nanapush's
spoken narratives are clearly derived from traditional Ojibwe narratives, which
they artfully revise and adapt to specific historical circumstances. As the hinge
between traditional Ojibwe oral narratives and the history of Ojibwe people
in the twentieth century, Nanapush thus offers a way of reconciling the
"magic" of Erdrich's series with its political and historical "realism."

NOTES

[1]Like the novels of William Faulkner (whose influence Erdrich has acknowledged),
her fiction involves multiple points of view and inconsistent, if not contradictory, narratives. Furthermore, her characters, like his, are related by complex family lineages

that are implicit rather than explained. (For genealogical charts, see Maristuen-Rodakowski (34) and Wong, "Adoptive Mothers" (178–79) as well as app. A, at the end of this volume. To make a valuable point about surrogate parenting, Wong juxtaposes charts of biological and adoptive relationships.)

[2]In the novel the more traditional tribal name, Anishinaabe, is used by Nanapush, but not by Pauline.

[3]Smith explores the trope of the trickster in the entire series; moreover, her account of the writing of trickster stories in various traditions—notably by Toni Morrison within the African American tradition and by Maxine Hong Kingston within the Chinese American tradition—opens up ways of making *Tracks* a point of entry into an important phenomenon of contemporary writing by women more generally.

Given that most tricksters—at least in those traditions known in print—are male and given the often extravagant phallicism of the male trickster, the deployment of tricksters by so many influential women writers is intriguing. For an account of this, see Jeanne Rosier Smith (21, 22). She points out that Erdrich's female characters—Pauline, Fleur, Lulu—also display trickster-like behavior.

For selections of trickster tales from various tribes, see Bright; Erdoes and Ortiz.

Finally, Smith, like Vizenor, is interested in the trickster as an aesthetic principle pervasive in postmodernism; this insight helps challenge the assumption of a radical divide between "primitive" oral traditions and "advanced" postmodern literature.

[4]Although the cultural codes are distinct, the cultures are not opposed. Erdrich delights in showing how characters may syncretically combine aspects of both, and one implication of Pauline's acculturation is of underlying affinities between them. In setting herself up as Fleur's nemesis, Pauline is not so much her antithesis as her Christian counterpart.

[5]Significantly, Nanapush refers to having once served as a negotiator-translator between Euro-Americans and Native Americans, and at the end of the novel, he takes up such a role again, in the attempt to retrieve Lulu from boarding school. He functions characteristically at the borders or crossroads of cultures.

[6]A standard account of the trickster is found in Babcock.

[7]For a rich exploration of the role of Misshepeshu in Ojibwe culture and Erdrich's fiction, see Brehm. For short, authoritative accounts of burial customs, see Vecsey, *Ojibwe Religion*; for a more far-reaching account of the Ojibwe worldview as a system, see T. S. Smith. A detailed account of Ojibwe beliefs and customs is found in Densmore, *Chippewa Customs*.

[8]At the same time, that some of the cultural codes are Christian rather than Ojibwe illuminates the way in which the novel reflects its characters' syncretism, breaking down any notion of an inherent and utter divide between these worldviews. One of the beauties of the novel, which my emphasis on Nanapush underemphasizes, is that Pauline's chapters mix references to Ojibwe and Christian culture in a way that defamiliarizes Christian culture as well: the magic of the novel's magic realism is not entirely a function of an unfamiliar Indian worldview. For an account of the often overlooked parallels between the worldviews of Nanapush and Pauline, who are usually seen as polar opposites, see Friedman's subtle account of the novel's syncretism.

[9]With Father Damien's retroactive sex change in a later novel, Erdrich has further complicated the gender binary of the earlier novel. For an illuminating account of Nanapush as a vital hinge between the living and the dead, see Brogan.

[10]Nancy J. Peterson offers a good succinct summary of the immediate historical

context: "The United States government initially disrupted tribal ways of life by establishing reservations so that the tribes were confined within strict boundaries while white settlers claimed more territory. Then the Dawes Allotment Act of 1887 codified a turn in government policy, making it relatively easy to divide up land formerly held communally on reservations and to allot it to individual Indians. The point of allotment was to convert tribes such as the Chippewa from a communal hunting and gathering organization to a capitalistic, individualistic agricultural economy. The allotted tracts were to be held in trust for twenty-five years . . . during which time the owners would be encouraged to profit from the lands (by farming, selling timber rights, and so on) but would not be required to pay property taxes. The goal was to use the trust period to assimilate the Indians into the 'white man's' way of life so that they would become productive capitalists, capable of assuming the responsibilities of landholding—such as paying taxes—without further governmental intervention. But in 1906 Congress passed the Burke Act, which allowed the commissioner of Indian affairs to shorten the twenty-five-year trust period for 'competent' Indians. Under this act, those deemed competent were issued a fee patent rather than a trust patent; they could therefore sell or lease—or lose—their allotments. Then in a 1917 'Declaration of Policy,' Commissioner of Indian Affairs Cato Sells announced that all Indians with more than one-half white blood would be defined as competent and thus would be made United States citizens and that they would be granted fee patents for their allotments. Although the professed original intent of allotment was to maintain Indian land ownership, the policy had the opposite effect. . . . Some Indians lost their allotments because they could not pay the taxes after the trust period ended; others were conned into selling their allotments at prices well below the land's value; still others used their allotments as security to buy goods on credit or to get loans and then lost the land after failing to repay the debts" ("History" 986–87).

[11]Perhaps the best account of this aspect of the novel is James Flavin's.

[12]Erdrich's description of *Love Medicine* (before *Tracks* was published) seems to me applicable to *Tracks*: "It also reflects a traditional Chippewa motif in storytelling, which is a cycle of stories having to do with a central mythological figure, a culture [hero]. One tells a story about an incident that leads to another incident that leads to another in the life of this particular figure . . ." (Jones 4). Finally, it should be remarked that these novels were produced in collaboration with her then husband, Michael Dorris, in a process that is rare and that may owe something to Native American orature.

[13]Nanapush is not an oral narrator because of an inability to write. Rather, after a Jesuit education and exposure to the blizzard of federal documents that enabled the dispossession of his people, he became suspicious of literacy and written texts. He does not, thus, simply perpetuate but revives and adapts oral traditions in a postcolonial context.

Tracking Fleur: The Ojibwe Roots of Erdrich's Novels

Amelia V. Katanski

In 1907–08, Frances Densmore traveled the Minnesota Ojibwe reservations, recording songs and collecting related cultural information for her 1910 ethnomusicological study, *Chippewa Music I*. Among the singers she encountered was a "unique personality," a woman named Manido'gicĭgo'kwe (Spirit Day Woman), who shared her love songs and what Densmore termed "love charm songs" with the ethnographer (148). Manido'gicĭgo'kwe is as magnetic a character for readers of Louise Erdrich's fiction as she was for Densmore. A photograph shows her to be a powerful-looking woman, her hair covered with a white scarf, her head thrown back in laughter, her face lighted by a fierce smile (fig. 1). Densmore describes the singer in terms that startle with their familiarity:

> On each side of her log cabin is a little lake. Back of it stretches the forest, broken only by a wagon road whose single track is marked by stumps beneath and drooping branches overhead. In this desolate place Manido'gicĭgo'kwe and her dogs guard the timber of her government allotment, the while she gathers roots from which she makes love powders to sell to the children of men. In her hand she usually carries a small hatchet. There is a smoldering fierceness in her small eyes, but her voice in speaking is low and musical and she laughs like a child.
>
> (148)

Lakes, timber, hatchets, love medicine, tracks, and that smile—Manido'-gicĭgo'kwe bears a striking resemblance to Fleur Pillager.

Whether or not Louise Erdrich modeled the character of Fleur on Manido'gicĭgo'kwe,[1] the similarities between this most vibrant of Erdrich's characters and a dynamic, powerful, historical Ojibwe woman provide a rich opportunity to understand more fully Erdrich's work. Tracking the "historical Fleur," making sense of some of the cultural and political forces that shaped her life—such as land policy and love medicine—by using Densmore's text, images, and recordings, along with other historical sources, will encourage students to research and understand the material realities turn-of-the-century Ojibwe people experienced, as well as appreciate the resonance with which Erdrich develops and reimagines historical people, events, and practices.

Figure 1. Manido'gicĭgo'kwe, or Spirit Day Woman. Photo reproduced with permission of National Anthropological Archives, Smithsonian Institution (photo no. 448)

"A Pack of Dogs": Allotment, Dispossession, and Tribal Factionalism

Manido'gicĭgo'kwe lived on the White Earth Reservation in northern Minnesota at the turn of the century.[2] According to Melissa Meyer's history, *The*

White Earth Tragedy, those decades were intensely turbulent for the Ojibwe, whose recently formed reservations were undergoing the process of allotment into small parcels of land that would be individually, rather than tribally, owned. This process and its ramifications constitute one of the central themes of Erdrich's novel *Tracks*. Allotment policy, passed into law in the Dawes Act of 1887, was a key component in the United States government's assimilation policy. Since assimilationists like Senator Dawes believed that "the last and best agency of civilization is to teach a grown up Indian to *keep* [property]," they championed allotment policy, which would act as "the entering-wedge by which tribal organization is to be rent asunder" (Prucha, *Americanizing* 29, 43).[3] This policy was obviously not born out of selfless concern for the progress of Indian people. "Surplus" land that remained once each tribal member received his or her 160-acre allotment was made available to white settlers and, in the case of Ojibwe land, to large lumber companies, who paid pennies per acre for resource-rich property.[4] Allotted land was initially placed into trust for twenty-five years, during which the land could not be taxed or sold. But under the Burke Act (1906), which allowed government officials to shorten or cancel the trust period, allotted land, too, fell quickly into the hands of outsiders. As Gregory Camp explains, revoking the trust status gave allottees the "responsibilities of citizenship," including taxation, and their status was often changed without the allottees' consent or knowledge. Thus their land titles "became known as 'force-fee patents,'" since the landowners would be forced to pay taxes or see their allotments sold at auction ("Working" 34). Allottees like Manido'gicĭgo'kwe, whose allotment featured coveted timber resources, constantly risked being cheated out of their land by lumber companies colluding with government agents and with tribal leaders who identified more with Euro-American culture and interests than with Ojibwe values (Meyer, *Tragedy*). White Earth Ojibwe lost ninety-three percent of their land base because of allotment and subsequent speculation and fraud (Meyer, *Tragedy* 229). At Turtle Mountain, the home of Erdrich's characters, nearly ninety percent of tribal members who received fee patent titles lost their land by 1920, only sixteen years after allotment began on that reservation (Camp, "Working" 36).

In *Tracks*, Erdrich uses Fleur's struggle to retain her land to retell the painful history of Turtle Mountain dispossession. Knowing about the widespread loss of resources—and the fracturing of community—that resulted from allotment policy enables us to comprehend more easily the tensions that run through Erdrich's text. Fleur Pillager was fortunate to have an allotment on the reservation at all, let alone a plot of land covered with valuable timber like Manido'gicĭgo'kwe, since the Turtle Mountain Reservation's land base was woefully inadequate for its population, and many allottees—like most of Margaret Kashpaw's children—were forced to take land as far away from the North Dakota reservation as Montana (Camp, "Chippewa" 401).[5] Some tribal members—especially single women, like Pauline—were promised money (which was never paid) instead of land, and thus were left with nothing (Murray 32). Soon after their land was allotted, Turtle Mountain allottees were surprised to find their ownership status changed from trust to fee patent title and to learn that they owed significant fees and taxes that they had little means to pay (Camp, "Working" 34–35). Father Damien shocks Fleur, Nanapush, and the Kashpaws when he shows them the agent's annual fee list. While Nanapush protests the "impossible" numbers, claiming, "I know about law. I know that 'trust' means they can't tax our parcels," Nector quickly explains, "If we don't pay, they'll auction us off!" (*Tracks* 174–75).

While Fleur, Nanapush, and the Kashpaws—who call themselves "old-time Indians"(180)—suffer to make their payments, the Métis, or mixed-blood, Morrissey and Lazarre families gain financial and political power by participating in the market economy of the reservation and hence are able to buy up foreclosed allotments. By highlighting the tension between these two sides, Erdrich demonstrates how differing cultural approaches to land ownership threatened to undermine the stability of allotment-era Ojibwe communities, from Manido'gicĭgo'kwe's White Earth to Erdrich's Turtle Mountain. Until the allotment era, Métis and "full-blood" families had lived together in the Turtle Mountain region for mutual protection and advantage (Murray 19).[6] As the community grew increasingly at odds over land ownership and dispossession, the split between "mixed-bloods" and "full-bloods" widened, however, changing from mutual tolerance to sometimes naked hostility. Nanapush describes the Morrisseys and Lamartines as "our best farmers" early in his narrative (37), but as "the bitterness between our families deepened" over the issue of a land-settlement offer that involved selling off timber resources, he describes the "mixed-bloods who profited from acquiring allotments that many old Chippewa did not know how to keep" (63) as "ferrets" (181), a "pack of dogs" (180), and finally, simply "our enemies" (178).

The terms "full-blood" and "mixed-blood" had less to do with genetics than with cultural affiliation in Ojibwe communities at that time. Those who acted according to conservative Ojibwe standards and who valued a communal economy based on the traditional subsistence cycle were known as full-bloods, while those who embraced individual ownership and measured their success against a white standard of wealth and achievement were considered mixed-bloods (Meyer, *Tragedy* 118). Manido'gicĭgo'kwe's cultural conservatism, including her performance of traditional songs and her practice of Ojibwe language and religion, aligns her with the full-blood community that became increasingly powerless and dispossessed as the assimilationist policies took hold. Like her historical counterpart, Fleur is closely associated with the cultural conservatism that Erdrich ascribes to the "old-time Indians," signified by her Pillager name. The Pillager band had the reputation for being "the most fearsome of the Minnesota Anishinaabe" (Meyer, E-mail), even declaring war against the United States in the 1890s.[7] Fleur's status as "the last Pillager" (*Tracks* 2), along with her ties to Misshepeshu, the lake manitou, aligns her with the fierce traditionalism of her ancestors.[8] In contrast to Fleur, Pauline Puyat actively decides to turn away from Ojibwe culture, declaring, "[D]espite my deceptive features, I was not one speck of Indian but wholly white" (137). And Eli and Nector Kashpaw, brothers frequently called twins, make opposite choices. As Nanapush relates, "As he grew older, [Nector] resembled Eli more in face and less in spirit. Whereas the elder brother never lost his tie to the past, the younger already looked ahead" (209). These choices and attitudes harden into factionalism—a threat to the community's survival that cannot be disentangled from land loss.

While Margaret rages against the reservation's Métis families, "enemies that she could fight, those that shared her blood however faintly" (173), and Fleur battles her fellow tribal members, first turning her powers on Many Women and Hat, who act as surveyors for the companies that wait poised to snap up her land, and next aiming her wrath at the Morrisseys and Lazarres, Nanapush is more concerned with the growing amount of foreclosed and sold land that has gone out of the hands of the tribe and is now owned by lumber companies and banks, "the land we would never walk or hunt, from which our children would be barred" (174). Through the figure of Nanapush, the trickster at the crossroads who has experienced a Jesuit education and served as a cultural mediator and translator without turning away from a tribal orientation, Erdrich asserts that factionalism must be overcome to save the land, and to save the community itself, which she metaphorically describes as a forest (184). Nanapush, Fleur, Eli, and Margaret, regrouping as "a kind of clan, the new made up of bits of the old, some religious in the old way and some in the new" (70), work to save the land through economic syncretism. Laboring together, they maintain a collectivist approach to resource management that strongly contrasts with the ideology behind allotment policy. This new clan attempts to raise money for fees by collecting cranberry bark and roots, which they sell to a tonic dealer. They thus enter the market economy on their terms, by continuing to participate in the traditional seasonal round of gathering and harvesting (*Tracks* 176; Meyer, *Tragedy* 80–81). In the end, this spirit of accommodation is betrayed by Nector, who is determined to profit through "foresight, shrewdness, greed, all that would make him a good politician" (209). Nector, like others who have turned toward capitalism, no longer fears or respects the Pillagers or their power and does not hesitate to sacrifice Fleur's land for his own profit by using the money they had collectively earned to pay off only the Kashpaw fees.

While Manido'gicĭgo'kwe remains frozen for us in the pose of resistance in which Densmore met her, brandishing her hatchet and holding lumber companies at bay, Fleur loses her land, and, in a shocking display of power, she fells the trees herself, crushing the men and equipment who took her land from her. Pushing her cart, made of wood from her land and bearing the clan totems of her ancestors, Fleur cuts deep tracks into the ground, marking the earth with the story of her dispossession and defiance as she leaves the reservation.[9] Though the trees surrounding Matchimanito crash to the ground, the forest that is the syncretic Nanapush clan still stands, even among the ruins of the community, leaving hope for the future. The novel ends with the image of Nanapush and Margaret holding Lulu, whom they had reclaimed from the government school. As Nanapush narrates, "We gave against your rush like creaking oaks, held on, braced ourselves together in the fierce dry wind" (226). Inventing a cultural syncretism still deeply rooted in Ojibwe values, this new clan survives, brought to life by Erdrich's deft ability to interweave history and metaphor.

Love Medicine: "An Old Chippewa Specialty"

While land loss and recovery play a central role in Erdrich's novels, love medicine is her unifying trope. Moses sells Pauline the love medicine that she uses to trap Eli in *Tracks*; Lipsha, too afraid to buy love medicine from Fleur, tragicomically makes his own in *Love Medicine*; and Lipsha and Fleur—the tribe's past and future—come together as Lipsha overcomes his fear in his own quest for love and belonging in *The Bingo Palace*. Love medicine is the medicine that heals and holds people together, and it is the power that keeps them going—their means to survival, as families and as Ojibwe people. As Lipsha plans to make a love medicine that will bring his grandparents Marie and Nector closer together, he reflects, "These love medicines is something of an old Chippewa specialty. No other tribe has got them down so well. But love medicines is not for the layman to handle. . . . You could really mess up your life grinding up the wrong little thing" (*Love Medicine* 241). Indeed, the practice of love medicine is a distinctive part of traditional Ojibwe culture, and Manido'gičǐgo'kwe's example provides instruction on the proper practice and uses of love medicine in a traditional context. As Densmore reports:

> In the working of a charm it is considered necessary to use both the proper song and the proper medicine. For that reason a small quantity of the medicine is furnished to a person who buys such a song. To accomplish the desired results this medicine should, if possible, come in contact with the person to be influenced, with some of his personal possessions, or with a small wooden effigy, which the person working the charm makes for the purpose. . . . In the working of a love charm it is customary to obtain a thread from the clothing of one of the persons to be affected, or, if possible, a loose hair. Two small wooden effigies are made, one representing a man, the other a woman, and the person

working the charm binds these together with the thread or hair. The effigies are then placed in a small bag, with some of the proper medicine. This bag is worn around the neck of the person working the charm, who frequently sings the song which is supposed to make the charm effective.   (*Chippewa Music I* 20–21)

Clearly, the practice of effective Ojibwe love medicine requires considerable knowledge and training. Manido'gicĭgo'kwe, undoubtedly a powerful woman who had achieved high rank in the Ojibwe's Midé religion, served her community by selling the proper medicines, joined to the proper songs, to those who sought her aid.[10] Though Erdrich admits that she is "uncomfortable discussing" traditional Ojibwe religion in her work (Chavkin and Chavkin 100) and wisely discloses only information that can be shared with a broad audience, her descriptions of Fleur suggest that, like Manido'gicĭgo'kwe, Fleur holds a place in one of the higher degrees of the Midéwiwin: she has a drum; she has a close relationship to a powerful manitou; and, like many high-ranking members of the Midéwiwin who were considered to have too much power for any one individual, she is feared for her potential to do evil.[11] Accordingly, when Nanapush describes the medicine he thinks Fleur has worked on Eli in *Tracks*, he details a traditional love medicine that could have come straight from Densmore's ethnography. He wonders

if Fleur had wound her private hairs around the buttons of Eli's shirt, if she had stirred smoky powders or crushed snakeroot into his tea. Perhaps she had bitten his nails in sleep, swallowed the ends, snipped threads from his clothing and made a doll to wear between her legs. (48–49)

Fleur, like her cousin Moses, practices a culturally conservative love medicine appropriate to her milieu.

Lipsha, Fleur's great-grandson and the confluence of all the families that populate Erdrich's novels—Pillager, Morrissey, Lamartine, Lazarre, and Kashpaw—represents the hybridity of contemporary Turtle Mountain people. His love medicine—a "charm" designed to bring his grandparents, Nector and Marie, together—branches out from his Pillager roots to encompass contemporary Ojibwe family life, wedding love medicine and humor as survival strategies. Since he "wasn't anywhere near asking Grandma to provide me all the little body bits" that traditional love medicine required, he decides to feed his grandparents the hearts of a pair of geese, since geese mate for life (*Love Medicine* 242). Lacking adequate skill to shoot the geese, Lipsha settles for frozen turkey hearts and as an added precaution, takes them to church to be blessed with holy water, bringing together Ojibwe traditions and Catholicism and valuing both. In what is ironically one of the funniest scenes in the book,

Nector chokes on the turkey heart, which Marie serves him on a bed of lettuce, and dies. Though Lipsha briefly loses his "touch," his healing power, after Nector's death his grandfather's presence does linger, as Marie acknowledges, saying, "It's the love medicine, my Lipsha. . . . It was stronger than we thought" (255). Laughter, the fearsome power of the Pillagers, is here appropriated by Lipsha, the gentle and confused clown who doesn't really even understand the power that he has, though he demonstrates to us his potential.

Teaching students something about the precision of traditional love medicine makes Lipsha's improvised ceremony even funnier because it highlights his simultaneous ineptitude, carelessness, and insight. His seemingly haphazard medicine actually mirrors Nector and Marie's first encounter, when they make love in sight of the convent while Nector's game—two geese—flop over his arm and stare at the lovers with their "frozen" black eyes (64). Nector gives Marie the geese as a reluctant sign of his attachment to her, and nearly fifty years later Lipsha chooses the geese as the love medicine that continues to bind them even beyond death. He proves himself a budding successor to Fleur, improvising an appropriate ceremony by drawing on all his cultural influences, thwarted only by the inexperience and fear he feels because he has not yet learned of his own roots and heritage. These patterns and repetitions of medicine and metaphor connect the generations of Erdrich's extended family of characters. As each branch grows, develops, and tells its story, we see the Ojibwe roots of these characters flourish and continue, changed, but still powerful, adapting traditional ceremonies to heal in the contemporary world.

The Center of the Drum

Manido'gicĭgo'kwe provides one remaining lesson for the readers of Erdrich's novels. As she sings her songs for Densmore, she accompanies herself on her drum, and she provides Densmore with the birch bark drawings that represent each song (fig. 2). Students can, in fact, listen to her songs on the recording Densmore produced as a companion to her book. Ojibwe singers, especially the powerful members of the Midéwiwin, used pictographs scratched onto birch bark as mnemonic devices that helped them teach and remember their songs, the source of their medicine, their culture. It is useful to think of these birch bark scrolls, which could be read by any knowledgeable member of the tribe (even by members of different bands who lived in communities that had lived apart for generations), as tracks—as the guiding markers that keep culture alive (Densmore, *Chippewa Music I* 15–18). At first, it may seem inappropriate to think of Fleur as the maker of tracks, since she is never a narrator in any of Erdrich's books. Though Fleur represents silence, she possesses "an awful quiet," "like the inside of a drum" (*Tracks* 212, 58). As the center of

Figure 2. Midé song writing. Reproduced with permission from National Anthropological Archives, Smithsonian Institution (photo no. 453)

the drum, Fleur is the silence in which all sound, all story resonates. The birch bark scrolls, devices of memory, keep the drum beating, reminding Ojibwe people of their common language, heritage, and power. Nanapush and Pauline follow Fleur's tracks to generate their narratives in *Tracks*, while in *The Bingo Palace*, Fleur's "tracked-up old cabin" is itself a birch bark scroll, its very walls inscribed with the words of history, memory, medicine, strength (272). The Turtle Mountain community has survived, aware (though sometimes subconsciously) of its depth of history and meaning. Even as we learn that the tribe will build a casino on the shores of Matchimanito, the tribal narrator of the last section of *The Bingo Palace* makes it clear that there is more going on at the casino than Vegas-style gambling. As Nanapush says, "[Fleur] was the funnel of our history" (*Tracks* 178), and as her cabin becomes a casino, the Ojibwe's contemporary gamble for cultural and economic survival, Fleur, who frequently gambled to save her land, will live on as the sound of the drum, the underlying beat, the root of Ojibwe culture that runs through Erdrich's novels—holding the soil together and feeding and sustaining life. This rhythm reminds the Ojibwe who they are, as the final words of *The Bingo Palace* explain: "Our lesser hearts beat to the sound of the spirit's drum, throughout those anxious hours when we call our lives to question" (274). Fleur is thus at the center of Erdrich's imaginative universe. She herself is the love medicine, the song, the scroll that holds that world together and helps Erdrich and her characters remember and create. Thinking about Manido'gicĭgo'kwe, Densmore's footnoted Fleur, in the classroom helps us remember that the metaphorically dense, mythically powerful Fleur Pillager is formed out of the strength and experiences of historical Ojibwe women. Looking at Manido'gicĭgo'kwe's photograph, listening to her voice, and learning about the struggles she faced to keep her land furnish a concrete point of contact that allows students to begin to unpack the layers of history and imagination that form the rich palimpsest of Erdrich's fiction.[12]

NOTES

[1]This is not to say, of course, that Erdrich is literally telling Manido'gicĭgo'kwe's story in her novels. The copyright page of *Tracks*, for example, flatly states, "Nothing in this book is true of anyone alive or dead." The novel is definitely not true to the life of Manido'gicĭgo'kwe, and in fact we know very little of the details of that life. But, as Michael Dorris said in a 1986 interview, his and Erdrich's characters sometimes incorporated elements of the lives and personalities of people they had encountered but were not based solely on particular individuals (Chavkin and Chavkin 41). Erdrich mentions in another interview that she uses historical documents such as tribal rolls for inspiration for characters' names, and her familiarity with historical documents is evident throughout her novels (Chavkin and Chavkin 227).

[2]Densmore includes Manido'gicĭgo'kwe's love songs in a table on melodic analysis of love songs from White Earth. She makes no other reference to Manido'gicĭgo'kwe's location (*Chippewa Music I* 155–56).

[3]The first quotation is from an 1884 address by Senator Henry Dawes. The second is from the 1885 platform of the Indian Rights Association. Prucha's anthology is an excellent source for understanding turn-of-the-century Indian policy. See also his *American Indian Policy in Crisis* for an assessment of the Dawes Act.

[4]See Meyer (*Tragedy*) for more on lumber companies and allotment at White Earth.

[5]See also Murray (esp. 32) and Camp ("Working") for detailed accounts of Turtle Mountain history and allotment.

[6]Murray explains that soon after Turtle Mountain was designated a reservation in 1882, Métis and full-blood community members were at odds over how land should be distributed. Métis families desired individual allotments, while full-blood families preferred to hold land in common. It is important to note that neither Murray nor Camp provides the same kind of sophisticated reading of socially constructed ethnicity at Turtle Mountain that Meyer achieves in her study of White Earth. Meyer's attention to "the historical process from which [dichotomous categories such as "mixed-blood" and "full-blood"] arose" (6) results in a nuanced history of ethnicity at White Earth that is, to date, unmatched in the scholarship on Turtle Mountain. While historical differences make it difficult to extrapolate extensively from Meyer's analysis to Turtle Mountain, Erdrich's own portrayal of mixed-blood and full-blood identities and relationships is far more complex than the racially oriented terms suggest, which is why elements of Meyer's analysis are useful here.

[7]In the 1890s, members of the Pillager band occupied Bear Island in Leech Lake, Minnesota, declaring war on the United States (Meyer, E-mail).

[8]For more information on Misshepeshu, see T. S. Smith.

[9]Fleur will return in *The Bingo Palace*, to win back her land in another calculated gamble.

[10]The religion itself is known as Midé (Grand Medicine), while the organization of the religion is called the Midéwiwin (Grand Medicine Society) (Densmore, *Chippewa Music I* 13). For information on the Midéwiwin, see Densmore and T. S. Smith, as well as Vecsey's *Traditional Ojibwa Religion and Its Historical Changes*, which is the standard text, though some now call it dated.

[11]T. S. Smith explains that Misshepeshu is associated with the higher orders of the Midé religion, and those who are able to use his medicine possess considerable power. But because of this possibly excessive power, "the members of the highest degrees were routinely understood to be practitioners of bad medicine," and having access to the medicine of Misshepeshu may play a role in this transformation (108–09). Even Nanapush worries that Fleur's powers may border on the malignant.

[12]Students must be cautioned, however, that a brief introduction to basic elements of Ojibwe culture does not make them *experts*. Like other native cultures, Ojibwe culture cannot be quickly learned, and it resists appropriation by outsiders.

Family as Character in Erdrich's Novels

Gay Barton

When teachers include in their syllabi the fiction of Louise Erdrich, one of the challenges that come to mind is helping students sort out who is kin to whom and how. Several sets of genealogical charts are available to help teachers keep these relationships straight.[1] The intricacies of family relationship in Erdrich's fiction, however, are far more than puzzles to be solved. In these novels, family is character. Paying special attention to the relationship between the character of family systems and that of individuals within these families contributes significantly to students' understanding of how Erdrich's characterization works.[2] Such scrutiny makes evident two aspects of this characterization: first, the Native perspective that individual character does not exist in isolation but is part of familial and communal systems and, second, Erdrich's conviction that Native people are not doomed, as mainstream stereotypes might suggest, but have the power to rewrite inherited stories. This essay illustrates these principles with examples from three early reservation novels often included in teachers' syllabi: *Love Medicine*, *Tracks*, and *The Bingo Palace*. I have chosen three examples: the Pillager heritage; the traits shared by three generations of Puyat women (and how these traits are altered); and one inheritor of multiple family characters, Lipsha Morrissey, whom two families' characteristics redeem from the seeming doom of the others. Once teachers begin to scrutinize connections between family and individual, they and their students will find additional examples, in these and other novels.[3]

One of the most powerful and persistent family inheritances depicted in these three novels, one that students should easily recognize, is the Pillager heritage. Pillager family traits—their shamanic powers; their wolf grin; their fierce passion; and their trickster-like qualities, especially their skill at gambling and their ability to escape seemingly hopeless situations—are passed through multiple generations, from Four Souls to Old Man Pillager to Fleur, then to Fleur's daughter, Lulu Nanapush, on down to Lulu's son Gerry Nanapush and grandson Lipsha Morrissey. When we meet Lulu in the *Love Medicine* story "The Island," she tells us that as she matures, she becomes more like her mother—"a Pillager kind of woman with a sudden body, fierce outright wishes, a surprising heart" (71). The brief sketch of Fleur in that novel does in fact show her to be, like Lulu, strong, fiercely independent, unmoved by what people think of her (101). But a fuller portrait of Fleur appears in *Tracks*, which depicts her not only as passionate and independent, capable of any extreme to save her land, but also as the inheritor from her Pillager ancestors of other family traits—an extraordinary power for healing and destruction; a special relationship with the lake manitou, Misshepeshu; and a cunning skill at gambling (7–9, 19–23, 31, 114, 175). The most remarkable of Fleur's powers is her ability to survive her own death, especially death by drowning (10–11, 212–13).

The *Love Medicine* portraits of Lulu, Gerry, and Lipsha reveal that they have, in turn, inherited these Pillager gifts. Lulu knows people's secrets without being told, as if, Lipsha tells us, she had "some kind of power" (333). Gerry is, of all Lulu's sons, the one who most fully inherits the Pillager traits, seen particularly in his uncanny ability to escape from prison (see esp. 172, 199–200, 285, 341). In his escapes, Gerry is described as "eellike" or "like a fat rabbit disappearing down a hole" (200, 209), descriptions suggesting the shape-changing attributes of his namesake, the Ojibwe trickster, Nanabozho. In Gerry's son, Lipsha, this Pillager power takes the form of Lipsha's healing "touch" (230–33). Gerry and Lipsha also share another form of the Pillager "touch," inherited through Fleur and Lulu—clever Pillager fingers, adept at "understanding" a deck of cards (354).

Another family system represents particularly well both the persistent power of family character and the freedom of individuals to rewrite their family story. This is the heritage of control and socioreligious ambition that is passed down through three generations of Puyat women—Pauline Puyat; her daughter, Marie Lazarre; and her granddaughter Zelda Kashpaw. The portrait of Pauline in *Tracks* reveals traits remarkably similar to those of the young Marie in *Love Medicine*, even though Marie grows up not knowing her mother's identity. Both women are members of less-respected, even despised, reservation families. Both want to rise socially through contact with the white world, specifically by becoming ultrapious nuns. Pauline flagellates herself with extreme penances in order to be a "martyr" elevated above the common lot (*Tracks* 192), and a decade and half later, Marie longs to be "a saint" to whom the other nuns must kneel (*Love Medicine* 43). Furthermore, just as Pauline, as

Sister Leopolda, is obsessed with controlling the young Marie, Marie controls her husband, Nector, determined to make him into something big on the reservation (*Love Medicine* 88–89, 154).

This mother and daughter, in turn, bequeath their ambition and their instinct for control to Marie's daughter Zelda. Zelda's social ambitions are reflected first in her own thoughts of becoming a nun (*Love Medicine* 10, 156) and then in her rejecting the love of an Indian suitor in favor of successive white husbands (*Bingo Palace* 46–48; *Love Medicine* 10, 12). In the opening story of *Love Medicine*, Zelda's controlling nature is evident in her relationships with her sister and daughter. But *The Bingo Palace* most fully develops the portrait of Zelda as an inheritor of her grandmother's obsessive desire to control others "for [their] own good" (118). What Lipsha Morrissey says about Zelda in this novel—"I remember to fear her pity, her helping ways" (13)—Marie might easily have said of Leopolda, who "helps" her daughter by scalding and stabbing her.

And yet, as this female Puyat heritage makes clear, in Erdrich's fiction family character is not absolute fate. In fact, the similarities between Marie and her mother highlight their differences. Marie's pathological family heritage makes it all the more remarkable that she develops into the nurturing mother we see in the later *Love Medicine* stories, a woman who provides for both her own children and countless "took-ins" (253) the stability she herself had lacked as a child.[4] Ultimately, Marie takes a route to sainthood opposite that of her mother, nurturing rather than annihilating her humanity. Near the end of *Love Medicine*, Lyman Lamartine, son of Marie's husband and her rival, has an epiphany of Marie as both saint and mother, with eyes like those of "a saint carved into the wood of a broad wall" and hair standing out on each side, "white and winged" (322). Even the iron-hearted Zelda, we discover at the end of *The Bingo Palace*, ultimately finds the power to alter her grandmother's destructive heritage of obsessive ambition and control. After a lifetime of freezing out love for fear of losing control like her father, one night, imagining herself to be dying, Zelda is seized by the realization that she is "sorrier for the things she had not done"—for *not* relinquishing control—"than for the things that she had" (242). She sees that the ever-chaotic emotion of love, like the fire in her father's pipe, is the element connecting heaven and earth (245).

Not only do individuals in Erdrich's fiction alter inherited family traits through their acts of will and moments of sudden insight, but the blending of multiple families in the heritage of certain characters facilitates their ability to rewrite their prevailing family story. Although a number of Erdrich's characters are points of intersection among different families, the most prominent "hinge of bloods," as Lyman Lamartine calls him, is Lipsha Morrissey (*Love Medicine* 318). From his mother's side of the family, Lipsha has inherited the blood of the "dirty" Lazarres and "no-good" Morrisseys (64, 86)—a heritage that has destroyed his mother, June Morrissey. In his initial narration in *Love*

Medicine, Lipsha represents himself as a typical Morrissey, a no-account, and Marie at times concurs, calling him "the biggest waste on the reservation" (230). Yet Lipsha's character is redeemed from the fate of being a no-good Morrissey by his inheritance from two other families. One is his connection with Marie and Nector Kashpaw as the adopted grandchild of their old age. As *Love Medicine* closes, Lipsha realizes that he is "lucky" that June had relinquished him to Marie, since he turned out far better than King, the son she had acknowledged (366–67). Lipsha's Nanapush (i.e., Pillager)[5] inheritance also serves to mitigate the Morrissey-Lazarre curse. When his father, Gerry, tells Lipsha in "Crossing the Water" that he is "a Nanapush man," Lipsha receives his first ever sense of true belonging (*Love Medicine* 366). This Pillager-Nanapush heritage of energy, spirit, and renewal empowers Lipsha not only to escape the Morrissey-Lazarre curse himself, at least in part, but also to bring the wandering spirit of his mother home at the novel's end.

Lipsha's portrait as a "hinge of bloods" is further developed in *The Bingo Palace,* a novel that accentuates all sides of his multifamily heritage. Both the reservation gossips and Lipsha himself emphasize his Morrissey-Lazarre tendency toward aimlessness and a wasted life (7, 73). At the same time, the novel deepens Erdrich's portrait of Lipsha as beloved Kashpaw grandchild, a heritage embodied in Nector's ceremonial pipe, which Marie gives to Lipsha rather than to one of her blood children (see *Bingo Palace* 28–29, 39; *Love Medicine* 260).

Yet *The Bingo Palace* depicts Lipsha primarily as a Pillager, inheritor of this family's medicine powers and its talent for survival. As an infant thrown into a slough, Lipsha, like Fleur, had survived death by drowning, a survival in both cases growing out of their family bond with the lake manitou, Misshepeshu. Zelda's puzzled question about Lipsha's early ordeal, "*So why weren't you drowned?*" (51), is answered by the vision in which he relives his drowning but also recalls a presence with him in the slough, a "lion-jawed" creature with "fins and horns" that rocks, cradles, and saves him (218). The connection between Lipsha and Fleur is made explicit when the two meet in the chapter "Mindemoya." Lipsha introduces himself as her great-grandson, and Fleur teaches him about love and the value of land (131–45, 151). Although the ending of *The Bingo Palace* is somewhat ambiguous, the last chapter suggests that Fleur's final legacy to Lipsha is a second survival of death, this time death by freezing (272),[6] the very element that had taken the life of Lipsha's Morrissey-Lazarre mother.

Just as Lipsha is twice saved from death by his connections to the Kashpaw and Pillager families, so also does this dual family heritage save him from the fate of becoming in truth a no-good Morrissey. In his vision, Lipsha comes to understand his mother's deadly legacy. Just as June had been abandoned repeatedly, left to freeze, left to starve (*Bingo Palace* 27–28; *Love Medicine* 86–87), she abandons Lipsha as an infant (*Bingo Palace* 217). And yet, as

Lipsha's narration in *The Bingo Palace* comes to a close, he seems to find within himself both the "staying power" of his Kashpaw grandmother (123–24) and an enduring Pillager strength as he determines not to repeat the Morrissey-Lazarre family pattern. Curling himself around the baby in the snowbound car, Lipsha muses:

> I know it will be a long night that maybe will not end. But at least I can say . . . here is one child who was never left behind. . . . At least he always had someone, even if it was just a no-account like me, a waste, a reservation load. (259)

Although Erdrich's characterization of her multiple protagonists is highly individualized, much of this individuation grows out of traits of the families to which these characters belong. And yet, despite the power of these family systems, her characters are not absolutely trapped within them but are able to vary the inherited patterns. Through her strongly realized individual characterizations Erdrich defies the dominant culture's stereotypes of Indian people, while at the same time her powerful depiction of family character illustrates how fully her fictional world is grounded in the familial and communal ethos of tribal life.

NOTES

[1]See appendix A, by Nancy L. Chick, at the end of this volume for charts that combine information from the various novels. Margie Towery fuses information drawn from Erdrich's first three novels and two early short stories into a single chart (116–17). Peter G. Beidler and Gay Barton include separate sets of charts for each novel (through *The Antelope Wife*) to reflect variations among the novels. Because of these changes in family structure from novel to novel, to avoid confusion teachers will want to convey to students only the genealogical information revealed in the novels on the syllabus.

[2]Teachers who wish to pursue further the connections among generations in Erdrich's families should see Connie A. Jacobs's chapter on family stories in her *Novels of Louise Erdrich: Stories of Her People* (esp. 134–45). This chapter provides the most extensive discussion of Erdrich's family systems to date. Teachers may also wish to consult Sarve-Gorham, "Power Lines"; Van Dyke, "Questions"; Wong, "Adoptive Mothers"; and Towery.

[3]One other example developed in the three novels being considered here is the heritage of "Kashpaw shrewd-mindedness" (*Tracks* 40) handed down through three generations of Kashpaw men. *Love Medicine* develops the similarities between Nector Kashpaw and his son Lyman Lamartine. *Tracks* goes back in time and hints at Nector's similarity to his father and reveals Nector's own self-serving shrewdness emerging in childhood. *The Bingo Palace* demonstrates how Lyman carries the self-centered aspect of his father's shrewdness to an extreme, as he turns himself into a "dark-minded schemer" (5).

[4]As it expands and alters the Puyat family story, *The Last Report on the Miracles at Little No Horse* increases readers' sense of this family lineage of bitterness and twisted relationships as being an inescapable curse. Thus the history added here makes even more remarkable Marie's ability to alter the pattern.

[5]Although the family of old Nanapush of *Tracks* is separate from the Pillagers, after Nanapush gives his name to Fleur's daughter, later "Nanapushes" are actually Pillagers by blood. Nanapush himself leaves no blood descendants. Lulu and her first three boys (*Love Medicine* 109) wear the Nanapush name by adoption.

[6]As Fleur takes the place of "the boy out there" caught in the snowstorm (*Bingo Palace* 272), technically the boy could be the baby in the snowbound car with Lipsha. The penultimate chapter reveals that a "hostage" has been found in good condition (268), and it is the baby who is the real hostage. Nevertheless, a reader of *The Bingo Palace* would feel it far more likely that Fleur is giving her life in exchange for that of her great-grandson than for that of an unnamed white baby. (Of course, readers who learn the rest of the story from *Tales of Burning Love* and *The Last Report on the Miracles at Little No Horse* discover the relationship between Fleur and this infant hostage. But *The Bingo Palace* itself gives no hint of this realtionship.) Furthermore, the opening chapter of *The Bingo Palace* suggests that Fleur may be waiting to die until she can find "a successor, someone to carry on her knowledge" (7). The only candidate the novel offers for this position, unlikely though he may be, is Lipsha.

Does Power Travel in the Bloodlines?
A Genealogical Red Herring

Nancy L. Chick

Students of Louise Erdrich's North Dakota novels—*Tracks, The Beet Queen, Love Medicine, The Bingo Palace, Tales of Burning Love,* and *The Last Report on the Miracles at Little No Horse*—will invariably struggle to map the Pillager, Lazarre, Morrissey, Kashpaw, and Adare family trees. The resulting genealogical sketches do not solve the frustration of attempting a chronological, linear, genealogical reading of these books.[1] My attempts with these family trees are included in this volume (app. A, p. 211), not to suggest definitive genealogies, but to illustrate the confusion in these maps and to encourage classroom discussion on the value of family trees in Erdrich's works.[2] What should emerge from such discussions is that these charts do not bring order to Erdrich's fictional universe, because this universe is not defined by blood relationships or the resulting blood quanta of mixed-bloods and full-bloods. Such family trees are tangled maps validated primarily by Euro-American political structures, not by the Native structures woven into the texts.

In *Tracks*, Pauline says that power travels in the bloodlines (31). Coming from perhaps Erdrich's least reliable narrator, Pauline's observation should serve not as confirmation of these relationships but as a warning to close readers. Determined to prove that she is no longer Native, Pauline and her statement about the path of power represent assimilation, the Euro-American push toward whiteness, and the erasure of the Native.

In the nineteenth and twentieth centuries, this push was carried out in many ways, not the least of which was the government's efforts to diminish the lands owned by Natives by dividing them into individual tracts and then, as in the specific case that is the historical basis for *Tracks*, manipulating the sale of those lands through the quantifying of blood. First came land allotment with the Dawes Act of 1887. This General Allotment Act divided tribal lands by distributing individual tracts to heads of families. Such private land ownership was intended to "civilize" the Natives, to teach them the American way of individuality, self-reliance, and a proper work ethic by ceasing tribal ownership and nomadic living patterns. The Dawes Act also specified that lands not granted to heads of families were designated surplus and sold to white homesteaders who would become the Natives' neighbors and teach them American ideals. A twenty-five-year trust period would theoretically give the families a chance to establish working farms and to become civilized before they were complete landowners, as well as protect them from losing their land. The allotment process, however, quickly diminished the amount of land owned by Native American tribes and converted it to land owned by whites. Then the

Burke Act was passed in 1906, canceling the Dawes Act's twenty-five-year trust on land titles and thus any protection from whites eager to acquire the remaining lands. The Burke Act opened the door for individual Natives to sell their lands, which dramatically sped up the loss of Native lands.

A careful explanation of the way this system was carried out and the lack of familiarity the Natives had with mortgages, the law, paper money, and even reading is essential to a historically accurate understanding of this period. The 160-acre tracts were not enough for a family to survive on, and many of the plots were not fit for farming, especially not year-round. As *Tracks* illustrates, it was not uncommon that the primary income of a family—sometimes the only way to survive—came from selling those individually owned plots of land or leasing them to large-scale agricultural or timber companies. Further, because it was not easy to survive on such small unarable plots, the allotment system made Natives vulnerable to fraud and land loss through the inability to pay taxes.

An understanding of the White Earth Reservation in northern Minnesota helps clarify the history played out before *Tracks* begins. Not only was there a tuberculosis epidemic on White Earth at the same time as it struck in the novel, but the specific history of land allotment is nearly identical. Like most other reservations after the Dawes Act, White Earth suffered tremendous land losses. Unlike other reservations, though, White Earth faced another specific threat lurking at its edges. In the novel, the timber companies are perched just beyond the boundaries of the reservation, waiting for tribal unity to weaken and individual families to surrender their lands once they are hungry enough. The same situation prevailed at White Earth, where the lumber companies were aided by legislation.

According to Richard H. Weil, the allotment process at White Earth was different from that at most other reservations because of the interests of these lumber companies and their effect on legislation. In 1904, the Clapp Rider and Steenerson Act granted an additional eighty acres of land to heads of families at White Earth, along with the right to sell the timber. In 1905, on the day of the new allotment, the tracts ran out more quickly than they should have because the process had been corrupted, and it was mostly full-bloods in the back of the line who were left without the timber-rich allotments (see Weil; Meyer).

Next, an Indian Appropriations Act was passed in 1906 with two amendments in Minnesota added by the author of the 1904 Rider and the former attorney for the local timber companies, Congressman Moses E. Clapp. The result of these Clapp amendments was that all restrictions on selling, taxing, or mortgaging mixed-bloods' past or future trust land at White Earth could be removed immediately at the allottee's request (Weil 77). The brief Clapp amendments had even further consequences because they had failed to define mixed-blood, so the Supreme Court finally defined mixed-blood as any degree of white ancestry (Weil 78).

As a follow-up to the Clapp amendments' references to mixed-bloods and full-bloods, a series of anthropologists were sent to the reservation to establish genealogical charts and a blood roll. The methods of designating a mixed-blood are significant: the anthropologists examined such physical features as hair, eyes, teeth, and skin. The results were dramatic. The blood roll decreased the number of living full-bloods to only two percent of the tribe, increased the number of mixed-bloods to ninety-eight percent, and significantly broadened the number of people eligible for land under the Clapp amendments (Weil 81).

The designation of blood quanta generally emerges from an impulse to erase the demonized image of the savage or a romanticized desire to save the Native through assimilation. Either way, it essentializes Native identity into one measured by blood. On White Earth, though, the designation of blood quanta was primarily economic. The mixed-bloods who received the recent allotments rich in timber were free to sell both the new *and* the original 1887 allotments to timber companies. Further, since a mixed-blood would now be any Native with even a drop of white blood, most of the tribe was vulnerable to the fraudulence and manipulation of the companies. It was clearly in the interest of those who wanted the resources on the allotted lands to designate as many mixed-bloods as possible. Within weeks of the amendments, over 250 mortgages had been taken out against reservation lands, and within four years, three-quarters of the allotments had been sold (Weil 79).

The effect of these designations was to render the mixed-bloods somehow less Indian and more white, because of the blood relationship with whites, as well as to imply that mixed-bloods were better able to negotiate the world of whites and play the games of business, commerce, and the American way. (Full-bloods first had to be designated "competent" to sell their lands.) These laws, genealogies, and blood rolls represent the steady attempt to replace the Native with white—not just by land grabbing but by literally and legally erasing a person's status as a full or true Native. Clearly, these genealogical charts and blood rolls—instruments of Western science, the United States government, and the lumber companies—served to harm the tribe by dividing the people by blood quanta and then by further dividing the lands.

This is the historical tension behind *Tracks*, the earliest setting for most of the families our students may try to map out in their own genealogical charts and blood rolls. However, Erdrich's stories are not merely jigsaw puzzles waiting to be pieced together in chronological time or mapped out in genealogical sketches. The privileging of linear time and blood relations that determine traditional family trees is not tribal in origin, and is certainly not the ordering mechanism of Erdrich's fictional universe. As Weil notes, the tribal meanings of mixed-blood and full-blood are not tied to blood quanta and specific lineage; to the Ojibwe, the degree to which a person maintained the traditional cultural and economic customs determined whether or not a person was mixed-blood. The tribe could consider even an assimilated white to be a full-blood, a designation at odds with the American legislative actions of the period (73). The loyalty to tribal unity, interests, and traditions was more important than specific racial makeup or family tree, contrary to what students today may understand. Reflecting this outlook, Erdrich (a mixed-blood herself) has created characters who are advocating not racial purity but instead loyalty to cultural tradition and preservation of their land, no matter whose blood flows through their veins.

Hertha D. Wong asserts that adoptive relationships represent a survival mechanism against tribal, family, and personal disintegration in a postconquest tribal reorganization ("Adoptive Mothers" 183). While this view is indeed applicable to relationships in Erdrich's novels, adoptions, extended families, and even extensions of the term *family* beyond bloodlines predate contact with Europeans (for examples see Van Kirk; White). Such practices had long been used to confirm social and economic alliances among tribes. This mode of bringing outsiders into the fold confirms the transformative, elastic construction of tribal families—a construction lost in genealogical charts.

Pauline's dictum that power travels in the bloodlines may be true in that the government's final power to acquire Ojibwe lands came with the designation of bloodlines and the lines between mixed-blood and full-blood. However, the common interpretation—that this quote reinforces the strength of blood relationships in the stories—is incomplete and incorrect. Erdrich's stories contradict the government's essentialist declarations by revealing that Indian-ness is not tied to blood quanta, nor is it passed down through the blood. If neither power nor culture travels in the bloodlines, then a genealogical chart becomes irrelevant and even misleading. Even an adoptive chart is incomplete. It is finally a narrative chart of who passes on stories to whom that is far more significant to the relationships in the novels and more helpful to students who are trying to decipher those relationships.

Such a chart would reflect a different set of relationships, even giving families to apparent orphans. For instance, in *Tracks,* the vision of Nanapush as the sole survivor of his family after the 1912 tuberculosis epidemic changes dramatically when we consider his narrative relationships. Just as his family dies, he becomes father to seventeen-year-old Fleur—also orphaned by the disease—by rescuing and nursing her and encouraging her with songs, eventually giving her stories to rely on (4, 7). Later, after Lulu, Fleur's daughter, rejects her mother for putting her into a boarding school, she also becomes Nanapush's descendant, as he even calls her Granddaughter (1). This direct address on the first page of the novel guides us to a different understanding of bloodlines, so his five chapters to Lulu serve as our eavesdropping on this narrative cultural parenting. We could also add Eli to the list of Nanapush's narrative children, making the elder far from the last Nanapush.

In contrast, Pauline's chapters reveal a narrative orphan. She rejects her family even before the tuberculosis epidemic, refusing to speak their language and hoping her father's concerns that she might "fade out" in the white town she moved to would become real (14). She is thus orphaned from her blood relatives and, more important, from her cultural heritage. She dismisses Nanapush and demonizes Fleur, learning nothing from the two characters who can teach Pauline the most. The only stories she seems to accept after a point are biblical, yet she takes them too literally, even distorting them to persecute Fleur and others, not surprising from a person untrained in stories. Of course, the other stories that she tells are often made up, exaggerated, and untrue. Further, unlike Nanapush's chapters narrated to Lulu, Pauline's chapters appear to be narrated to no one, suggesting that she passes her stories on to no one. She may become a mother, but only biologically. She is certainly no narrative mother to Marie.

Reading this way, through the lens of narrative relationships rather than of bloodlines, requires our students to reevaluate their definitions of culture and how it is passed on. It encourages them to focus on storytelling, on the stories themselves, and how the stories are read or heard, instead of viewing relationships according to essentialist definitions of race or culture. The resulting charts would look less like the linear parentage of genealogies than a web of narrative relationships fanning out from a character to everyone who passed on the myths, stories, tales of their heritage. This is the map we should have our students sketch as they read, an assignment that helps them step outside of their Euro-American worldview of scientific quantifying of blood and linear genealogies, into the Native view of tribal identity, narrative parenting, and stories as the blood of the culture.

NOTES

[1] I am indebted to my assistant Jen Anderson for sorting through my tangled and illegible genealogies and putting them into computer format.

[2] I am particularly wary about giving the impression that the charts included in appendix A are supposed to be fully "correct" or authoritative, not only because the information on these families changes with new revelations in each novel (and Erdrich clearly is not finished with these families) but also because of the point of this essay. These charts are not reflective of the Native or mixed-blood worldviews expressed in Erdrich's novels.

"Patterns and Waves Generation to Generation": *The Antelope Wife*

Alanna Kathleen Brown

The Antelope Wife, published in 1998, demonstrates Louise Erdrich's profound belief in the integrative power of stories to hold together the chaos and buoyancy of human lives. Although Erdrich continues to address the difficult subjects of sexual neediness, alcoholism, even suicide, it is the exploration of abject self-pity, blind jealousy, possessive lust, and longings that cannot be satisfied in this life or the next that is remarkable about this novel. Erdrich has the extraordinary ability to put into words confusions of the heart so deep that they can only be expressed, not unraveled. What balances the starkness of her insights is Erdrich's wonderful Indian humor, her belief in serendipity, and a calling to love that will not be denied.

There are three strategies that unite what on first reading might be experienced as an awkward dispersion of narrative voices. The first and most obvious organizational tool is the four-part movement of the novel, more like acts of a play than a continuous narrative. In part 1, some early family histories are introduced and juxtaposed against Klaus Shawano's kidnapping of the Antelope Wife in modern times. The love triangle of Rozin; her husband, Richard; and her lover, Frank, is also introduced. This unit ends with a surprising turn of events when Frank develops cancer, and Rozin and Richard's treasured daughter, Deanna, is inadvertently asphyxiated. Part 2 introduces us to a mother's profound grief at the loss of a child and Richard's and Klaus's descent into urban drunkenness, twisting in their despair and constant longing. Deanna's twin, Cally, also nearly dies, from a fever, but is saved by the comic and irrepressible Almost Soup, her reservation dog. A number of years pass before the events of part 3 take shape. This is a hopeful unit after significant personal tragedies have befallen many characters. Cally, as a young woman, returns from the reservation to Minneapolis in search of identity and meaning. Her mother, Rozin, also returns, to pursue a law degree, and in a terrifying scene where a carnival ride goes out of control, she breaks loose into her profound love for Frank. Their subsequent wedding day, however, is severely disrupted three times by Richard, the ex-husband, who cannot release Rozin. In a terrible final and ironic effort to control his world, Richard shoots himself to death in front of the newlyweds on their wedding night. Part 4 depicts Rozin's heart-rending struggle with the windigos, the spirits of her dead child and first husband, who haunt her. The love and the discoveries in this final movement for all the characters create surprising and satisfying resolutions. For a brief time, the patterns of the present, the electrifyingly beautiful ways in which lives weave and unweave themselves and then become unstrung and must be beaded again, are clear.

The metaphor of beading, as reflected in the series of questions that end the text—"Who is beading us? Who is setting flower upon flower and cut-glass vine? Who are you and who am I, the beader or the bit of colored glass sewn onto the fabric of this earth?" (240)—is the second unifier. The unexpected plot twists and changing narrative perspectives, combined with the constant references to beading activity, unhinge readers from commonplace narrative developments and resolutions and guide them to watch how people attempt to sew others into their storylines. All the characters disrupt as well as harmonize with the longings and family destinies working themselves out through the narratives. In truth, we human beings are, at once, the beaders and the beaded of our lives.

The third unifying device, however convolutedly revealed, is the intricate involvement of seven generations of families. The various narratives encompass about a century and a half of human activity, stretching from the mid-1800s to the Indian life of Gakahbekong (Minneapolis, Minnesota) in the 1990s. Two lines of descent are particularly important. The most prominent is that of Rozin's family and the seven generations, outlined below:

1. Elderly woman (killed by Scranton Roy in a military raid on a peaceful Ojibwe village)
2. Midass, married to a Shawano man (survives the Blue Coat massacre)
3. Blue Prairie Woman, later named Other Side of the Earth, married to a Shawano man (breast-feeds the dog named Sorrow when her baby girl is lost; is a lover and beloved of the deer people; leaves her surviving family to look for the lost daughter)
4a. Baby girl, later named Matilda (carried away on the back of a dog in the Blue Coat raid; raised as a young child by Scranton Roy; later adopted by a band of Antelope; Antelope Wife is her descendant)
4b. Mary and Josephette (Zosie) (the first set of twins, whom Other Side of the Earth leaves to search for the lost daughter)
5. Mary Shawano and Zosie Roy, both involved with Augustus Roy (the second set of twins, who are the grandmothers in the text)
6. Aurora and Rozin Roy (the third set of twins; Aurora dies at age five of diphtheria; Rozin first marries Richard Whiteheart Beads and then Frank Shawano)
7. Cally and Deanna Whiteheart Beads (the fourth set of twins; Deanna dies at age eleven of car asphyxiation)

The other critical lineage is that of Scranton Roy. The numbers in parenthesis before the names of the characters indicate which of Rozin's seven generations the Roy characters generationally match.

(2) Quaker parents who live in Pennsylvania

(3) Scranton Roy (the young soldier who kills the elderly Ojibwe woman; defects from the military chasing after the Indian baby cradled on the dog; nurses and names the baby Matilda; marries Peace McKnight)

(4) A son (born to Scranton Roy and Peace McKnight before Peace dies in childbirth)

(5) Augustus Roy, married to Zosie Roy, lover of Mary Shawano (Augustus suffers a suspicious death; the twins are murder suspects)

(6) Aurora and Rozin Roy (the two lineage lines combine)

(7) Cally and Deanna Whiteheart Beads

Although little is said of Frank Shawano or his brother, Klaus, the ancestors of Rozin did marry Shawano men. The text also makes clear that Richard Whiteheart Beads is descended from the young pregnant woman who received the ruby-red whiteheart beads Augustus Roy gave to Midass in exchange for marriage to her great-granddaughter Zosie. But genealogy is not merely located in human lives in *The Antelope Wife*. As the title affirms, human beings are not isolated from the other beings who surround them.

While contemporary Euro-American literary criticism uses the term "magical realism" for what I discuss in this essay, that term distorts the Ojibwe worldview. What those from Western civilization would describe as the impossible or miraculous is understood as a part of experiential and historical reality in Ojibwe culture. Blue Prairie Woman loved and was loved by a deer as a young woman. Her acceptance by the deer community and her protection of them is incorporated in the special song Other Side of the Earth sings, which calls the antelope to protect Matilda, the young daughter, when the mother realizes that she has found her stolen child only to die. The Antelope Wife, alias Sweetheart Calico or Mrs. Klaus, and her daughters are descendants of Matilda and the Antelope People. While Rozin does not know that she and the Antelope Wife are related through their mutual great-grandmother, Blue Prairie Woman, Rozin does know the story of the deer love and understands that along with Ojibwe blood, she is a descendant of an Ivory Coast slave, "a bastard son of a bastard daughter of a French marquis" (35), a windigo ("bearwalker, bad holy dream-man" [35]), and the deer people (55–59).

More comic in treatment, but no less significant, is the descent of Almost Soup, the wry and insightful commentator on dog survival in a human world. Almost Soup is descended from Original Dog, named Sorrow, who was the puppy nursed by Blue Prairie Woman when her breasts were swollen with milk for the lost child, and who will later be killed to sustain Matilda's survival. Again and again in the text we see the generosity of our fellow beings acting on behalf of human beings. A deer warns Blue Prairie Woman of the coming Blue Coat attack, and thus she has time to attach her child's cradleboard to a camp dog for a getaway. The antelope accept Matilda into their band. Almost

Soup draws Cally's essential spirit self into his safekeeping when Cally's fever brings her close to death. Windigo Dog harasses besotted Klaus with raunchy jokes and personal attacks that force Klaus to see what a poor excuse for a human being he has become. Later Windigo Dog, or perhaps another dog, jumps at and is hit by a lawn mower in the critical moment that saves the blades from cutting through Klaus's face. For Erdrich, human beings express the divine no more than all the creation around them. As she affirms at the beginning of part 2, "Neej," human beings "are as crucial to [the beading of the pattern] as other animals. No more and no less important than the deer" (73).

The spirit connection between two-leggeds and four-leggeds is explored in one of the primary love stories that drive the novel. Love is a complex and multifaceted power in *The Antelope Wife*, and Klaus and Sweetheart Calico establish a core antithesis that many people experience at the heart of passionate love. For Klaus: "Earth and sky touch everywhere and nowhere, like sex between two strangers. There is no definition and no union for sure" (21). For Antelope Wife: "It was so powerful, her traverse of boundless space. Time is endless in the heart, where sky meets earth" (222). Klaus can only keep her close by binding her wrist to his with a material called sweetheart calico, violent acts, the seduction of alcohol, and obsessive focus. Who is the woman who has aroused such ardent desire? Why is the book named for her?

The best way to unfold that identity is to pay attention to how Antelope Wife is physically described, how Klaus and Cally change in their responses to her, and what little we discover about her through her own actions and words. Like June in *Love Medicine*, Antelope Wife is enigmatic, someone who triggers profound responses in the mind and heart, but who herself says little. The descriptions of her at once communicate her physical appeal and other-worldliness, especially for those living in the metropolis of Gakahbekong. We first see Antelope Wife and her daughters through the eyes of Klaus. They are "[c]lassy, elegant they set a new standard of simplicity" (23). When he watches them dance at the Montana powwow, "they are light steppers with a gravity of sure grace." Antelope Wife holds a fan of feathers of a red-tailed hawk, birds who "follow the antelope," and her cry is that of "the high keer of the stooping hawk—a lonely sound, coldhearted, intimate" (24). He decides to kidnap her away from her sleeping children, for "[h]er breath has the scent of grass and her hair of sage. I want to kiss her forever" (30). Later descriptions draw attention to a "sloping deer-haunch bottom" (46), "her black stiletto heels like shiny fork prongs" (105), and a perfume that "smells like grass and wind" (107).

Her own actions when in Gakahbekong continue to communicate the crisis of a confused, "cracked apart," caged antelope spirit. When she first realizes that Klaus has somehow stolen her away, "she knows she is caught" and fights to get free, "breaking her teeth on the tub's edge" in the process (30). When trapped in Klaus's life back home in the city, she randomly calls Montana 406 prefixes, hoping to reach family and friends, but she doesn't understand how to use the telephone. She tries to run away, is gone for days at a time, but finds "that no matter how fast or how far she walked, she couldn't get out of the city. The lights and car panic tangled her" (52). Klaus had been able to steal her away using knockout drugs. He keeps her hooked to him through alcohol, but ultimately, no matter what he does, what he believes, what scenarios he tries to inscribe for her and himself, Antelope Wife remains aloof. "Klaus, she never dreamed about or remembered. He was just the one she was tied to, who brought her here" (51).

For Klaus, Antelope Wife is his "nibi," his water. "I only want to be with her, or be dead" (22). "I'll do anything for her. Anything except let her go" (30). In a revealing but ironic statement Klaus also says of himself, "Wait, I say, digging for the real me, which I can't find. Where is it and where am I and worst of all who?" (48). What attracts him to Antelope Wife is also what he fears in himself: "I'm just a city boy. . . . I don't know what you people do, out there, living on the plains where there are no trees, no woods, no place to hide except the distances. You can see too much" (33). Interestingly, the unshaped but observant Cally is also drawn to, but fears, Auntie Klaus. "I can't stop thinking of her and I see things. I see her in my deepest thoughts. I dream. . . . Her scent is like sun on my back, like cool rain, like dust rising off a waterless, still, nowhere-looking road" (108). In another penetrating comment about Antelope Wife, she states, "For she alters the space of things around her and she changes the shape of things to come" (106). But is Antelope Wife such an active agent? Or is it rather that her presence for some can arouse the awareness of loss and incompleteness, and thus of longing for the essence of who she is?

The resolutions of Klaus's and Cally's conflicts surrounding Antelope Wife reveal a great deal about who they are, but also about who Antelope Wife is. Klaus must go through a program for detoxification, acknowledging the violence of kidnapping and drugging his beloved Sweetheart Calico and of literally binding her to him to ensure that he will be loved. He must face the pain that his Sweetheart Calico "[l]ives in another body, walks in a different skin. Thinks different thoughts I can't know about. Wants a freedom I can't give" (155). But he will discover that he can release her. He will untie the false romantic vision he has been telling himself to hold on to her, and he will ultimately go on the long walk to where city and countryside meet in order to free her. Cally's process is a different one. In the face of all the powerful personalities that surround her, she struggles to validate her own experience, to become her own person (118). Initially, she is filled with many more questions than answers (121). But her process of self-discovery is among the most important in the book. When Cally suddenly hears the word *daash-kikaa* ("cracked apart") that her great-great-great-grandmother cried out when being bayoneted by Scranton Roy, the breach among the seven generations can be healed, and Cally steps into her naming power (4, 196, 213). In her coming to self-awareness about who she is as a person, who she is in relation to family and her people, and in Antelope Wife's gift of Matilda's indigo-blue beads to Blue Prairie Woman (Cally's sacred Indian name), the family "cracked apart" so many generations ago is momentarily made whole. Readers are given the opportunity to comprehend the multiple facets of what Indians call "a long story," to understand not only how that story is resolved in modern times but also how the initial disruptive violence has played itself out through the seven generations again and again (Augustus's mysterious disappearance; the kidnapping of Antelope Wife; the death of Deanna, whose Indian spirit name is Other Side of the Earth; the four sets of physical twins, as well as Richard and Frank, people who are at once one and divided in their love for Rozin). It is Cally who finally understands that as a "namer" she has been sent here "to understand and to report . . . Gakahbekong. The city. Where we are scattered like beads off a necklace and put back together in new patterns, new strings" (220).

As readers, we may wish that Klaus's and Cally's growth through their interactions with Antelope Wife might not be costly to her. But they are. Antelope Wife is a special being in the world, a descendant of the original peoples, and her enclosure in the isolation, neediness, and fears of modern city life wound her. When freed, she knows which direction to go, but "stumble[s] over the uneven ground. . . . a staggered leap, a fall, an attempt to run" on her way home at last (230). We can only wish her a spiritual recovery as she finds her way.

The other major love story does end joyously despite the odds. It is the tale of Rozin Roy, Richard Whiteheart Beads, and Frank Shawano. As Rozin lets us know, she never asked to be a wife with a lover (40), but her intimacy with Frank is so complete that "once it started, the closeness, it became continual and I at once lived within him just as he came alive in me so that wherever I go and whatever I do I am making love to him" (41). In contrast, her experience of Richard is with a love that is "deep clawed, hungry." His neediness is so constant, his moods are so variable, that Rozin learns to lie so that she can "at least control his anger by keeping him satisfied at the appearance of his world" (58). The differences in the love the two men offer are stark. Of course, Rozin gravitates to Frank, a womanly hearted man, generous, nurturing, passionate, loyal, devoted, responsible. But Richard cannot imagine or permit Rozin's loss.

Others' comments about Richard reveal a great deal about his character. Thinking of his alcoholism and his hold on a bottle, his daughter Cally recalls that "[it] was difficult to get anything away from him at all" (197). Klaus speaks of "Whiteheart's imaginary surround" (43) and of the toxicity of his character (50). At his death, Zosie states the psychological as well as physical truth when she tells Rozin, "He never came to, Richard. He never made it" (185). In fact, Richard is a dark coyote figure, one so totally self-absorbed that he only brings chaos and tragedy to himself and others, though he perceives himself to be the abandoned one, the victim of circumstances or of those he loves. He needs control, denies responsibility, and trusts that his charisma will carry him through whatever confronts him. But Frank is too immediate, too caring, too vulnerable, too honest (as his name implies) to be toyed with or diminished. Frank knows himself, and he has tasted perfection. He wants to bring that completeness into form once again as a baker, as a lover, as a human being: "I make the staff of life. . . . That is my calling. But I will never stop attempting the blitzkuchen" (117). His tenderness and love, acceptance and strength, in caring for his brother, Klaus; his sister-in-law, Sweetheart Calico; his sister, Cecille; his beloved's daughter, Cally; and most certainly in his devotion to Rozin when she is in utter despair, haunted by the windigo ghosts of Deanna and Richard, compose an extraordinary portrait of a loving man. Because he is so true, Rozin knows that their love can keep Richard "alive and keep him safe" (193) in the collective consciousness of all their lives. Theirs is a triumphant, even comic, ending.

Louise Erdrich begins the novel with a world torn asunder for the Ojibwe. The crisis is so severe that names and meaning cannot hold together. Blue Prairie Woman / Other Side of the Earth must choose among children, among lives. She does recover her daughter, but only to die soon after. Nonetheless, since a language of connection and a spiritual worldview still survive, Other Side of the Earth can call to the Antelope People to aid her daughter. The spaces reflected in her two names seem as if they would have no meaning in the modern world of Gakahbekong, "where everything is set out clear in lines and neatly labeled, where you can hide from the great sky, forget" (25). But yearnings deeper than consciousness bring people's "colliding histories and destinies" together (197). As Erdrich well understands, "It is longing makes us do the things that we should not. Even longing for the good, for love" (227). When Klaus kidnaps his beloved Antelope Wife and ensnares her in the city, he both reveals his need and frustrates it, for one cannot experience boundless space while fearing exposure and emptiness. Klaus will do the inward work he needs to do; Richard will not. "Into all of our lives there comes a great uncertainty to foil us. Either, as is the case so often, we retreat in fear to guard what we know, or we shrug off those worn skins and go forward" (197). In Frank and Rozin's love, in Cally's self-discovery, the Ojibwe world centers itself again, this time in the throbbing heart of the city where so many Indians now live.

An Indigenous Approach to Teaching Erdrich's Works

Gwen Griffin and P. Jane Hafen

It is their turn now,
their turn to follow us. Listen,
they put down their equipment.
It is useless in the tall brush.
And now they take the first steps, not knowing
how deep the woods are and lightless.
How deep the woods are.
                    —Louise Erdrich, "Jacklight"

In her poetry and fiction Louise Erdrich has created an enduring voice of survival and resistance that is based on her Ojibwe tribal identity experiences. In teaching her works, we try to establish a context for Erdrich that values the ideas of Native scholars and authors and represents our own survival as Native Americans. We use a combination of academic training and personal experience to encourage students to increase their cultural sensitivity to and awareness of the issues in Native literature.

This style of criticism resists those literary and political agendas that often subvert tribal voices in favor of dominant ideologies that rarely recognize or affirm the experiences of American Indian people. For example, to emphasize the ultimate extermination of the "Vanishing American," John Neihardt ended *Black Elk Speaks* with the famous quote, "There is no center any longer, the sacred tree is dead" (230), a statement Black Elk did not make.[1] Likewise, Catherine Rainwater mourned the tragic demise of Gerry Nanapush and Lipsha Morrissey in the ambiguous final chapters of *The Bingo Palace* ("Ethnic Signs").[2] These conclusions presume a destructive notion of "assimilate or perish" and do not reflect modern Native views. To foster a more inclusive literary dialogue, Craig Womack (Muskogee Creek) observed that "Native viewpoints are necessary because the 'mental means of production' in regards to analyzing Indian cultures have been owned almost exclusively by non-Indians" (5). Therefore, an indigenous approach to teaching Native literature will begin to incorporate what Indians have to say about themselves.

As tribal peoples, we need to tell our own stories and develop critical processes that will help readers engage with Native literature while respecting tribal-specific cultures. The Native studies scholar Robert Allen Warrior (Osage) has noted, "In comparing our histories and our contemporary lives with those of other American Indian people, we see the complexities of our various pasts and have an opportunity to learn how other people have confronted the same problems we face" (123). Openness to learn from the experiences of others is part of the process of dialogue. As Native readers and scholars, we are aware of particular cultural aspects of Native literature that others may not readily recognize. As a result, when we are part of the dialogue, we can all begin to appreciate the broadness and complexities of these texts. What makes the inclusion of Native voices in this exchange significant is what Warrior calls a "pro-Indian awareness of our own strength" (123).

As critics and teachers of Erdrich's works, we all have a responsibility to explicate the text and examine the imaginative process Erdrich uses as she weaves complex Ojibwe tales. However, an indigenous approach recognizes intellectual sovereignty (Warrior's "pro-Indian awareness") and emphasizes what Gerald Vizenor (White Earth Chippewa) refers to as "survivance," the capability of survival and endurance (*Manifest Manners*). Native peoples share a history of significant, deliberate loss of culture and language through federally sponsored initiatives such as the reservation system, boarding schools, and relocation. Consequently, this characteristic of survivance is extensive in Native literatures but often ignored by non-Native readers who are unaware of the complexities of overcoming what Erdrich called "cultural annihilation" ("Where" 23). Our goal in the study of Native writers is to provide students and teachers with the tools necessary to uncover the sources, the cultural points of view, of the stories and poems they read and thereby to better talk about the significance of Native writing, survival, and tribal-specific identities.

Despite the ever-increasing amount of information available on the Internet or through television and movies, the knowledge many of our students have about American Indian peoples is often faulty. On the basis of their experiences with popular movies like *Dances with Wolves* or television programs like *Doctor Quinn, Medicine Woman* and the stereotypes promoted in today's culture, most students come to Native literature classes armed with what they believe is factual information about all Indians. Consequently, students have difficulty comprehending the extended family relationships and circular time elements in Erdrich's writing. They lack an awareness of an Ojibwe point of view as opposed to a Taos Pueblo or Dakota or German point of view— unfortunately, for many of these students an Indian is an Indian is an Indian.

The methodologies we employ in teaching Erdrich vary somewhat but have the same objectives of recognizing tribal voices and contextualizing Ojibwe points of view for readers so that they can begin to appreciate specific Erdrich texts. While we are not Ojibwe tribal members, we do benefit from what Louis Owens (Choctaw-Cherokee) calls a "remarkable degree of shared consciousness and identifiable world view" (20), which exists among us even though we are from diverse tribal and cultural backgrounds. This collective experience enables us to focus on issues distinct to teaching Native literature that center on the complexities of being Indian and the issues surrounding tribal identity. Duane Champagne (Ojibwe) points out, "Non-Indian scholars are usually driven by theoretical or disciplinary issues that abstract segments of Indian history or culture for analysis, and often do not reflect the study of a culture as a holistic entity" (183). Our approach attempts to introduce students to some of the important tribal elements in Erdrich's works.

Tribal Context

Elements that constitute a context for reading Native authors include a people's history, literature, religion, traditions, and geographic location or place. Studied separately, each element provides only a partial view of a culture. Viewed together as sections of an integrated foundation, they begin to present an outline of a specific tribal worldview.

Students should begin their introduction to Erdrich and her tribal identity with the works themselves. While her work may be linked with that of other writers of loss—for example, Jewish or African American authors—Erdrich's stories are about indigenous survival. She explains, "Contemporary Native American writers have therefore a task quite different from that of other writers" ("Where" 1). "In the light of enormous loss, they must tell the stories of contemporary survivors while protecting and celebrating the cores of cultures left in the wake of the catastrophe" ("Where" 23). Accordingly, her writing portrays differing points of view about Ojibwe culture, from very traditional to very disconnected experiences, each one a valid representation of Ojibwe life.

The culture and characters portrayed in Erdrich's poetry and fiction represent a range of contemporary Ojibwe people, their environment, and conditions. From the descriptions of Turtle Mountain Reservation in *Jacklight* to the communities in Erdrich's first five novels (*Love Medicine, The Beet Queen, Tracks, Tales of Burning Love, The Bingo Palace*) to the language and myths of *The Antelope Wife*, students can begin to appreciate the diversity that is Ojibwe culture. The survivors in her writing—runaway boarding school children forced to wear green dresses "the color you would think shame was" (*Jacklight* 11), some characters who are displaced and alone like June Morrissey—endure by being brought back to the geography that informs their tribal identity. Erdrich explains, "In a tribal view of the world, where one place has been inhabited for generations, the landscape becomes enlivened by a sense of group and family history" ("Where" 1). That connection to the land is preeminent in Erdrich's writing and in all Native writing.

Erdrich herself represents diversity, as varied influences interact with her Turtle Mountain Ojibwe heritage. The poetry of *Baptism of Desire* depicts how Erdrich syncretized elements of Catholic faith and German tradition with Ojibwe culture. *The Crown of Columbus*, written with Michael Dorris, intertwines the atmosphere of the academy with Native experience, and *The Blue Jay's Dance* portrays a writer's world and mothering feminism.

Nonetheless, to prevent students from elevating Erdrich to a position of possessing an ultimate and singular voice of the Ojibwe and to reinforce the idea of multiple voices among tribal communities, we often include works of other writers from the same cultural background. The narrative of Ignatia Broker (*Night Flying Woman*) provides a good framework of the old ways and stories present in Erdrich's writing. The essays and novels of Vizenor, the novels of David Treuer (*Little, The Hiawatha*), as well as the poetry and short stories of Jim Northrup (*Walking the Rez Road*), also contribute contemporary views of Ojibwe life. The works of these writers extend information about Ojibwe culture and broaden the dialogue of Native literature.

Paula Gunn Allen (Laguna Pueblo–Lakota) reminds us, "The significance of a literature can be best understood in terms of the culture from which it springs, and the literature is clear only when the reader understands and accepts the assumptions on which the literature is based" ("Sacred Hoop" 3). Each reader brings different assumptions to the text, depending on his or her own given culture, upbringing, and contact (or lack thereof) with Indian people. To create a common background for our class, we incorporate a group project that can be used in conjunction with any of Erdrich's novels.[3] The project introduces students to a tribal context and allows them to discover for themselves aspects and concepts of Native American studies. Spoonfeeding background information to students would be simple, and there are ample resources. However, to even begin to think about tribal perspectives, most students need to make major paradigm shifts. To engage them beyond mere intellectual exercise, instructors must consider the methodology and process to be as crucial as the content. Our teaching strategy allows students to engage the complexities of Ojibwe tribal interweavings in Erdrich's works.

Group Assignment

Each class member is assigned to a group. The group researches information about Ojibwes that includes the following components: an origin myth, the traditional tribal name, a summary of tribal culture, a description of the tribe's geographical location, significant tribal historical events, and current tribal status. The results of the assignment are presented orally to the class. The group decides on the method of presentation, which may include panel discussions, game show formats, cooking demonstrations, and attempts at material culture exhibits. Part of each student's evaluation is based on how well the group coordinates its information and recognizes the diverse points of view in Erdrich's texts. Additionally, each member of the group prepares a seven- to nine-page essay that correlates the information from individual research or addresses critical issues pertinent to the Erdrich work selected. Students use MLA style and documentation and include a bibliography of all resources for the essay and the presentation.

By working in a group, individual students are challenged to reassess natural tendencies to assume there is only one way to look at a text or only one valid idea of representation. Although they cannot enter into or completely understand the culture of tribal communities, they may begin to see some parallels in group dynamics where differing opinions or multiple approaches to solving a problem may occur. Because information in their particular research categories overlaps, students also begin to see the integrated intricacies of tribal cultures.

From this project, students should learn that several versions of origin stories exist for the Chippewa/Ojibwe/Anishinaabeg. They should also recognize that the stories may have been told by non-Indian translators and must be recontextualized. Nevertheless, these traditional stories shape the Ojibwe worldview and are alluded to in various Erdrich texts. The apparent discrepancies and multiple versions of stories the students uncover in this part of the exercise bear witness to the fact that there is diversity not only among the more than five hundred Indian nations in this country but also among the various bands of Ojibwe. In addition, identifying the traditional tribal name, Anishinaabeg, allows students to encounter the significance and power of naming among the Ojibwe bands, within families, and for Erdrich's characters. Erdrich exemplifies this power in *Love Medicine* with Moses Pillager's name in "The Island" (82) and Margaret Kashpaw/Rushes Bear (96).

The summary of Ojibwe tribal culture may encompass many components including traditional and contemporary social structures, gender divisions and constructions, material cultures, foods, dwellings, and arts. Students often discover that in some secondary literatures discussions of cultures primarily focus on male behaviors or employ racist or prejudicial language. This discovery provides a good opportunity to examine the role of historical or anthropological texts in creating and perpetuating negative stereotypes of Indian peoples. Allen points out that "the most favored theme in novels about Indians by non-Indians is the plight of the noble Indian who is the hapless victim of civilized forces beyond his control" (*Sacred Hoop* 77). Stereotypes of "Vanishing Americans" are presented in classic works such as Oliver LaFarge's *Laughing Boy*, Frank Waters's *The Man Who Killed the Deer*, and James Fenimore Cooper's *The Last of the Mohicans* (*Sacred Hoop* 74).[4] Erdrich writes against these stereotypes by creating strong characters like Fleur Pillager, who defies the conventions of "Indian princess" and "squaw" in *Tracks*, and Nector Kashpaw, who reinvents and reclaims his own version of popular Noble Savage imagery in "The Plunge of the Brave" chapter of *Love Medicine* (see Hafen, "Let Me").

Students can also learn about land issues and tribal distinctions through descriptions of geographic locations. Discussion of land is frequently connected with Ojibwe historical events, such as the White Earth timber scandal. In 1897, the White Earth band lost a quarter of a million acres of timberland, taken by the State of Minnesota as tax payments. These forfeitures were ruled illegal in 1977 by the Minnesota State Supreme Court, and in 1985 the federal government offered to "settle" the losses for $17 million, or the 1910 value of ten thousand acres.

In addition, a historical review helps students connect past to current and future events. For example, early Ojibwe encounters with Jesuits illuminate the influence of Catholicism. The 1934 Indian Reorganization / Wheeler-Howard Act is the foundation for Nector Kashpaw's role as tribal chairman in *Love Medicine*. Similarly, students profit from research on the tribe's current status by recognizing, particularly regarding *Tracks*, that American Indians are part of contemporary living cultures, not historical relics. Powwow cultures and gaming issues may be connected with *The Bingo Palace*. An examination of Ojibwe arts can illuminate the beading tropes in *The Antelope Wife*, and an analysis of economic statistics can correlate with *Love Medicine*. Creative students sometimes contact various Ojibwe bands for current and more detailed information.

By the time the students complete the oral presentation and the essay, they should be able to read the works of Louise Erdrich with sensitivity to tribal issues. Accompanied by a survey of other Ojibwe writers, they can also place Erdrich's writings within a larger cultural context and begin to recognize the Ojibwe tribal elements of her works. The study of these literatures helps students acknowledge tribal voices, endurance, and survival. While we have used this method to teach Native literature over a period of several years, Womack provides a good description of our perspective on a "new" Native criticism as one that "emphasizes unique Native world views and political realities, searches for differences as often as similarities, and attempts to find

Native literature's place in Indian country, rather than Native literature's place in the canon" (11).

When our approach to teaching Erdrich's works is successful, students gain insight into the uniqueness of Ojibwe culture and awareness of Ojibwe points of view. They understand that multiple Ojibwe voices exist in contemporary and historical texts in testimony to their survival. They have the tools they need to begin to expose the fallacy that "an Indian is an Indian is an Indian."

NOTES

[1]Julian Rice notes Neihardt's intentionality in *Black Elk* (qtd. in Wiget 215): "Neihardt's fictive terminations include some of Black Elk's most widely believed emotions: 'you see me now a pitiful old man who has done nothing, for the nation's hoop is broken and scattered . . . and the sacred tree is dead' (*Black Elk Speaks* 270). But his actual last words recall his youthful desire for revenge before returning to tribal protection: 'the next day we were supposed to make peace. We made a law that anyone who should make trouble in the fort (agency) should be arrested and tried and if found guilty he would be punished. Two years later I was married' (*The Sixth Grandfather* 282)." (See also Alexie, *Indian Killer* 58.)

[2]See also Judith Freeman, whose book review of *The Bingo Palace* ends, "Instead, both characters are consumed in a storm of mystical imagery, and disappear into a white and disturbing void."

[3]The group-project approach was developed from a discussion on teaching Native literature with Craig Howe (Lakota).

[4]These texts are regularly part of college reading courses. Additionally, Cooper's Indians become prototypes of the vanishing Noble Savage.

Sites of Unification: Teaching Erdrich's Poetry

Dean Rader

Most readers of Louise Erdrich's novels are well aware of the complex thematics of her fiction. Cultural loss, the burden of the past, the sense of renewal, the support and endurance of family and community connect *Love Medicine, Tracks, The Bingo Palace*, and even *The Last Report on the Miracles at Little No Horse*. In each of these works, Erdrich explores how characters deal with the tensions between the individual and the communal; how public and private expectations, transgressions, and responsibilities get reconciled over the course of a life, a generation, a century. In her poetry, Erdrich articulates these questions with a startlingly intense bimodal desire. By this I mean that her poems tend to work on two distinct levels at once—they feel shockingly personal and profoundly tribal. Because the lyric poem lends itself to a particularly intimate voice and because poetry still carries the impulse of chants and prayers, I argue that even though this bimodality exists in her fiction, it finds its most acute articulation in Erdrich's poetry.

Above all else, Erdrich's poems are about desires—desires to unify seemingly opposing ideas, worldviews, and gestures. These desires may come from Erdrich's endeavors to reconcile significant dualities in her own life, such as her Ojibwe and German American ancestry and her interest in both Ojibwe and Catholic religions. Rather than totally embrace one system of belief or one religion, Erdrich seeks hybridized visions that coalesce elements from both. Similarly, Erdrich extends this desire for unification to her poetry. Instead of writing a typical Western lyric or re-creating American Indian oral performances, Erdrich merges aspects of both into one unique poetic expression. Through poetry, Erdrich combines modes of cultural dwelling, enabling her to reside in two worlds at once, a gesture that serves as a metaphor for many Native Americans and Native American communities who feel torn between Anglo and Native cultures.

Not only does Erdrich seek unity within individual poems, but she also seeks a unified vision articulated by each of her books of poems. So, as a kind of broad introduction to her poetry, I offer a quick overview of her books, a strategy that sets the stage for my readings of her poems and for more detailed explorations of her poetry in the classroom. Erdrich's first two individual collections of poems, *Jacklight* and *Baptism of Desire*, appeared five years apart. Though *Jacklight* was published in 1982, the same year as *Love Medicine*, most of the poems were written in 1977 and 1978. Essentially divided into four sections—"Runaways," "Hunters," "The Butcher's Wife," and "Myths"—*Jacklight* contains forty poems, most of which focus on the themes suggestive of the sections in which they appear. The only poem not to appear in one of these sections is the title poem, which begins the book set off from the rest in its own self-titled segment. The other sections focus on Native issues, particularly on how to conciliate potentially divisive relationships between whites and Natives, Natives and the land, and the realities of the present and the constant presence of the past.

In an interview in 1986, Erdrich claimed that she would not publish any more poems, in part because she thought her poetry had become too private. Nevertheless, three years later, her second and only other collection of poetry appeared, *Baptism of Desire*. While *Jacklight* garnered a number of positive reviews, *Baptism of Desire* did not fare as well, perhaps because of the book's intensely private tone. In a kind of endnote to one of the sections, Erdrich remarks that most of the poems in the book were written between two and four in the morning, while she was pregnant. Not surprisingly, these poems possess an interiority and intimacy that is missing from *Jacklight*. Formally, though, the books mirror each other. Like *Jacklight*, *Baptism of Desire* is divided into four sections of poems and one section in which only one poem appears; however, none of these sections bear titles. Indeed, it would appear as if titles are unnecessary, since many of the poems work to reconcile the tensions of Catholicism, faith, deliverance, and, as the title of the book suggests, desire.

While it seems unlikely that many professors teach both books in the same course, it is worthwhile to talk about the two in relation to each other. To me, *Jacklight* works more like an epic poem, whereas *Baptism of Desire* functions like a lyric. The thrust of Erdrich's first book is tribal, communal, and mythic; it invokes Ojibwe myths, rituals, language, spirituality, and a sense of history and solidarity. In the poem "Jacklight" the point of departure is two Ojibwe words, and in poems like "Windigo," "Rugaroo," and "Old Man Potchikoo," Erdrich recasts critical Ojibwe myths. *Baptism of Desire* works differently. These poems are personal, even mystical. At times, they feel like prayer. In essence, the *Jacklight* poems begin inward and radiate outward toward a narrative, public space, whereas the poems from *Baptism of Desire* seem to begin outward in a system like the church or Catholicism and spiral inward toward a more lyrical, more private space. Hence her books read like two maps charting routes and means of passage between public and private worlds. And just as this desire to unify two distinct worlds gets played out on the macro level of the two books, so it gets played out on the micro level of the individual poems.

It's often dangerous to define someone's poetics in terms of recurrent themes or traits; thus I should acknowledge that Erdrich's poetry is not limited to the strategies I sketch below. Instead of seeing these suggestions as taxonomies, I use the following methodologies as springboards to a larger pool of interpretations that illuminate the poems more fully than I can do here. That said, I would like to explore how individual poems unfold into sites of unification. In these texts, we find Erdrich coming to terms with seemingly contradictory issues: public and private spheres, Anglo and Native cultures, human beings and nature, nature and civilization, human beings and the divine, the sacred and the secular, poetry and prose. In "Jacklight," for instance, the speaker seeks a union between those who inhabit the woods and those for whom the woods are the boundary to otherness. For Erdrich, the woods represent not only cultural peripheries but also the liminal areas of language itself, as stated in the poem's epigram linking hunting, violence, and sexuality. Referring to "Jacklight," Erdrich claims that "if our relationships are ever going to be human . . . men have to follow women into the woods and women likewise. There must be an exchange, transformation of power shared between them" (Interview [with George] 243). If the "we" in the poem represents women, then Erdrich clearly associates females with animals and nature, while associating men with hunters and their mechanized and violent world.[1] Of course, we are also supposed to imagine the "we" in the woods as Natives, likened to animals through their desire for concealment from white killers. In this poem, students tend to want a hard and fast corollary for the "we"; they want the speakers to be either women *or* Indians *or* animals. I try to explain why it is important for Erdrich to conflate the three, how an amalgamation of these entities enables the poem to inhabit, concurrently, the realm of politics, art, history, humanity, and the environment.[2]

Similarly, in "Windigo" and "Rugaroo," also from *Jacklight*, Erdrich calls attention to the dangers of drawing strict boundaries between human beings and nature. In both poems, Erdrich creates a dangerous character bent on stealing people's bodies and souls. In "Rugaroo," the antagonist is a man who drinks Sterno and Vitalis, a kind of hunter, like the men in "Jacklight," who want to ferret out the hidden other. Similarly, the Windigo, a flesh-eating spirit with a man buried inside it, is driven by a hunger to consume. Reminiscent of William Butler Yeats's "The Stolen Child," "Windigo" turns on the tensions between wilderness and civilization. In both poems, a child is lured away by seductive sylvan creatures. Here, the Windigo speaks like a lover: "Oh touch me, I murmured, and licked the soles of your feet. / You dug your hands into my pale, melting fur. // I stole you off" (79). But as in many Native American stories, the trapped person is released. Here, both the child and the Windigo are transformed through contact with each other. "Windigo" and "Rugaroo" dramatize the rupture between wilderness and civilization, even if the wilderness is within. With some help, students should be able to see how "Rugaroo" and "Windigo" serve as metaphors for a kind of monstrous pursuit to devour or eradicate Indian cultures, lifestyles, and myths. Additionally, students might be asked how these poems serve as explorations for a kind of mystical connection with the natural world, an approach that participates in literary and poetic history when grounded in the tradition of the pastoral poem.

Two other poems, "The Woods" and "The Strange People," also enact moments of union between human beings and nature. The speaker in "The

Woods" actually embodies earth by wearing the woods themselves, transforming physical ritual into spiritual excursion. By the end of the poem, through a kind of sylvan mysticism, body and tree become one. Likewise, in "The Strange People," Erdrich fuses body and doe, a trope that she later expands in *The Antelope Wife*. In this poem, Erdrich plays with the concept of shapeshifting, a facility that allows people to turn into animals and animals into people. Because the doe, a trickster, possesses the ability to move from animal to human being, she comes back from the dead, after being murdered, to perform an act of revenge on her killer. No doubt, this retaliatory act mirrors more complicated historical and cultural desires for requital against the encroachment and aggression of whites.

Erdrich localizes this white or male tendency toward violence in the iconic image of John Wayne in her famous "Dear John Wayne" (*Jacklight* 12–13) a text that in my mind is one of the best and most important American poems of the last fifty years. A tour de force of public and private tensions, the poem weaves dialogue from Wayne's character into the text of the letter itself, so that not even Erdrich's language escapes Wayne's influence. Wayne's imposition onto Erdrich's text mirrors the ways in which Erdrich and her friends are unable to escape the culture and technology that Wayne's image embodies, just as her ancestors could not elude the drive for cultural domination that brought the white settlers, and, by extension, Wayne and the cinema to Ojibwe territory in the first place. The words that Wayne speaks are words of eradication, removal. Erdrich's description of the wrath of the white settlers against the pagan Indians not only finds resonance in many biblical narratives but also is seemingly justified by scripture. In tone and theme Wayne's words evoke a myriad of Old Testament admonitions:[3]

> His face moves over us,
> a thick cloud of vengeance, pitted
> like the land that was once flesh. Each rut,
> each scar makes a promise: *It is*
> *not over, this fight, not as long as you resist.*
>
> *Everything we see belongs to us.*   (12)

In passages like Ezekiel 25.17 ("And I will execute great vengeance upon them with furious rebukes; and they shall know that I *am* the LORD, when I shall lay my vengeance upon them") and Exodus 22.24 ("And my wrath shall wax hot, and I will kill you with the sword; and your wives shall be widows, and your children fatherless") one hears the language of the angry father before enacting punishment on the infidels, a language that gets reencoded in Wayne's. Like the face of God, from which there is no hiding, the dark gaze of Wayne, a virtual panopticon of judgment and retribution, remains a force from which the idea of escape is an illusion. Wayne is an icon for a certain type of American; thus what he says on the large, white screen that expands into the sky and into the wilderness is certainly more significant than mere movie dialogue. His large pale face speaks for America, and Erdrich is profoundly disturbed by what she hears. I like asking my students if Erdrich's representation of Wayne alters their perception of the actor, Hollywood, and the act of watching a western, and I try to draw their attention to Erdrich's wonderful reversal: the representation of Wayne and white cowboys as the savages. Again, Erdrich links the personal experience of watching the film with larger cultural and political issues that the film provokes. Without question, she seeks a text, a poem, a letter that unites the performative power of Native oral expression with the cultural influence and mass appeal of a John Wayne western.

But what really makes "Dear John Wayne" worth closer study is how Erdrich's desire for thematic unity gets mirrored formally. First of all, Erdrich adopts the classic positionality of the lyric speaker—the first-person persona. In this case, she positions herself as one of us: she becomes a member of the audience, approaching a John Wayne movie from the outside, just as we approach her poem. Even though the poem is a letter written to John Wayne, the curious pronoun usage in the next-to-the-last line—"he" as opposed to "you"—suggests that the speaker is now addressing someone else, perhaps her friends, her community on the reservation, perhaps herself. The dual signification is underscored when we reread Wayne's comments in the same stanza. They, too, seem particularly personal, as though they are simultaneously spoken by hundreds of white men from the past and future and are aimed directly at the group of Indians on the hood of the Pontiac. As speaker, as poet, as character in the poem, Erdrich yet again unifies the disparate elements of the poem but also of her own life. Similarly, through her use of the lyric "I" and the communal "we," Erdrich is able to connect writer and reader—a gesture that evokes the dialogic and interactive structure of Native orality.

Beyond Erdrich's compelling enactment of the lyric's penchant for dual signification, "Dear John Wayne" is a case study on the use of poetic form and technique. For instance, buried in the poem is a remarkable apostrophic moment. The lyric poem enjoys a long history of the apostrophe, a poetic figuration in which the "speaker directly and often emotionally addresses a person who is dead or otherwise not physically present" (Murfin and Ray 21). Here, Erdrich addresses the departed John Wayne, *"The eye sees a lot, John, but the heart is so blind"* (12); however, unlike most apostrophes, in which the speaker unburdens himself with a positive revelation, the object of Erdrich's poem is an object of critique. Thus in "Dear John Wayne," Erdrich turns poetic history on its head. She uses a canonized poetic device derived from western European literary tradition to undermine a canonized Anglo American icon. What's more, the poem is an excellent example of a contemporary dramatic monologue. *A Handbook to Literature* describes a dramatic monologue as a poem in which the "character is speaking to an identifiable but silent listener at a dramatic moment in the speaker's life" (Holman and Harmon 158). Without question, this moment on the Pontiac is a turning point for the poet, but not as significantly so as is the moment of the poem. What I love about "Dear John Wayne" is that Erdrich, unlike most practitioners of the dramatic monologue, does not silence the object of her address. She provides Wayne with dialogue, a gesture typical of Native discourse in general.

Lastly, the poem is a kind of anti-elegy. Rather than celebrate or mourn John Wayne's death, "Dear John Wayne" problematizes Wayne's life. The cumulative effect of all this is that Erdrich deftly employs the classic tropes and gestures of western European poetic form for yet another dual purpose. On the one hand, she creates a beautiful poem whose architecture echoes Browning, Milton, and Shakespeare. On the other hand, she employs the machinery of established literary institutions to call into question the cultural machinery that could produce an icon like John Wayne, creating a provocative fusion of Native oral discourse and western European poetic strategies.[4]

As I note above, Erdrich engages Wayne through dialogue, and, not surprisingly, many of the poems in *Jacklight* reveal a dialogical subtext, most notably enacted in a Native-colonizer conversation in which the poet seeks not obliteration but hybridization. In the poem "Captivity," for instance, Erdrich problematizes the colonial project. A fusion of "Dear John Wayne" and "Jacklight," "Captivity" recasts the Mary Rowlandson narrative and reverses the male-female and Native-Anglo power dynamics.[5] In Erdrich's revisionist lyric, Rowlandson begins to identify more closely with her Indian captors than with her puritan culture, transposing the traditional relationship of colonizer and colonized. Thus Native culture and its ability to transform personal (and cultural) identity becomes the object of desire, not Anglo culture. Susan Perez Castillo rightly notes that when Rowlandson begins to see her captor as a person instead of a stereotype, she crosses a threshold into power and liberation ("Construction"). As a result, Erdrich's poem emerges as a model of what can be accomplished by grafting Anglo and Native worldviews.

Besides these instances, I think it is important for students to consider additional gestures of unification. For instance, what drives Erdrich's fusion of animal, female, and Native sensibilities? It would appear that she wants to explode any system that limits individual potential and cultural enunciation. Instead of viewing men and women, whites and Indians, and public and private worlds as binarisms that rend individuals and communities, Erdrich's poems underscore larger attempts of collaboration and transformation.

Even more interesting is how in "Captivity," Erdrich merges historical fact with personal conjecture, creating a text that takes notions of poetic license to provocative lengths. Consider the poem's epigram:

> *He (my captor) gave me a bisquit, which I put in my pocket, and not*
> *daring to eat it, buried it under a log, fearing he had put something in*
> *it to make me love him.*
> —from the narrative of the captivity of Mrs. Mary Rowlandson, who
> was taken prisoner by the Wampanoag when Lancaster, Massachusetts
> was destroyed, in the year 1676 (26)

According to my research and that of Robin Riley Fast, this passage does not
appear in either the American or the British version of Rowlandson's narrative,
a fact that raises questions about history, documentation, and the liberties of
poetic creation. What's more, Erdrich's poem suggests that the speaker (not
necessarily Rowlandson) is not only attracted to her Native captor but actually
hints at a sexual liaison between the two (Fast 190):

> It was so tender,
> the bones like the stems of flowers,
> that I followed where he took me.
> The night was thick. He cut the cord
> that bound me to a tree.
>
> After that, the birds mocked.
> Shadows gaped and roared
> and the trees flung their sharpened lashes.
> He did not notice God's wrath.
> God blasted fire from half-buried stumps.
> I hid my face in my dress, fearing He would burn us all
> but this, too, passed.   (26–27)

This is the language of seduction, the language of personal expression and
liberation. This is the language of private desire in the face of public punishment. This is the language of lyric poetry.

It is not, however, the language of history. In poems like "Captivity," "Indian
Boarding School: The Runaways," and "The Butcher's Wife," Erdrich locates
the poem in a historical topos; however, while the texts may bleed history,
they do not conform to historical fact. They suggest how history is as subjective
and indeterminate as poetry itself. For instance, it will probably not occur to
most readers to question whether the epigraph from "Captivity" actually
appears in Rowlandson's narrative, just as it will not occur to most readers to
question the historical accuracy of Rowlandson's accounts of her Indian captors. In my mind, Erdrich is not simply mimicking Coyote, the infamous
Native trickster figure, but, as in "Dear John Wayne," she is trying to combat
the objectivity of historical and cultural artifact with subjective art. As Fast
suggests, it would appear that Erdrich,

who plays freely in the poem itself with incidents and language from the *Narrative*, is beginning with an intentionally ironic invention: ironic in that, if we accept the epigraph at face value (as most readers must), then we have begun our reading by replicating earlier readers' likely acceptance of Rowlandson's assumptions.[6]   (190)

If history is not objectification but interpretation and, more important, conversation, then Erdrich has added her voice to the larger project of historical discourse.

Another irony of this poem is that as in "Dear John Wayne," the first-person narrator of "Captivity" lends the text a spoken rhythm hard to match in prose or film. The primacy of the lyric "I" feels more immediate, more personal and authentic than Rowlandson's constructed persona of unwavering Christian devotion and certainty. The speaker's voice, then, takes on the incantatory pressure of Native orality. On a related note, a final irony is Erdrich's play on the concept of captivity. In the next-to-last stanza, the speaker suggests that, culturally and existentially speaking, not just she but all Anglos are being held captive by a kind of cultural imprisonment:

> Rescued, I see no truth in things.
> My husband drives a thick wedge
> through the earth, still it shuts
> to him year after year.
>
> . . . .
>
> And in the dark I see myself
> As I was outside their circle.
>
>   (27)

Erdrich suggests here that immersion in a Native community makes seeing the world from only an Anglo perspective simply impossible. One cannot look at John Wayne anymore and not think of Indians. Mary Rowlandson cannot look at her husband, her family, her god, and not think of Indians. What before the poems may have seemed opposite now seems integrated.

In each of the poems discussed so far, Erdrich uses the lyric poem as a site of cultural positioning, that is, she wants to connect Indian culture to that which may have been lost. "Indian Boarding School: The Runaways," for instance, explores how Natives might reconnect with place and ritual. Here, young Indian children muse over being transported back to their "home" after having been tracked down by the local authorities. Erdrich does a good job of evoking the sense of confusion and frustration (and the irony) of being transported by whites back to a place to which they have been removed—also by whites. By necessity, home becomes an interior space impenetrable to exterior forces. Thus in *Jacklight*, as in *Love Medicine*, Erdrich links the absence of home to the presence of being an Indian or, more specifically, to rituals that connect a tribe and a place. P. Jane Hafen ("Sacramental") argues that poems as various as "The Woods," "Chahinkapa Zoo," "The King of Owls," "The Red Sleep of Beasts," and "The Strange People" contain gestures or artifacts that become ritualized. These acts of ritualization unite the Ojibwe with the spiritual realm and the cycles of history and, despite the sense of chaos and dissolution of the present, provide structure, order, and performance. A useful classroom strategy involves asking students to locate and explain ritualized moments in these poems. What is behind Erdrich's desire to meld personal symbols with Ojibwe ritual? Ultimately, we can read the poems in *Jacklight* as mini-rituals themselves, performative enactments of a relation between physical and spiritual realms. Erdrich is able to find in ritual the loop that unites public and private, sacred and secular.

Erdrich further problematizes the marriage of the sacred and the secular in her remarkable poem "Christ's Twin" from *Baptism of Desire*. Here Erdrich provides a vision of Christ's violent, primal, and savage doppelgänger. Erdrich's representation of Christ's other corresponds to early pejorative Christian representations of Indians, similar to those informing Mary Rowlandson in "Captivity." The poem contains further Native inscriptions through its theme of twinning. As some students may know, twins are among the most common trope of Native mythology, and, as in many myths, the twins in Erdrich's poem possess opposite traits. Where Jesus is pious and gracious and passive, his twin functions as a sort of trickster with tendencies toward violence and excess. Through the figure of Christ, Erdrich not only unites poles of human nature but also blurs the boundaries between Christian and Ojibwe religions.

Ironically, though, in "Orozco's Christ" (the poem directly following "Christ's Twin"), this characterization of Christ's twin applies to Christ himself. The title is from a painting by the Mexican muralist José Clemente Orozco; Erdrich's disfigured Christ rips his own flesh, chops down the cross, and rolls the boulder sealing his tomb over Mary herself.[7] Erdrich underscores this notion of twinning through the side-by-side placement of the poems within the book and through the realization that Christ is his own doppelgänger, suggesting that even though Anglo and Native spirituality may seem worlds apart, they are essentially two sides of the same coin. Without question, Erdrich identifies with Orozco's vision of Christ, perhaps because of the similarities between Orozco's representation of Jesus and Native representations of spirits and beings. It would appear that Erdrich uses the two Christs as yet another means of dramatizing and uniting Native and Anglo perspectives. Through her motif of the two Christs, Erdrich seems to be working through her desire to bridge the seemingly unbridgeable gap between Anglos and Indians by linking humans and the divine.

Uniting the two Christs reveals an overarching desire for inclusion and significance that does not subsume identity. The book's title, *Baptism of Desire*, refers to the Roman Catholic concession granting the sacrament of baptism to a person who cannot perform the act itself but who desires it. Indeed, there is evidence that desire for unity is itself a kind of unification, a thematic Erdrich pursues in the poem "The Sacraments." Dividing the poem into six sections that correspond to the six holy sacraments, Erdrich adroitly layers Native spirituality, Catholic mysticism, Native and Catholic ritual, and personal desire. Perhaps more than any other poem in the book, "The Sacraments" dramatizes Erdrich's contradictory attitudes toward Catholicism. Neither repudiating nor accepting Catholicism entirely, she evokes the powerful elements of the religion that make it for her both repellent and dynamic: "God, I was not meant to be the isolate / cry in this body. / I was meant to have your tongue in my mouth" (22). No question, these are provocative lines, as the speaker questions her own isolation but desires physical union with the divine. I have found it helpful to discuss the erotics of this section and also the sense of longing and desperation permeating the poems. In "The Sacraments," Erdrich seeks a kind of metaphysical unity with the Christian God in ways she does not with Ojibwe deities. Perhaps this poem seeks a kind of crossbred god, a deity in which Catholic and Ojibwe desires find reconciliation.

Those familiar with *Love Medicine* can easily imagine the lips of Marie Lazarre burning with the words from the passage above, just as one might find on her lips the litany of desires in "Fooling God," the most commonly anthologized poem in *Baptism of Desire* and the first poem in the collection. The speaker, most likely a young girl, obsesses over what she must do to fool or please God in order to "taste the everlasting life" (4). In "Dear John Wayne," Erdrich characterizes Wayne as a prosecutor, a warden, and a hunter, a portrayal not unlike God in this poem. And, like Wayne, such a powerful, mythical figure exudes undeniable allure. Understandably, students find the diminished self troubling in "Fooling God"; however, I like contrasting the speaker of that poem with the speaker of "Ritual," the final poem in *Baptism of Desire*. Functioning as bookends, these two poems reflect a progression, a growth, perhaps even a baptism, from the reality of a child into the potential of an adult or, more specifically, a mother. Often, students imagine the speaker of the poems as the same person, the speaker in "Ritual," grown and pregnant. One gets the feeling that she is taking steps to ensure that her child will not be tormented by the need to fool any god. To this end, the tension and alienation of the opening poem fades into a sense of contingency, contemplation, and completion. The human ritual of childbirth gives the speaker the unity and connection she has desired.

With some coaxing, students should notice a shift from *Jacklight* to *Baptism of Desire*. In her first collection, ritual gets dramatized in decidedly Native terms, through collective ceremony; however, in *Baptism of Desire*, ritual is transformed into something more private. Ultimately, in both books, we uncover a poetics of connection that unites the poet to her community and to the divinities she desires.[8]

When teaching Erdrich's poems, it is worth asking how they differ from her prose. What do her poems do that her prose does not? Or, what can she accomplish in poetry that she cannot accomplish in prose? Since the ontology of the lyric poem is grounded in connection and contingency, I would submit that Erdrich sees poetry as the genre in which she is best able to reconcile issues that tend to get parsed in her fiction. Some of my most successful classroom moments have come when I have used the poems and prose as sites of intertext and interaction. For instance, in "The Butcher's Wife," Erdrich explores the German American side of her family through a cycle of poems on the immigrants Mary and Otto Kröger. These European American characters and several others resurface two years later in *The Beet Queen* and even later in part 2 of *Baptism of Desire*. Also, I often use *Jacklight* to explain or contextualize Ojibwe gestures in *Love Medicine* and *Tracks*, since the most overt connections, "A Love Medicine" and "Family Reunion," appear in permutated forms in *Love Medicine*. Even though these texts can help shrink the thematic abyss that often separates poetry from prose, the more provocative sites of union may transpire in the realm of genre. In both *Jacklight* and *Baptism of Desire*, Erdrich devotes space for sections of prose. These prose segments, stories of the lovable trickster Potchikoo, further blur the boundaries between prose and poetry, personal and communal narratives, and public and private expression. To me, these segments function as metonyms for larger issues of hybridization and amalgamation. For Erdrich, Western history and theology have bifurcated Native culture, the body's relations to the natural world, even her ethnicity. Erdrich wants to conflate the dualities of otherness.

Additionally, I wonder if Erdrich includes the prose pieces as a means of uniting completely different kinds of public and private spheres: prose and poetry. If poetry is profoundly personal and prose clearly more public, perhaps Erdrich sees these poetically rendered myths as the bridge between the two. That Erdrich finds her means of unification in indigenous stories, myths, and tales—the means by which one engages the divine—is no surprise.

In both books, Erdrich enters into various dialogues: dialogues with her own internal voices, dialogues with Ojibwe tradition and history, dialogues with the divine, and dialogues with us, the audience. It is through these dialogic acts that she finds sites of unity. For her, poetry is also dialogue, a means of communicating and connecting, and therein lies much of the joy of reading and teaching poetry.

NOTES

[1]See Carter Revard for more on "Jacklight" and what he calls the "conflicts in American culture between human and animal" (173).

[2]Contrasting Erdrich's poem about nature with classic pastoral poems like Thomas Gray's "Elegy in a Country Churchyard" or even James Wright's "A Blessing" may foreground the subtextual tension of Erdrich's lyric.

[3]Not surprisingly, John Wayne appears as a kind of deity in a poem by Sherman Alexie. In stanza 8 of "My Heroes Have Never Been Cowboys," Alexie's brother seems to equate Wayne's cultural omnipotence with the cosmic equivalent: "Looking up into the night sky, I asked my brother what he thought God looked like and he said, 'He probably looks like John Wayne' " (*First Indian* 102). All evidence points to Erdrich's poem serving as inspiration for Alexie's. In fact, stanza 6 of the poem begins, "*Win their hearts and minds and we win the war*" (102). This italicized line alludes in both form and content to the last four stanzas of "Dear John Wayne."

[4]Through this fusion of Native orality and classic western European poetic forms, Erdrich participates in what I call "engaged resistance." For more on this term and for a longer reading of "Dear John Wayne" as a culturally revolutionary text, see my essay "Word as Weapon."

[5]In 1675 or 1676, Mary Rowlandson (1636–1711), the daughter of a wealthy landowner and the wife of a minister in Lancaster, Massachusetts, was taken prisoner by the Wampanoag tribe as a kind of last resort to hold onto their lands against British advancement. For eleven weeks, she was a captive among the Wampanoags, though never really mistreated. Seven years after her return to Lancaster, she published *A Narrative of the Captivity and Restoration of Mrs. Mary Rowlandson*, a first-person account of her captivity. It was among the most popular texts of seventeenth-century America and Great Britain.

[6]It should be noted that, for years, I assumed this passage appeared in the *Narrative*. Only through a coincidence of teaching the *Narrative* in an American literature course at the same time that I was writing a draft of this essay was I prompted to search for the passage. I also suspect that Alexie assumes the passage appears in Rowlandson's *Narrative*, as he uses Erdrich's epigraph as the epigraph for his poem, also entitled "Captivity." Teaching Erdrich's "Captivity" and Alexie's "Captivity," in which he argues that the reservation system holds Indians captive, allows for a wonderful moment of Native poetic intertext (see Alexie, *First Indian* 98–101).

[7]While a student at Dartmouth, Erdrich would have seen *The Epic of American Civilization*, the magnificent twenty-four-panel mural by Orozco. Panel 21 is entitled *Modern Migration of the Spirit* but is better known as *Christ Destroying His Cross*. Dartmouth has made an image of the panel available on its Web site (www .dartmouth.edu/~library/Orozco/panel21.html). Another page with commentary and a similar Orozco painting (which I suspect is the inspiration for this poem), actually titled *Christ Destroying His Cross*, can be viewed at http://home.t-online.de/home/ametas/orozco.htm.

[8]In 2003, Erdrich published *Original Fire: New and Selected Poems*, a book that collect most of the poems from *Jacklight* and *Baptism of Desire*, though in a different arrangement. The new poems, including one entitled "The Seven Sleepers," continues the themes of unification, birth, and the search for the divine.

"And Here Is Where Events Loop Around and Tangle": Tribal Perspectives in *Love Medicine*

Paul Lumsden

With multiple narrators telling stories from different synchronic positions, *Love Medicine* is an unusual novel. Many critics suggest it is a collection of thematically linked short stories that does not follow the multifarious requisites of a novel. However, the function of its narratological structure, where no single voice or point of view takes hierarchical position over another or dominates another voice in the novel, approximates or embodies the oral tradition and the role of the storyteller in this tradition, a role that pulls together the community. I call this view a tribal perspective. And as is suggested in the title, *Love Medicine* invites attention to the medicinal qualities of storytelling. "[S]torytelling constitutes both theme and style. . . . [A]s a series of narratives or chapters/stories shared with the reader, the work as a whole becomes a kind of 'love medicine' of forgiveness and healing in its own right" (L. Schneider 1).

In this essay, I discuss ways for English instructors to appreciate and understand the effects of the multiple narratives and multiple narrators of Erdrich's *Love Medicine*. I do not discuss the individual chapters of the novel; rather, I describe the steps I take to conceive, present, and teach the narrative function of the novel. In the process, I suggest ways to provoke students to think of the novel as an integrated work of fiction that draws on the Western tradition of narrative and, more important, unites it with a Native American oral tradition.

I teach *Love Medicine* in an introductory university English class to primarily non-Native students and devote about nine hours of class time to it. My introductory lecture and prefatory remarks provide general background information on Native cultures to emphasize Edrich's relation to the Native American Renaissance. To illustrate some of the many contributions of Native Americans to North American culture, I refer to Joseph Bruchac, who suggests that we think of Native Americans not as a homogeneous group but as over four hundred different languages and cultural groups ("Four Directions"), and I cite the anthropologist Jack Weatherford, who in *Native Roots* highlights how the American colonists were helped by Natives. Joseph Epes Brown's *The Spiritual Legacy of the American Indian* has been valuable as well.

By the time we get to *Love Medicine* in the course syllabus, I have exposed students to narratives such as Nathaniel Hawthorne's "Young Goodman Brown," Joseph Conrad's "Heart of Darkness," William Faulkner's "A Rose for Emily," and a play such as Shakespeare's *The Tempest*—all of which provide an effective segue into *Love Medicine*. Generally speaking, the narrative patterns in the preceding, conventionally taught works differ from the one we see in *Love Medicine*. The former narratives are constructed around a journey motif, which can be used to illustrate a departure from what we have read and a transition between that and *Love Medicine*: in those works the protagonists leave their homes and in the process gain experience, while in *Love Medicine* the Native protagonists have gained experience of various kinds and are now returning home.

William Bevis has noted that the movement in several Native American novels displays a characteristic he has labeled "homing in" (580). "Home" is the last word in the first and last sentence of *Love Medicine*. The journey of a Native protagonist is not, as St. Jean de Crèvecoeur wrote of Americans, the journey of one who leaves the old to take the new (46), but the reverse. The process of "homing in" involves realignment with the traditional Native world. It also involves the immersion of readers who are unfamiliar with Native culture and Native cultural reference points into territory they may not understand. Non-Native readers thus participate in constructing and understanding contemporary Ojibwe culture (see Rainwater, "Reading"). Readers share the experience of being brought into a new home, of learning family stories (21). Non-Native readers are brought into a fictitious Native community and exposed to Native characters whose values, traditions, and cultural ethos differ from their own.

Readers of *Love Medicine* are frequently in an uncomfortable position in this novel. Alcoholism, sexual promiscuity, death, guilt, rage, poverty—these causes of suffering are depicted throughout the novel, and readers often find themselves mediating between violence and humor. Early in the novel, for example, Gordie tells a joke about "An Indian. A Frenchman. A Norwegian," and as he tells the joke, King beats his wife. We are not allowed to enjoy the humor, and if we do, we are still aware of the visceral brutality of King's shrieking and of glass breaking (34–35). To recoil from the violence or to laugh at the punch line of the joke: how should the reader reconcile these opposing responses? One approach is to consider this narrative manipulation as a reflection of the demands put on the reader to integrate information presented by an oral tradition.

The structure of *Love Medicine* provides insights into what the oral tradition is and how it works in the novel. Oral tradition generally refers to how familiar narratives and the spoken language manifest themselves in a written form through a narrator's voice, wordplay, and gaps in the plot—resulting in a mutual creation that takes place between the teller and the audience. I define the oral tradition by demonstrating to my students their role in constructing events of the novel. The most apparent manifestation of the oral tradition is the episodic plot structure and the various speakers. Paula Gunn Allen suggests that "traditional tribal narratives possess a circular structure, incorporating event within event, piling meaning upon meaning, until the accretion finally results in a story" (*Sacred Hoop* 79). The episodic plot is less important than the effect of multiple voices. Being told a story allows the listener to participate as a member of a group. Walter Ong observes, "When a speaker is addressing an audience, the members of the audience normally become a unity, with themselves and with the speaker" (74). Moreover, the multiple narratives and multiple narrators draw attention not to individuals but to the community itself, to the way that the telling of the tales unites the community.

Erdrich asks readers to follow narrative structure in ways many students find unfamiliar. To help them understand the cultural ethos in *Love Medicine*, to conceive a perspective of a world different from their own, I draw attention to the various speakers, or voices. Of the eighteen narratives in the novel, all but five are told in the first person, and the reader shares in the intimacy of being told an event directly by the teller—through "[p]rivate, personal narratives . . . [that have] the feel of gossip and confession" (Ruppert, *Mediation* 133). This method of storytelling brings readers into the confidence of the teller, as they are brought into this fictional community.

Because many of the chapters are narrated in the first person, the reader becomes familiar with the thoughts and feelings of members of this fictional Ojibwe tribe. The reader becomes a complicit participant who constructs events; knowing the intimate details of the characters' lives, the reader ultimately makes the connections that the various characters in the novel cannot make. The accomplishment of this novel is that it reinvents an oral storytelling tradition, presenting a tribal perspective. The effect is not divisive, nor does it alienate a non-Native reader. It makes the reader the mediator who unites the community. The oral tradition is apparent in the novel through its structure and the demands put on the reader.

To demonstrate the importance of creating community through the oral narration, I draw students' attention to those chapters in the novel written in the third person, which emphasize the alienation of the protagonists from the values of the Native community. In "The World's Greatest Fisherman" June is "killing time" in North Dakota (1). In "The Bridge," Henry Lamartine blends his past, fighting in Vietnam, with the present, having sex with a young Albertine. In "Lulu's Boys" Beverly Lamartine comes back to the reservation from the Twin Cities, where pursuing "great relocation opportunities" he sold books door-to-door (109). The narration stresses how awkward Beverly feels on the reservation and how far removed he is from his community. Looking at Lulu's boys, he notes, "Clearly they were of one soul. Handsome, rangy, wildly various, they were bound in total loyalty, not by oath but by the simple, unquestioning belongingness of part of one organism" (118). In contrast, Beverly feels he is not part of any group.

Traditional oral narratives require the listeners to integrate and understand disparate information as they hear it. Although it is impossible to create an oral story for a reader, Erdrich comes close, by having narrators from five families—Nanapush, Lamartine, Lazarre, Morrissey, and Kashpaw—and a time frame that spans the years from 1934 to 1984, although not in a straight-forward, sequential order. The reader is asked to integrate the different voices and the stories told by numerous characters and to draw the significance out of these stories. In many respects, the narrative follows a structure used by Nector Kashpaw in "The Plunge of the Brave" when he describes how he started his romantically "burning" relationship with Lulu Lamartine: "And here is where events loop around and tangle" (128). Nector's circular, inter-twining metaphor illustrates Erdrich's narratological frame for the novel and exemplifies the oral tradition.

Once students have a way to focus on the episodic structure of the novel, to distinguish the different effects of first- and third-person narratives, to understand their role as readers and the effect of traditional narratives, all of which draw attention to how "[o]rality communication unites people in groups" (Ong 64), they are prepared to appreciate the tribal perspective of the novel. The accomplishment of the narrative is that it represents an oral storytelling tradition that focuses not on the individual tellers but on the tribal perspective. For non-Native readers *Love Medicine* may be the first time they encounter Ojibwe culture from the inside and the first time they are required to integrate multiple narratives and multiple narrators. The narrative is medic-inal, creating community for the listening readers. To Lydia Schultz, Erdrich makes what is "unfamiliar to many readers—Chippewa people and their expe-rience—familiar by allowing them into the minds of numerous characters" (93).

Tracking the Memories of the Heart:
Teaching *Tales of Burning Love*

Debra K. S. Barker

As she reflects on the power of the narrative act, Louise Erdrich explains that a story told in its proper context brings people together in a powerfully intimate way: "At the telling of it we would be lifetime friends. . . . It would be a new story and an old story, a personal story and a collective story, to each of us listening" ("Where" 43). In *Tales of Burning Love*, the fifth of her North Dakota novels, Erdrich dramatizes the power of storytelling not only to draw individuals into a circle of community but also to achieve several other purposes, which my students and I explore in our discussions of this novel. In this essay, I first offer a detailed analysis of the novel's characters, conflicts, and major themes: the power of narrative and the power of love to transform the major characters in the book. To date, there has been relatively little critical analysis of the novel, so this section should provide useful foundational material for those teaching the novel for the first time. Second, I introduce key issues and topics that my students and I have discussed and debated in developing our interpretations of what we see Erdrich accomplishing with this novel. Finally, I guide the dynamic of our classroom toward community building and the sharing of stories, texts, and ideas so that students may experience the pleasures and enrichment of sharing a collective story that they have worked through for themselves. The framing idea that guides my analysis and approach to teaching the novel is this: we cannot live well either without love or without the power of the story offered as a gift to heal the heart and draw us back into the arms of kinship and community.

Themes, Knots, and Threads of the Novel

In *Tales of Burning Love* Erdrich returns to her favorite themes: the centrality of family and community, the recovery of tribal relations, the dialogic enactment of the oral tradition, and, yes, love, in its range of emanations from the erotic to the spiritual. The novel's title is hyperbolic in one sense yet apt in its evocation of the element of fire, which pervades the narratives, much as water and earth dominate the imagery of *Love Medicine* and air, *The Beet Queen* (Nowick 70). Linking the novel's embedded narratives, fires, heat, and electricity transform many characters' lives, effecting transmutations and bringing several characters through the passage from life to death—both literally and figuratively.

The novel opens to reprise the first scene of *Love Medicine*, with June

Morrissey drifting into the Rigger Bar in Williston, North Dakota, in response to an invitation from "Andy," whose real name we learn is Jack Mauser and who will figure as the central character in *Tales*. The novel is set in and around Fargo and Argus, North Dakota, towns already familiar to us from Erdrich's earlier novels. Fourteen years and four wives later, the first of whom was June Morrissey, Jack is presumed dead in a house fire. His former spouses, leaving the funeral home together, find themselves stranded in an unexpected blizzard, much like the one that had claimed June's life. To keep themselves awake and thus alive until help arrives, each woman relates the story of her relationship with Jack, adhering to Dot Adare Nanapush Mauser's strict criterion: the story must be hot enough to "scorch paper, heat up the air!" (206).

These stories serve as the structural frame of the novel, while the conflicts recounted point up the strength and complexity of the women whom Jack has brought into his life. In the course of hearing their stories, we learn as much about Jack as we do about the women and come to recognize how his life has been a process of dying and renewal, until he can come to avoid making the self-destructive choices that have fractured not only his life but also the lives of the people who care about him. On some level Jack has known that a woman's love would be instrumental in his quest to solidify his sense of identity. He also acknowledges needing "the grounded feeling of connection" (55). Musing over his need for an architect to help him develop his construction projects, Jack relates an architectural analogy to the conception of his selfhood: "I do things from plans. I make them real. I could do it for myself if I could get a guy that could design me. But since that's not possible, I've always relied on women. Somewhere inside I think—they're women, they should know" (158). Just as women have the natural power to conceive new life, Jack's wives likewise wield the power to call forth various dimensions of his personality. Thus each marriage signifies a symbolic return to a new beginning and a fresh blueprint for the genesis of a less conflicted self. Each set of wedding vows, each new start, presents Jack with a clean slate, as it were, an opportunity to renew and redeem himself for the woman who does not know all the facts about him, that he is Indian, for instance, or that he has married as many women as he has. With each new wife he has a new identity and thus a renewed hope that his future self will be happier, wealthier, and more successful than his past ones. Jack's vows and resolutions, however, echo the promises and renewed good intentions of those who dream, drink, and gamble to excess, buying off the consequences of their actions with promises to reform and make amends.

In *Tales of Burning Love* the blueprints for transformation, for Jack as well as for his four wives, are encoded in the stories the women share in the stranded Explorer, as well as in the background narratives Erdrich's third-person narrator relates to us readers. Jack's is a trickster story, for instance, recounting the lies, pain, and betrayal he has doled out to nearly everyone in his life. Noting the defining characteristics of trickster, the Ojibwe writer Gerald Vizenor points out, "Trickster is capable of violence, deceptions, and cruelties; the realities of human imperfection" ("Naanabozho" 162). Rootless and homeless, Jack reminds us of the original trickster from the Ojibwe creation story in which the Creator sent four spirits to his suffering people so they might learn "wisdom and medicine." The fourth spirit, Nanabush, is a shape-shifter and an orphan, sent specifically to bring healing and to teach his people to behave kindly toward one another. Though often foolish, he prompts human beings to knowledge of proper conduct, as well as knowledge of self (Johnston, *Ojibway Ceremonies* 165).

The night of storytelling in the stranded Explorer assumes the dimensions of ceremony as each wife in turn shares her private knowledge of Jack, venting anger, picking through rare moments of tenderness, weeping at the loss of promise, opening to self-knowledge. Not until they purge festered emotions and articulate the dimensions of Jack's character that they each knew, however, can they accept one another, make peace, and realize a kind of catharsis. In this way language and storytelling are "medicine" in a traditional sense to heal emotional wounds and knit the bonds of community. The narrator explains that after this point, the women release their "antagonism" to form a "tentative sisterhood, and in that, there was a sad wisdom." In sharing "the denser bread of analysis," they link in their stories Jack's "moods, manners, and betrayals," forging a unique type of "intimacy that rivals any lover's union" (200–01).[1]

The storytelling ceremony draws these women from their disparate worlds of individual suffering into a little community unified by their collective history with Jack. Their stories enable them not only to survive the blizzard but also to heal and come to self-knowledge about what they want and need from a love relationship. The second wife, Eleanor, for instance, has been going through the motions of living her life, devoting herself to intellectual pursuits and loveless sexual conquests. Evading the terrors of failure and intimacy, she struggles to control her unabated desire for Jack as well as her demand for certainty in life.

Her relationship with Jack, emotionally intense and fraught with the violence of their mutual attraction and ambivalence about emotional commitment, prompts her to investigate the ostensibly selfless love of saints for God. Her questions bring her to Our Lady of the Wheat Priory, where she hopes to interview the legendary Sister Leopolda. Although Jack sets her on this journey for answers, Sister Leopolda is the one to tell her that she has been looking in the wrong places. While separated from the Explorer, wandering in the blizzard, Eleanor has a vision of the now deceased nun, who has come to guide her both to safety and to a realization of what she has been searching for all along. Sister Leopolda declares, "You want abiding rightness, assurance of your course. You will *not* find all that in a man" (373).

Later as she prepares to write her book on Sister Leopolda, Eleanor reflects on miracles, truth, and faith, finally coming to terms with her fear of failure and her need to transcend her chronic self-absorption. Rather than intellectualize love as an operational construct in her research, she is moved by her love for Jack (and her conversations with Sister Leopolda) to recognize her fear of emotional commitment and reawaken the courage to give unconditional love.

The fourth wife, Marlis, who finds love with the third wife, Candice, transforms from a manipulative, con-artist trickster-consort to a loving and vulnerable woman. In the role of a trickster nemesis, Marlis first exploits, seduces, and tortures her "mark," Jack, who inadvertently repays her by getting her pregnant and awakening in her the need for the intimacy of a love relationship. As the layers of moral corrosion peel away from her nature, Marlis emerges from this mutually abusive, conflicted relationship with Jack, a mature woman now capable of creating a new family with Jack Junior and Candice, with whom she ultimately finds her home.

The birth of Jack Junior brings Marlis to a newly realized capacity for unconditional love and opens her heart to a relationship with Candice, who has herself only now found real love in her relationship with Marlis and Jack Junior. The power of love in their lives has brought out the best in both their natures, as they focus less on themselves and more on the child and family they wish to nurture. Clearly, without Jack they probably would not have met, and they certainly would not have the treasured love of their lives, their baby son.

The themes of love, death, and transformation are inextricably linked in the novel, illuminating for us a truth that frequently recurs in American Indian stories: human beings cannot truly thrive when they are emotionally disconnected from home and community. Through love and the power of the words they share with one another, each character in the novel ascends to a certain degree, experiencing the transmutation of the darker, more destructive qualities of the human personality. Kathleen Sands, as she reflects on the marriage of language and love in *Love Medicine*, speaks to the same relational dynamic at work in *Tales of Burning Love*: "Love is so powerful that it creates indissoluble ties that even outlast life, and ultimately it allows for forgiveness. . . . Erdrich's characters are lovers in spite of themselves, and the potion that works to sustain that love is language . . ."(41).

Having used language as a potion of seduction more than once, Jack functions as a catalyst for change, much in the same way the traditional Naanabozho figure has done in tribal stories. Living, dying, resurrecting, wandering from life to life, marriage to marriage, Jack prompts each of his wives to experience for herself the power of love and self-transcendence. What Eleanor and Dot come to realize about the power of love, for instance, is not only its persistence but also its attending demands of courage and self-reliance in the face of unabated longing. After marrying Jack to appease her longing for a love relationship, Dot finally accepts that for her there can be no other life partner than Gerry Nanapush and that a life alone would be more satisfying than one with Jack and his "net of complications" (414). Her love for Gerry is transcendent, she concludes, musing, "It exists in a finished world, beyond the reach of common sense. That's how I love Gerry, and that is that, that is all" (417). She comes to realize, moreover, that she does not require Gerry's physical presence in her home for her to feel fully alive; she is, in and of herself, complete and stronger than she has ever been. Through their experiences of sharing Jack's life, his wives map the territory of love and desire, in the meantime discovering core values that are not only tribal but also universal in their applicability to those who seek community. Love and stories can guide us to those moments of epiphany, or insight, in which we can confront our shortcomings and mistakes, heal, and then transform to become the best human beings we can be. To facilitate epiphany, however, we need to transcend ego and suspend self-involvement, even if briefly, in order to realize a distance from pain, confusion, and desire. Each wife, transformed by her relationship with Jack, recognizes and experiences intense, unconditional love, emerging from her ordeal stronger and more capable of loving and living cooperatively within her relationships.

Jack's moment of transformation occurs at the climax of the novel, when June's spirit comes to guide him through the blizzard as he searches for his infant son. A shimmering specter in her wedding dress, June leads him to the car sheltering both of their sons, Jack Junior and Lipsha Morrissey, who had inadvertently kidnapped the child when he stole Candice's car. Operating as a type of narrative frame, the two blizzards—the first that takes June's life at the beginning of the novel and the second that threatens the lives of Gerry, Lipsha, and Jack Junior, the people she and Jack love—shock Jack into resuming and then concluding his mourning for June's death. The narrator explains, "Jack was now beginning to see, just catching at the design of his life. Bits and pieces of understanding he had carefully collected and hidden from himself were magically assembling" (380). Reunited briefly with June's spirit, Jack experiences "the bloom of loss" (380) and is now capable of resolving his grief over her death and perhaps of taking responsibility for the momentary callousness that enabled him to watch her wander into the storm to die.

With Jack's story Erdrich dramatizes for us the process by which language and the narrative act have the power to rearticulate a life fractured by acts of selfishness, self-indulgence, and deception. For after years of treating the people who care about him only a little less badly than he treats himself, Jack squandered his moral and spiritual integrity. Having loved and hated him since they first met, Eleanor long ago recognized that he was not a whole person, saying, "I love him but there's something missing in him" (82). As he reads the newspaper story of his wives' survival and rescue from the blizzard, Jack finds an odd comfort in being remembered and mourned by the circle of women who know him most intimately. Symbolically, in their shared stories of Jack from the various stages of his life, the women have reintegrated or consolidated him with their love. The narrator tells us, "It was as though his whole life had come together without his knowing it or having to feel responsible, though he was" (404).

With his return to the native soil of the reservation, Jack—carrying his infant son—begins to feel a psychic reintegration, transformed by love, his wives' stories, and his stirring response to the land as the Ojibwe part of his soul, long dead and buried, resurrects itself. Earlier in the novel Erdrich links Jack's indifference to the earth to his denial of his Ojibwe heritage, echoing Eleanor's recognition of Jack's emptiness. The narrator comments, "Since the Ojibwa part of Jack was inaccessible, he was a German with a trapdoor in his soul, an inner life still hidden to him" (153). Jack's inner life stirs with the resurrection of his long-repressed memories of his Ojibwe mother and his recognition of the earth that holds the bones of his ancestors. We're told, "Even though the old people, his mother, called the land leftovers, scraps the whites didn't want, she loved the place. Now Jack was hit by feeling for it. Memories came to him in his weariness, pure and strange" (401). By allowing himself to open his spirit to the land, he is now at a point where he can recover the Ojibwe part of him that originally drew him to June Morrissey, that yearned for the sense of completion that a union with her had promised.

Not only is Jack redeemed from himself, likewise is Sister Leopolda—and in a manner that would have appealed to her voracious appetite for drama. The admittedly lurid title of the novel promises stories of unabated passion, and to a certain extent the novel delivers on this promise, most unexpectedly in the embedded narrative that reunites us with Sister Leopolda, who is now 108, a rumored candidate for sainthood, and as tormented by frustrated desire as she was when we first met her in *Tracks*. Reflecting on what she perceives to be the old nun's longing for spiritual fulfillment, Eleanor concludes that saints are "humans in the sickness of desire" (446). Sister Leopolda, elaborating on her love for God, whom she compares to a faithless husband, lectures Eleanor: "[You] ask me what love brings? Can't you see! No relief to love, no end, no wave, no fall, only a continual ascension. . . . My prayer is a tale of burning love" (52–53). To the end Sister Leopolda's relationship with God remains fraught with egoism, incessant demands, and high drama.

Nevertheless, with her eventual immolation by lightning and her subsequent apotheosis, her prayers for God's recognition are indeed finally answered through the power of storytelling. Years of rumors of miracles occurring in and around Argus prompt Father Jude Miller to write Bishop Retzlaff, alerting him to the possibility that Sister Leopolda's legend could put Argus on the map as the Lourdes of the upper Midwest. He explains, "[T]here is something well worth investigating in the entire design and history of persons, places, and even objects surrounding the now deceased Sister Leopolda . . ." (443).

Recognizing an opportunity to capitalize on the sensational stories of bleeding statues and miraculous healings, Lyman Lamartine hopes to make Argus a religious tourist trap by persuading Eleanor to write Sister Leopolda's story and thus prompt her eventual beatification. Sister Leopolda will thereby find redemption as she ascends forever into the body of local mythology as the first mixed-blood saint of Our Lady of the Wheat Priory.

Clearly, in *Tales of Burning Love* the ties of love and passion weave a web of relationships knotted with memories and stories, connecting the living and the dead, the sacred and the mundane, the present and the past. The return of June's spirit and the reaffirmation of Dot's love for Gerry bear witness to the power of love to endure separation, regardless of whether that separation is wrought by prison sentences or death. The love of Sister Leopolda for God—fraught as it is with passion and thwarted desire—also bears testimony to the strength of the human spirit to endure for decades the silence and apparent indifference of the object of one's passion. Nevertheless, daily, until her death at 108, she fashions her prayers, "tale[s] of burning love" she calls them (53), the language potions set out as offerings for the recognition of God.

Indeed, all the characters are somehow redeemed by love—Eleanor, Marlis, Candice, Jack, Lawrence Schlick—but they have to go through fire, some literally, some figuratively, to undergo the alchemy of transmutation. In this novel, love—like narrative—is dynamic, recursive, life-affirming, and endlessly renewing, offering the most comfort when it can be shared. Erdrich shows us yet again a cultural value the luckiest of us are taught—or must learn the hard way: both stories and the experience of genuine, heartfelt connections have the power to redeem us from the worst in ourselves, provided we can surrender the ego and prepare for the fires of experience.

Tales *in the Classroom*

One of the most significant goals of my Indian literature courses involves my bringing students to respect and even appreciate the important conventions of Native literatures, such as the oral tradition and the cultural perspectives of various Native writers. Like many non-Indian students living in Indian country, a number of my students feel ambivalent about Native people. They can also be reticent about publicly discussing their reactions to a Native perspective, whether that perspective comes from a text or from me, a Lakota professor. Given these realities, my course design attempts to engage my non-Indian students in cross-cultural understanding and community building. I begin by helping them understand the value and power of the oral tradition, demonstrated not only in *Tales of Burning Love* but also in daily classroom activities designed to prompt dialogue, questions, their own stories, and the sharing of ideas in response to assigned readings.

I have taught this novel successfully both in my contemporary American Indian fiction course and in a major-author course devoted to Erdrich's fiction and poetry.[2] As I work to maintain a student-centered dynamic in the classroom, I guide that dynamic by focusing on key critical and cultural issues that emerge from questions and discussions of the text, as well as on the major conflicts and themes of the novel.

Texts

With the exception of *The Beet Queen, Tales of Burning Love* is not as suffused with Ojibwe cultural information as are Erdrich's other North Dakota novels. Nevertheless, we spend some time talking about the history and locations of the Ojibwe reservations in Wisconsin, as well as in North Dakota and Minnesota. Peter G. Beidler and Gay Barton's *A Reader's Guide to the Novels of Louise Erdrich* and Hertha Wong's casebook on *Love Medicine* both provide useful maps and family trees for the characters in Erdrich's novels. (See also the genealogical charts in appendix A at the end of this volume.) Allan Chavkin's *The Chippewa Landscape of Louise Erdrich*, a collection of critical essays on the issues and values enacted in the first five novels, also provides valuable critical commentary on *Tales*. For cultural background, I direct students to two texts that focus exclusively on Ojibwe history and culture: *The People Named the Chippewa: Narrative Histories*, by Gerald Vizenor, and *Buried Roots and Indestructible Seeds: The Survival of American Indian Life in Story, History, and Spirit*, edited by Mark A. Linquist and Martin Zanger. Connie A. Jacobs's book *The Novels of Louise Erdrich: Stories of Her People* provides a critical overview of *Tales*, while at the same time situating it in relation to Erdrich's other novels.

Students are particularly interested in the connections between *Tales* and the other novels, so I suggest teaching *Tracks, Love Medicine, The Last Report on the Miracles at Little No Horse*, or just the chapter "Saint Marie" from *Love Medicine* before assigning *Tales*, thus helping students trace the web of relationships running throughout the novels. Those intertwining relationships of history and blood, a theme unifying the North Dakota novels, reflect a feature of Native culture that holds true in life on many reservations today.

Another feature of Native culture is the belief that if an individual's stance is relational and participatory within a group, rather than individualistic and self-involved, positive outcomes occur, whether that outcome is a healing within a ceremony or the communication of an important idea through a story. In a biography of Joseph Eagle Elk, a revered Lakota medicine man, Gerald Mohatt maintains that stories have the power to heal when a narrative operates as a "process" involving not only the storyteller but the listeners as well: "We enter together into a story and move through it together. We punctuate it. We fill in the gaps" (Mohatt and Eagle Elk 195). In this way the narrative process facilitates healing by redirecting the consciousness of individuals from themselves to the story and the task at hand, in this case the healing ceremony. At the same time the process fosters an intellectual and emotional engagement, a dynamic that I think is crucial to the successful teaching of *Tales of Burning Love*. Bearing this in mind, I ask students to form discussion communities of four to five people, so that they may more easily become acquainted with one another and feel less self-conscious about sharing their ideas in small-group and larger class discussions. I then provide an introduction to Erdrich's work and tribal nation.

Praxis

After presenting biographical and cultural background on the author and her tribal nation, I distribute lists of questions for the discussion groups, directing them to explore the formal features of the texts before moving on to extrinsic or cultural issues. As a class we do explore the contrast between linear and circular narrative structures, focusing on *Tales*' elliptical and recursive style; the unfolding of the novel mirrors the dynamic of Native oral traditions and the looping paths of memory. I ask students to keep a reading journal as we discuss the novel; thus they create for themselves an archive to which they return to engage their connections and insights as they occur, participating in this way in Erdrich's storytelling process. Since *Tales* is a rather lengthy novel that students enjoy discussing, I occasionally ask the discussion groups to take turns initiating our conversations, using insights from their reading journals or a series of questions they or other members of the class have devised.

A group might also engage the class in discussing a critical article that I have suggested, one of which is Jack Forbes's "Colonialism and Native American Literature." Forbes speaks to a question often raised about novels like *Tales*, namely, How is this an "Indian" novel? He points out the differences between the expectations of Indian audiences and non-Indian audiences as they come to Native texts. Though both audiences may enjoy reading about the mystical dimensions of Native cultures, for instance, some non-Indian readers may not find instances of humor or the topics of politics or love or sex as compelling, or even relevant to their notions of what they think Native people ought to be writing about (21).

The last time I taught this novel, one non-Indian student criticized the text for not being "as Indian" as *Tracks* or the other novels in our course, giving me the opportunity to caution readers about coming to this or any other Native text with particular ethnographic agendas or stereotyped notions about what constitutes an authentically Indian text. After I remind students that every text is unique, just as every tribal nation or national background is unique, we discuss the necessity of not imposing one's own cultural and aesthetic assumptions or expectations on the artistic expression of writers from other cultural backgrounds.

Native students and Native educators alike can appreciate Erdrich's treatment of certain realities we struggle with: the issues of white privilege, internal oppression, and passing in the white world, all of which were introduced in earlier novels with the characters of Pauline Puyat and Marie Kashpaw. In *Tales* these issues are dramatized with Jack's ambivalence about his Ojibwe mother and his initial lie to June about his name and his birthplace. Moreover, with a friend's early reference to June as Jack's "squaw" and Marlis's dismissal of Jack's first wife as "that Indian" (204), Erdrich reminds us of the racism that remains pervasive not only here in the upper Midwest but everywhere Native people are marginalized, ostracized, or treated as colonial subjects.

Clearly, Jack's practice of passing as a non-Indian reflects the extent to which white supremacy has insinuated itself into Euro-American ideology, where language and systems of white privilege are concerned. As Jack contemplates the substantial loan he has negotiated at his bank, he marvels over the incongruity of an Indian being entrusted with a vast amount of money by a Euro-American lending institution. "Here I am," he thinks, musing over his check, *"an Indian."* The narrator goes on to explain:

> That part of his background was like a secret joke he had on everyone. His crews. His banker. Asshole clients. Even his own wives. He'd thought, strangely sometimes, when walking through those bank lobbies, *the hell with all of you. Your doors would swing the other way if you knew who I am!* (151)

For Jack, passing becomes an act of resistance to the institutionalization of white privilege that has historically marginalized Native people, as it does to this day. As a non-Indian, Jack can enjoy the unquestioned acceptance and participation in commercial ventures that Euro-Americans take for granted, never conscious of how their whiteness opens doors ordinarily closed to most people of color. Indeed, only a person of color would stop to notice the connection between unearned privilege and race, given that for most Caucasians in America, their race has generally never posed a barrier, a problem, or even a matter of comment. White is accepted as normative; color is deviant.

Erdrich is here dramatizing the imperative of the decolonization of the Native imagination, which begins with the acknowledgment of the internal oppression that often occurs as one confronts racism and internalizes shame. In this novel, to become a whole person Jack must recover his Ojibwe identity, as well as dismantle the colonial ideology he has internalized over the course of his life: for instance, land is merely real estate, and Anglo bankers do not readily loan hundreds of thousands of dollars to an American Indian. For

Native people generally, this process of decolonization begins with the claiming of their names, their relatives, and their stories.

To help students explore the issues of race and privilege in the novel, I assign readings by Greg Sarris ("Reading") and David Mitchell ("Bridge"), both of which speak to the unique challenges Native people face, negotiating identity issues within a white-dominant culture in which their minority status is never forgotten. As we discuss the admittedly sensitive topic of white privilege in Euro-American culture, I draw readings from two excellent anthologies, *White Privilege: Essential Readings on the Other Side of Racism*, edited by Paula S. Rothenberg, and *Off White: Readings on Race, Power, and Society*, edited by Michelle Fine et al.

While discussing cross-cultural reading strategies for readers from the dominant culture, we do talk about the dynamic of learning and creating knowledge through an accretive process, rather than from a linear or deductive one. This process is demonstrated through our growing comprehension of Jack's character after hearing the successive stories of his wives, each of which provides a slightly different perspective on his strengths and flaws. Each story likewise broadens our understanding of not only the novel's structure but also the interconnection of its conflicts. The student discussion groups adapt quickly to this conscious reading strategy and come to enjoy participating in the narrative process, retrieving and then contextualizing stray bits of information as they reconstruct Jack's and his wives' stories. Consequently, students find themselves better prepared to move on to more complex narrative structures, like those in Leslie Silko's *Ceremony*.

Questions that reoccur in class discussion often concern the discrepancies between the facts of *Tales* and those of the preceding novels, most frequently the accounts of the scenes of June's death from the novel and from *Love Medicine*, as well as such details as the discrepancies of the ages of Lipsha and Sister Leopolda. I remind students about the features of the oral tradition that allow for the variations a story undergoes as it is related over and over again. I tell students that when I am at Rosebud, my family reservation in South Dakota, and listening to a story, the person relating a story often qualifies it, saying, "This is the way I learned the story" or "This is what I was told." Culture, particularly oral culture, is a living, dynamic phenomenon; quite naturally we can expect transitions, adaptations—even amendments to previously established narrative details.

What Erdrich tells us again and again throughout the North Dakota novels is that stories and relationships are integral components of our lives; stories are memories of the heart. They heal us and teach us and connect us to one another in life-enriching ways. Moreover, our capacity to love is predicated on our finally embracing our own stories, our fundamental selves, as well as our home places, wherever they may be. This is wisdom for us all, Native and non-Native alike, which is why I think Erdrich's novels resonate so powerfully in the classroom. A cache of stories blending pleasure, humor, and pain, *Tales of Burning Love* not only explores the miraculous spectrum of human love but also reminds us to be as fully alive as we can be while we are here and to be mindful about connecting all the lives we live with all the people we love.

NOTES

Portions of the material in this article appeared in a paper I presented at the Anishinaabeg of the Great Lakes Region Symposium on History, Culture and Contemporary Issues. University of Wisconsin-Eau Claire, 30 September 1999. I would like to thank the University of Wisconsin–Eau Claire Office of University Research Internal Grant Programs for providing the support that helped make this project possible.

[1]For a reading of the wives' relational bonds as reflective of those of Oshkikwe and Matchikwewis of the Ojibwe story cycle, see K. Stokes.

[2]Given the sexual content of the novel, I would hesitate to teach this text at the secondary school level.

Academic Conversation: Computers, Libraries, the Classroom, and *The Bingo Palace*

Sharon Hoover

Most undergraduates who come to one of my beginning literature classes do so with immature skills, little knowledge, and even less confidence in taking part in academic conversation. They have developed few means of engaging a text and rely mainly on their own feelings. Teaching *The Bingo Palace* can bring together the students' need to learn academic skills and their need to learn to respect and enjoy literature.

Reading is a complex activity that students can improve far beyond what was expected of them in precollege schooling.[1] Students should understand this complexity and realize that much of their success in college, in their career, and in their social life will depend on the sophistication with which they read and converse with others about their reading. This statement may sound gratuitous, but it is one I think instructors of all disciplines, including literature, need to keep in mind. Part of our job as teachers is to enable students to be skillful readers after they leave our classes.

In this essay, I outline techniques I find particularly useful in approaching Louise Erdrich's *The Bingo Palace* with students while keeping in mind the larger purposes of teaching literature. I have used these techniques with many different novels but never with the delight I felt in combining them with a reading of *The Bingo Palace*. The setting and characters of *The Bingo Palace* are somewhat familiar to students, since gambling on reservation land has been in the news for years. Lipsha makes many crazy adolescent moves, but at the same time, his life and community are particular and important components of the story. Students usually sense that they need more cultural information and that they need to read carefully and thoughtfully if they wish to contextualize Lipsha's choices. Students in my classes also enjoy relying on one another's information and insights to build their bases of knowledge and comprehension. The interactiveness of the class activities soon helps them feel more like members of a community, albeit a community grounded in the American academy.

This essay outlines three specific activities: computer interactions, a related library project and report, and engagement in academic conversations. I allocate from eight to twelve fifty-minute sessions to classroom conversation on *The Bingo Palace*, depending on the class, adjacent assignments, and available time in the semester.

Computer Interactions

These remarks are based on fifteen years of experience using the computer for classes. All the while, our university was constantly changing hardware and software. Because available resources vary widely and change frequently, I explain the types of interactions I have used, rather than critique particular programs. Each instructor needs to work with his or her instructional technology group and its leadership to determine how best to use available resources. The most helpful aspects of my university's system have been consistent faculty, student, and administrative commitment to a joint instructional technology group and the camaraderie among users.[2]

When I first began to use interactive computer conversations in my literature classes, I set up one account for each class and different files within that account for each novel. All students could access the account. The students and I sometimes found it annoying that two students could not write to the account at the same time; otherwise the process worked well for over a decade. Students were required to write one entry a week, anytime before the last class of the week. They were strongly urged to write as early as possible in the week, and they learned that reading other students' entries would often stimulate their own responses. I have not required that any student type in an entry on a particular day because, although access to computers on our campus has improved greatly, students who work or live off campus may find it difficult to access a computer on certain days.

As the university introduced Web-based instructional approaches, I found the computer entries worked less well for me. A system of prompts requesting from the students the book they wished to make an entry about, the date, and their user identity ensures that students' responses are entered into the correct file with complete information. I found, however, that the more structure that was introduced, the less spontaneous and creative the student entries were. The results became so disappointing that I dropped the requirement altogether for a short time. Part of the problem may have been that many other instructors were using variations of class on-line writing. Students would enter and leave discussion of the novel without reading entries by other students, which may have been appropriate for another class or professor, yet was contrary to and undermined our purpose in holding conversations. The university has recently adopted Blackboard, which may be more adaptable to my goals. The key for me is to work constantly with technical staff members so they understand my classroom goals and I understand the limitations and possibilities of the programs I am using.

In my beginning literature classes I direct students to "talk" online and to make their entries spontaneous yet thoughtful enough to spark conversation about an issue in the novel. I tell them not to worry about presentation, just as they do not worry about it in rough drafts. In my experience, overemphasis on good writing at this point stifles imagination and risk taking, which in turn stifles growth in thinking. I have not found that this attitude results in sloppy writing. Students usually want to express their ideas clearly and succinctly so that their peers understand and respect their work, but they want to do so without editing themselves heavily, so that they can complete this part of the assignment expeditiously. Editing comes later in the process, and students in my classes submit more formal assignments in more formal language. Initially we are generating questions, reflections, and ideas. At first, students often record straightforward questions, such as How does Lipsha's childhood affect his adulthood and his relations with other characters? What is his attitude toward money and what is Lyman's and how do they differ? One student asked her classmates online:

> I'm wondering why Lula's son, Lipsha's father, was imprisoned. How are all the characters related and how are their lives intertwined? Will Shawnee marry Lyman or Lipsha? What significance does the Bingo Palace have? Should we keep in mind the author's life and wonder if it plays a part in her novel? How and why does Zelda control the actions of people she is close to?

Those of us who have read Erdrich's novels can sense the prescience of these questions, and later, at appropriate times, I remind students of them. The questions impress the students much more when they are voiced by one of their peers trying to complete an assignment than if I introduce them. Students begin to recognize that they can direct their reading in profitable directions to talk with their classmates about a work. The computer conversation also motivates students to speak who do not usually initiate comments in class, it allows for many more conversations than the classroom does, and it records those comments so all students can access them later.

Students include unedited copies of their individual entries in their class portfolios. At each individual conference, I ask to view the student's entries in sequence, and the student and I talk about the nature and depth of the entries and about what alternative kinds of questions the student might try to explore. For instance, I may suggest that the student try to form questions at different levels of abstraction or questions that more directly reflect class discussions we have had.

Some professors assign code words or numbers to students so that no one else in the class can identify the writer. I have never felt the need for that, and I believe it would defeat the pedagogical purpose of having students engage in academic conversations. Students in my classes almost always sign their entries. That way other students, stimulated by the online conversation, can engage them in conversations regarding the novel outside of class. I have found students willing to raise and discuss racist or sexist issues online that they are timid about bringing up in class. Once the issues are opened, however, everyone seems to have permission to talk about them.

The entries are valuable, too, for giving me insight into the strengths and weaknesses of the students individually and as a group, so that I can better plan class sessions. A few minutes on the computer before class allows me to see how the reading is going, what students have been thinking about already, and where it may be profitable to begin the day's discussion.

Library Project and Report

In addition to encouraging students to have individual reactions to the reading and to share their insights, I want to encourage them to find information that will help them develop more informed responses. Reference searching can help students begin to comprehend geography, landscape, demographics, history, cultural allusions, economics, and politics relevant to the novel. None of these concepts is easy to grasp within a tradition, because they are familiar and unquestioned; and none is easy to grasp from outside a tradition, because they appear different to the outsider while they are assumed to be natural to people within the culture. Book researching is an intellectual, not an experiential, way of learning, but in our culture students must learn this method of study. Sharing stories in class by those who have experience in other cultures, geographies, and religions is pedagogically important, too. It helps convey the emotional ties people have to cultural concepts, encourages students to search out and appreciate experiences, and allows them to articulate orally to a group something they know. Such sharing helps prepare them to read research sources as they also seek intellectual ties to the stories. An instructional reference librarian introduces the students in my classes to using the library and calls their attention to various specific sources that may inform their reading. These include atlases, timelines, specialized dictionaries and encyclopedias, journals, pamphlets, government documents, statistical abstracts, newspaper articles, and the Congressional Record. Students then select some topic that has caught their attention while they were reading the novel or during the librarian's talk and begin to research it.[3]

Each student is responsible for entering one single-spaced paragraph (about half a page or 250 words) of specific information that might be important in understanding the novel. I set up a particular computer file for this information that students can easily use, helping them learn to recognize that different purposes in writing require different styles. This assignment requires students to use a more formal writing style than they use in their more spontaneous entries. The entry begins with a descriptive topic phrase and ends with a full and accurate bibliographic reference in *MLA Handbook* style. The student then summarizes the information he or she has found. Here are snippets from a student entry:[4]

> Lipsha's performance is referred to as "one of those sad reservation statistics." This led me to find something out about how Native American children fare in school.

The student reported the dropout and suicide rates she found for Native American children and for the general population. She also presented the "problems" "experts" identified as contributing to the rates.[5]

Another student snippet:

> Because of the import of that pipe being put together by non-Indian hands, I thought I would search for more detailed information on pipes and the significance they can have.

Other student research has had to do with gaming, dancing, powwows, family structures, land use and ownership, the Dawes Act, the timber industry in former Ojibwe land, the history of the Ojibwe, and many different animals— fox, owl, skunk, parrot, and so on. I constantly ask students to tie their research findings to the text. After reading about pipes, some student is usually keen to say that Lipsha's response to the border guard's letting the feather on the pipe touch the floor suggests that Lipsha respects the grandfather's traditions and that Lyman's willingness to gamble with the pipe shows that perhaps he does not. Another student usually counters that Lipsha's and Lyman's behavior seems at times to be respectful of their cultural traditions and at other times not. The next questions, of course, are when and why these differences occur. Such conversations lead back to the text, keeping our attention on the possible implications of our information while reading the text.

In-Class Academic Conversations

In an essay titled "Reading between Worlds: Narrativity in the Fiction of Louise Erdrich," Catherine Rainwater argues that readers must supply "extratextual information" (407) to help them ponder how the conflicting codes of the Ojibwe world and those of the dominant United States culture affect their attempts at interpretation. Extratextual information includes all that the students learn through the computer conversations, the library work, the work they may be doing in other classes, or stories in the daily newspapers.

Extratextual material includes storytelling, too. If there are students in the class with differing cultural backgrounds and the classroom culture is one in which storytelling as a basis for culture has been valued, students may tell stories from their own cultures. Stories put human, emotional, and imaginative faces on codes, kinship, religions, and concepts of time. A student from East Timor once characterized the war in Timor as a story of Indonesian and American involvement in Timor so that the United States could control the straits between it and Australia. The students could feel his emotion as he described the deterioration of the life he had known there. An American student retold the story of a United States newspaper article that characterized the struggle in East Timor as Indonesians fighting Indonesians, about what he wasn't quite sure. These different renditions of the war highlighted for us the very different points of view from which they came. Sometimes students will tell moving stories grandparents or other relatives have told them about concentration camps, internment camps, or political collapses. Students can often tell personal stories of discrimination and racial profiling. Occasionally, a student who has experienced the death of a friend from another culture or religion can tell about the differences in heartfelt beliefs and rituals. The relationships between these stories and issues in the novel need to be made explicit so that students can begin to consider them consciously.

The computer interactions and the library work, like the storytelling, are not ends in themselves. Students invariably write about orality and community in the computer conversation, and I use those entries to spark a classroom conversation about community. Students may ask such questions as:

> What does it mean that the narrative voice in chapter 1 is "we"?
>
> Is the collective voice a tribal voice?
>
> Is everyone related to everyone? How? When? Why?
>
> These people's lives seem to revolve around everyone else's and the ways in which the lives interact. Does the "we" imply that what happens between Lulu and her son affects all the others, even if they don't know it?
>
> When the narrator changes—for instance, to Lipsha in chapter 2—the style changes. What does the style change communicate to us?
>
> Lipsha reflects on the way he feels outside the circle and on his experiences away from the reservation and away from the other characters. Are his feelings and his other experiences related to the feelings and actions of other characters in the novel?

In the classroom conversation, a student quotes a sentence from the novel: "But we start with one person, and soon another and another follows, and still another, until we are lost in the connections" (5).

I introduce some extratextual material I have found in an essay about Native American philosophy, engagingly titled, "If You Think about It, You Will See That It Is True," by Vine Deloria, Jr., Standing Rock Sioux. Deloria says that in the moral universe in which he is immersed "all activities, events, and entities are related" (47). There are "no ultimate terms or constituents . . . only sets of relationships" (48). Each of us is related to every other one and to every other entity. Our individual responsibility is to develop our own "self-knowledge and self-discipline" (51). Lipsha struggles with adjusting to this aspect of his culture. He must find his place and identity in the circle, the dance (*Bingo Palace* 9); he must sort out for himself his relationship with the load of "[h]istory, personal politics, tangled bloodlines . . . around us" (17). Lipsha "must recognize that obtaining what we want at the expense of other forms of life or of the earth itself is short-sighted and disrupts the balance that the whole fabric of life requires" (Deloria 51). Some of the students usually argue that Lipsha must see Shawnee Ray as a person with her own inherent rights and Lyman as the person he is in the history in which he lives. Lipsha should expect neither to be what he might want of them—a lover or a rescuer. His actions exist in relationship to all others. In other words, Lipsha has to find, through his experiences and interactions in the world, his own responsibility to Shawnee, to Lyman, to Redford, and to all other entities and actions, such as Russell Kashpaw, the Montanan, the white baby, Fleur, the skunk, the bingo game, and Lake Matchimanito.

Some of the extratextual material I want to introduce to the class I structure early in the semester. Part of the semester's assignments is to read one text not on the syllabus and report on it to class, relating significant similarities or differences with the books we are reading as a class. The intent is for students to learn that when they pick up a book to read, they are not reading it in a vacuum of background. Some of the books I suggest to students are other novels by Erdrich, if they have not read them. Near the end of the time we spend on *The Bingo Palace*, I ask those who have read other novels by Erdrich to give a collaborative report on the genealogy (blood-related and not) they find in the novels. Their report is always rich, not only with the relationships they find (they always present various sorts of diagrams) but also with the views of the nature of those relationships. The class responds with many highly focused questions that lead to lively discussion of who is related to whom and who has cared for whom and who has responsibilities to another, and so on, eventually culminating in the realization, as one student put it, that "everyone has a story, the stories get all mixed up, and that makes it a community." Other students want to push the ideas further and express the thought that community also means caring about oneself and others—"and skunks," another student will add.

I distribute to the entire class Erdrich's essay "Skunk Dreams," a story of a night on a football field in North Dakota where she goes with her sleeping bag to work off an adolescent funk. This encourages students to consider the complexities of which they were previously unaware between an author, a character, and a totem. When a skunk, searching for a cozy bed, makes a nest at the back of her knees, she contemplates "the sharpness and number of skunk teeth" and "the high percentage of skunks with rabies," and she and the skunk fall asleep together peacefully. In the morning, however, a dog stirs the skunk, and "when the skunk lets go, . . . [she's] surrounded by skunk presence: inhabited, owned, involved with something you can only describe as powerfully *there*" (112). We should, Erdrich says,

> [t]ake comfort from the skunk, an arrogant creature so pleased with its own devices that it never runs from harm, just turns its back in total confidence. If I were an animal, I'd choose to be a skunk: live fearlessly, eat anything, gestate my young in just two months, and fall into a state of dreaming torpor when the cold hit hard. Wherever I went, I'd leave my sloppy tracks. I wouldn't walk so much as putter, destinationless, in a serene belligerence—past hunters, past death overhead, past death all around.   (120)

After reading the essay and talking about the characteristics of the skunk as Erdrich outlines them, the students are impatient to talk about Lipsha's various habits indicated throughout the novel. Most of them conclude that the skunk is an excellent spirit animal for Lipsha.

Other students point out that Lipsha wishes for a different vision, maybe one of "some horses who split the sky with their hooves, or a bear, an eagle with a bald head and long brown wings to carry me a saying to mess with Lyman's mind" (220). Lipsha does not change and grow easily, they insist, as his yearning for a stereotypical vision attests. Before Lipsha can become himself, he has to argue his way through the experiences of his entire vision, bringing to them everything he knows.

> It's not completely one way or another, traditional against the bingo. You have to stay alive to keep your tradition live and working. . . .
> And yet I can't help wonder, now that I know the high and the low of bingo life, if we're going in the wrong direction, arms flung wide, too eager. The money life has got no substance, there's nothing left when the day is done but a pack of receipts. . . . Our reservation is not real estate, luck fades when sold. Attraction has no staying power, no weight, no heart.   (221)

The way is neither forward nor back. Lipsha tells himself, as he settles into his long night of cradling the baby close to his heart, "There's no return to what was. . . . An unknown path opens up before us, an empty trail shuts behind. . . . Before the nothing, we are the moment" (258–59). The only moment that exists is now. All the other moments are within it. The tenor of the students' conversations has become broad ranging and probing, yet directly tied to the novel.

The nebulosity surrounding Lipsha's meeting with his parents and his night with the baby set the students conversing on the computer to wondering about June's appearance, the wild ride through the snow, and Gerry's disappearance. One student writes:

> What does anyone make of the meeting between Lipsha, June, and Gerry? Looks to me as Gerry's gone to be with June and Fleur has taken Lipsha's place—grudgingly—humor to the end! But, wow, and how is this related to June's giving Lipsha the bingo cards and Shawnee's dream at the end? Yeah, I want to hear a lot of entries to answer these questions.

Another student writes:

> If, in the kinship system of the Ojibwe, one who saves another becomes the guardian/father/mother, then Lipsha and the baby will always be related and Lipsha will be responsible for him. What would that mean?

Such questions on the computer, even before we get to class, stimulate students (and instructor) to reach beyond easy responses and self-limiting information to consider issues such as liminality, synchronicity, and ambiguity. The students' conversations come to engage deeply the complexities Erdrich has woven into a tale that is rewarding to read (sometimes with a belly laugh) and memorable in many of its details. The students have become thoroughly familiar with a contemporary American novel that reveals a young male bildungsroman. Now, too, I feel comfortable that the students have improved their skills in ways that will help them read any other novel, in or outside their culture, with greater understanding and joy.

NOTES

[1] I sometimes ask upper-division students to study the multipage *Oxford English Dictionary* definition of *read*. Memories of that assignment serve as a reality check whenever I glibly instruct students to "read the next fifty pages."

[2] I wish to credit the Instructional Technology Group at Alfred University.

[3] This project's success depends not only on the instructor's enthusiasm for learning and sharing information but also on the skill and enthusiasm of the librarian. The librarians with whom I work read the novel, read reviews of the novel, and prepare thoroughly before the class appears in the library. The librarians pull fascinating materials off shelves all over the library and organize their thoughts so that they can tell students how to access materials reasonably, if not always easily, both from the shelves and through the university's technology. Many of the writing-center tutors have been through this process too and can provide the students with additional help.

[4]The entries from students have been edited for length, not for content, and typographical errors have been corrected. I have also omitted students' names. My thanks go out to all the many students who have shared my efforts to make the study of this novel a richly rewarding activity. Special thanks to Adam Bessell, Meredith Jackson, and Danielle Ohlson.

[5]The quotation marks result from our class conversations about the term "problem" and about the limitations of sources.

Gender and Christianity: Strategic Questions for Teaching *The Last Report on the Miracles at Little No Horse*

Peter G. Beidler

In early 2001, Louise Erdrich published *The Last Report on the Miracles at Little No Horse*, a long novel with a long title. It covers some eighty-six years, a wider expanse of time than she covered in her earlier novels in this series set on or around a reservation in the northeast quadrant of North Dakota. This new novel is connected most intimately with *Tracks*, though it also has connections with *The Beet Queen, Love Medicine, Tales of Burning Love, Four Souls*, and, though tangentially, *The Bingo Palace*.

In *The Last Report on the Miracles at Little No Horse* Erdrich seems to want to tie up some of the loose ends left dangling in other novels. It answers such questions as how, precisely, Napoleon was murdered; who the parents of Jack Mauser are; how Marie Kashpaw finds out who her real parents are; where Fleur goes when she leaves the reservation and sends her daughter off to boarding school at the end of *Tracks*; how Nanapush initially gets connected with Margaret, one of the wives of his old friend Kashpaw; how and when Nanapush dies; how Nector Kashpaw gets connected with Bernadette and the record copying that he bends to the advantage of his own family; what happens to Jude Miller after the Beet Festival; whether Lulu has any more flings after she moves to the senior citizens center; whether Sister Leopolda is likely to be named a saint; and so on. Of course, the biggest question the novel answers is who Father Damien is and whether he is, in fact, as good a friend to the Ojibwe as he had appeared to be in *Tracks*.

The two initial questions teachers have to face are whether to teach this novel at all and, if they do, whether it can work as a stand-alone novel in its own right or requires the context of one or more of Erdrich's earlier novels. My feeling is that students reading the novel will not fully get it unless they have read at least one other novel by Erdrich. To be sure, because the central character, Father Damien, is at best a shadowy figure in the earlier novels, the story of his life is almost entirely self-contained in this novel. And, yes, Father Damien's life—from 1910 until his death in 1996—absolutely defines *The Last Report on the Miracles at Little No Horse*. The novel begins with his life as a young woman named Agnes DeWitt, who leaves her role as a novice nun, enters a common-law marriage to a German immigrant farmer near Fargo, becomes the wounded hostage of a bank robber who eventually murders her husband, assumes the robes and role of a dead priest named Father Damien Modeste, and takes the train north to the Ojibwe reservation called Little No Horse. All that takes us from 1910 to 1912. For the next eighty-odd years, this woman impersonating a male priest lives at Little No Horse.

Father Damien's actions and emotions are at the center of the novel. Toward the end of his life, knowing that he is near death, Father Damien writes confessional letters to the pope. Those letters, augmented by the visit of Father Jude, who is investigating the possible candidacy for sainthood of Sister Leopolda (formerly Pauline Puyat), lead to the connected recollections that make up most of the novel. So the novel does work as a self-contained unit and can be read with tolerable ease as the story of the strange life of Father Damien. Some chapters will seem not to fit very well with that story— the tale of the stolen car and the tale of the moose "hunt" come to mind— but there is enough interest in Father Damien and his life and death that those chapters will seem to many readers like bonuses rather than interruptions.

Readers' pleasure in the novel, however, will be significantly enhanced if they know some of the characters referred to in the earlier novels. Those who have seen the saintly trickster Nanapush in earlier novels will understand and love him better here. Those who have seen the diabolical Pauline Puyat before will appreciate better the ironic absurdity of any misguided attempts to canonize her. Because *The Last Report on the Miracles at Little No Horse* is especially enriched by a knowledge of the history of these two antagonists, readers would be well served by an earlier reading of *Tracks*, where the contrasts between Nanapush and Pauline are reflected in the alternating chapters told from their two opposed points of view.

My recommendation is that if teachers can assign only one other Erdrich novel to help enrich their students' reading of this one, it should be *Tracks*. In *Tracks* we get the reactions of Nanapush and Pauline to the people and events that seem bent on destroying the way of life the Ojibwe have known for generations. If it is possible to assign a third novel, it should be *Love Medicine*. In *Love Medicine* readers find out about the history of Lulu and her many husbands and lovers and about her affair with Nector, the husband of her friend and antagonist Marie. Knowing about that history helps explain why Father Jude, after a life of celibacy, in his later years throws that life away by falling in love with the octogenarian Lulu, intoxicating still after so many years.

That Father Damien is really a woman who binds her breasts and pretends to be a priest for more than eighty years is of enduring interest in *The Last Report on the Miracles at Little No Horse*. Her being a woman casts into relief much that we know about Erdrich's characters and themes from her earlier novels. Damien's secret is not a matter of suspense in the new novel. We find out that secret, after all, in the prologue to the novel, where the priest, now more than a century old, gets ready for bed:

> Then, with slow care, he turned off the bedside lamp and in moonlighted dark unwound from his chest a wide Ace bandage. His woman's breasts were small, withered, modest as folded flowers.   (8)

The suspense in the novel, then, is not whether Father Damien is a woman but which other characters will find out the truth and what damage they will do with that information. At least four other characters do discover the secret—Nanapush, Father Gregory Wekkle, Mary Kashpaw, and Sister Leopolda—but they all have their own, quite different reasons for keeping the secret. What we readers do with the secret leads to one of the two central issues—gender and Christianity—that teachers will want to invite their students to talk about. In the remainder of this essay, I present a range of questions teachers may find useful in generating class discussion of the two issues.

Gender

The gender issues raised by *The Last Report on the Miracles at Little No Horse* fascinate readers of both sexes. The implications of a woman's filling, and filling creditably, what is traditionally a man's role are vital to an understanding of the novel, and students want to talk and write about them. Teachers might want to begin with the simple issue of believability.

Could the central event really happen? That is, could a woman pass as a man for all those years and fool almost everyone? Erdrich has anticipated that question in her "End Notes" to the novel: "Those who question the possibility of lifelong gender disguise might read *Suits Me: The Double Life of Billy Tipton*, by Diane Wood Middlebrook" (357). *Suits Me* (1998) is the strange story of a woman named Dorothy Tipton who lived much of her adult life successfully passing as a male jazz musician named Billy Tipton. Billy even married five times and apparently managed to keep the secret from all but the one wife who, after their divorce, found Dorothy's birth certificate. The biography has many photographs and is based in part on interviews with Billy Tipton's wives. Billy's secret was discovered by medical examiners only after his death in 1989 at age seventy-four—a death hastened by the fact that he could not seek medical help without revealing that he was a woman. None of the three sons he had adopted with one of his wives knew their "dad" was not a man. Does the story of Billy Tipton make it more believable that Father Damien, who, after all, never had to fool any wives, could conceal the physical signs of his womanhood under the flowing black robes of a priest? Like Billy Tipton, Father Damien is concerned that his secret not be found out. Near death he thinks, "Time at last to end the long siege of deception that has become so intensely ordinary and is, now, almost as incredible to me as it will be to those who find me, providing I let that happen" (342). To ensure it does not happen, he burns certain letters and documents and then goes off alone to drown himself in Matchimanito Lake. But secrets have a way of coming out. One might ask students, How does Father Damien's desire for secrecy differ from Billy Tipton's? How does Erdrich's writing a book about Father Damien's secret differ from Middlebrook's writing a book about Billy Tipton's?

Leaving aside the issue of whether Agnes could get away with it, one might bring up the question of why she decided to spend her life passing as a man. The answers are not clear, and it would be instructive to see what kinds of ideas students come up with. The Billy Tipton story is not much help. Billy Tipton apparently decided to pass as male for two reasons, first so that he could have some hope of success as a jazz performer, which was pretty much a man's profession, and second because he liked the intimate company of women. Probably neither of these reasons apply to Agnes. There is no solid evidence that Agnes had ever wanted to be a priest or was annoyed that the priesthood was open only to men. The power of the priesthood is the last thing she seems to want, though Father Damien does get satisfaction in using that power by helping the Ojibwe. And there is even less evidence that Agnes ever wanted to be intimate with other women. Indeed, she seems very much to have enjoyed her physical relationships with Berndt Vogel and Father Gregory Wekkle. Her orientation is clearly heterosexual. Does Erdrich provide an acceptable alternative motivation to explain Agnes's decision to pass as a man?

Some critics, such as Daniel Mendelsohn, consider the creation of the secretly female priest just a literary device. In an early review of the novel Mendelsohn writes:

> Agnes/Damien's secret identity and the ongoing moral crisis it creates is meant to provide *The Last Report* with a meaningful narrative frame, but it's really just a gimmick. Gender, deception, concealment—none of these is ever really linked in a profound way to the numerous stories you get here; if Father Damien had been a man all along, the novel wouldn't be any different.

On the surface, of course, Mendelsohn's statement is plainly incorrect. If Father Damien had been actually rather than just apparently a man, the novel would have been far different. The tension created by Father Damien's secret influences virtually every character interaction and theme in the novel. Is there any sense, however, in which Mendelsohn's statement might be accurate?

Might one argue, for example, that Erdrich's having Father Damien pass as a man introduces a feminist theme to *The Last Report on the Miracles at Little No Horse*? Does Erdrich seem to want to drive home a point by having the second (false, female) Father Damien Modeste apparently do a better job of being a priest than the first (true, male) one would probably have done?

Agnes apparently is a successful priest. Is her success in some ways attribut-
able to her being a woman rather than a man? How can we know? Why is
she more comfortable as Father Damien than she was as Sister Cecilia? Father
Damien writes letters to the pope. Do we see in the novel also Erdrich's
implied letter to the Catholic authorities that women should be admitted to
the priesthood and not be relegated to the role of nuns?

Another way of considering the possible feminist theme of the novel is to
discuss the additional respect that Father Damien gets from Kashpaw just
because he is a man: "the driver treated her with much more respect as a
priest than she'd ever known as a nun" (62). And what about the subtle con-
descension that Father Gregory shows her once he finds out that she is a
woman? "He was unaware of it, but in all worldly situations, where they stood
side by side, he treated her as somehow less" (303). Father Damien even
wonders if he himself has somehow come to be condescending toward women:
"Did she patronize women too, now that she'd made herself so thoroughly
into a priest?" (303). Does Erdrich mean to suggest that Nanapush's low-key
acceptance of Agnes's attempt to pass as a man is healthy, or is Nanapush the
most antifeminist character in the novel? Finally, how do we assess the tone
of Father Damien's list of ten ways (excerpted below) he uses as a way to
convince others that he is really a man, not a woman?

    1. Make requests in the form of orders. . . .
    3. Ask questions in the form of statements. . . .
    8. Advance no explanations.
    9. Accept no explanations. . . .   (74)

Is the central "secret" of the novel, then, a strategy to get readers to think
about feminist issues?

Erdrich does seem to want to show that women can do work traditionally
associated with men. Not only can Agnes be a successful priest, but Mary
Kashpaw can chop wood and dig ditches more energetically than any man
does, Mashkiigikwe is the best hunter in the family, and Margaret is the hunter
who finally brings the moose down. If women can do the work of men, is
there any need for men at Little No Horse? If so, what is it? Does Erdrich
balance the slate by showing that men can do the work traditionally associated
with women? If this novel had been written by a man, would it have as consistently depicted men as foolish, weak, arrogant, self-centered, deaf, lazy, and
useless? Is the pope himself among these men, and if so, what does that say
about Erdrich's attitude toward Christianity? That last question takes us to
the second large issue in *The Last Report on the Miracles at Little No Horse*.

Christianity

Ever since the fourteenth century, when writers like Boccaccio popularized satiric presentations of church officials, literary writers have been trying to improve the Christian church by offering positive representations of good clerics and satiric representations of clerics who are variously corrupt, uncelibate, insensitive, selfish, or greedy. Geoffrey Chaucer in the *Canterbury Tales* criticized not so much the Catholic church itself as the less-than-perfect officials who were supposed to bring the benefits of Christianity to the people. In *The Last Report on the Miracles at Little No Horse* we find a similar concern with religion and especially its less-than-perfect officials. Teachers of the novel will probably want to help their students explore the nature of Erdrich's views toward Christianity in general and Catholicism in particular.

What is Erdrich's attitude toward the pope himself in *The Last Report on the Miracles at Little No Horse*? Why does she portray eighty years of popes in such a negative light? The novel presents the popes as a series of men off in Rome who never quite answer the heartfelt questions from the men and women out in the field working to convert pagans. When Father Damien finally does get a letter from Rome, it is too late because he is already dead, and it reports little more than that Father Damien's letters have all been lost from the Vatican files. Then, too, this is a religion that considers beatifying the murderous Leopolda. It is obvious to readers that Sister Leopolda is a lying, self-aggrandizing, blackmailing, child-beating murderer. What does it say of the Catholic hierarchy that it sponsors an investigation to see if she is holy enough to be canonized?

Are there positive aspects of the portrayal of the various Catholic priests in the novel? Do we see enough of the original Father Damien Modeste to know whether he would have been a successful priest at Little No Horse? What about Father Gregory? Are we to admire him or despise him for succumbing to his desire for Father Damien? Does Father Jude's resistance to the truth about Sister Leopolda mark him as a fool? Is his falling in love with Lulu at the end proof of his weakness and lack of celibacy, or is it, really, the one completely natural thing that he does in his life? And then there is Father Damien himself. One could read the novel as suggesting that he is a good priest in direct proportion to the number of Catholic rules and principles he ignores. Are we concerned that by performing a series of illegal marriages, baptisms, and last rites and by illegally hearing confessions and easily absolving sinners, Father Damien is endangering his people's immortal souls? Or is the easy forgiveness Father Damien practices meant to be an example to the rest of us that we should all be ready to forgive not only our own worst secret sins but also the worst sins of others?

And speaking of sins, how does that black dog function? Is the dog the

Judeo-Christian devil come, with his foot in Father Damien's soup, to tempt allegorically the good Christian in the wilderness? In the Christian tradition it is supposed to be evil to make a pact with the devil, yet Father Damien does just that when he offers his own life, and presumably his soul, in exchange for Lulu. Does that make him a hero or a fool, damned like Faust? What are the implications—and of course the biblical allusions—of Father Damien's command to the dog, "Get thee behind me" (308)? Or is this dog just a crazed hallucination on Father Damien's part?

No reader can fail to notice the role that music plays in this novel. Sister Cecilia's erotic love of the music of Chopin, which she sometimes plays naked, takes her away from the convent in Fargo and into the arms of a stolid German farmer. And later she selfishly spends money she stole from a bank robber not to help the Ojibwe directly but to purchase a Steinway piano. Since the church already has what appears to be a perfectly good old upright piano, are we to see the Steinway as evidence that the church and its priests waste money on luxurious consumer goods? Or is purchasing that piano an expression of Father Damien's devotion to the world of art and so one of his noblest acts in the novel? Does it matter that the money came, ultimately, from the bank accounts of ordinary rural investors to whom Agnes might have returned it? And what are we to think of those snakes that seem drawn to Father Damien's playing?

What does the novel suggest about Erdrich's views on Christianity versus the paganism that Christian priests were supposed to wipe out? Why does Erdrich make Nanapush, for all his oversexed trickster foolishness, into such an attractive old man, so helpful to others and so in tune with the environment? Why does Father Damien make such a point of telling the pope that the "esoteric forms of worship engaged in by the Ojibwe are sound, even compatible with the teachings of Christ" (49)? Father Damien even speaks of having converted to paganism himself and says that after he dies, he looks forward more to seeing the men and women in the Ojibwe heaven than those in the Christian heaven. Are the various conversions in the novel, from bank robber to priest, female to male, nun to priest, Christian to pagan, less conversions than mergings, less rejections of one side than a blurring of boundaries?

There is much more, of course, for students to talk about in *The Last Report on the Miracles at Little No Horse*. The two large issues I outline here, however, take students to the heart of the novel. Father Damien is the key to this story, but we cannot understand him without understanding the way Erdrich uses him to say something about the role of women and the role of Christianity in modern Anglo and Ojibwe society. The questions I have posed here should help students and teachers approach these important issues.

Collaboration in the Works of Erdrich and Michael Dorris: A Study in the Process of Writing

Tom Matchie

One of the unique phenomena in the history of literature is the way two married writers, Louise Erdrich and Michael Dorris, combined their talents as writers to produce several great pieces of literature. Students of these two authors will want to look closely at that collaboration, not only to better understand the writers' lives and fiction—two factors "not long separated" (Jones 4)—but also to get a special look at the collaborative writing process itself. Erdrich once commented that many people wonder "What happens?" and "Who does what?" (Schumacher 176) in that process. Innumerable interviewers have asked these questions. One critic thinks it is almost impossible to imagine that writers of their caliber could suppress their egos to enhance the quality of each other's writing (see Cryer 84). But that is what Dorris and Erdrich say they did, so a study of how their joint enterprise came about is worthwhile. Students need to reflect on what the two writers say in their many interviews, as well as research what they went through in producing a particular piece. What I do here is trace the historical evolution of their art, paying attention to changes in their thinking and techniques as they developed as writers over about a thirty-year period—from the early 1970s through and beyond (for Erdrich) Dorris's death in 1997.

Students might approach this study by asking several questions, which involve stages. First, how did the act of writing influence the way these two came together as a married couple? The relationship between Erdrich and Dorris at Dartmouth, where they met, is now legendary. He was teaching there in the early 1970s; she took his class, graduated, and later returned as a writer-in-residence while he was on leave in New Zealand. While he was abroad they corresponded, largely about literature, even exchanging stories and poems for each other's perusal. In one sense, then, their marriage preparation was to a great extent literary. Both liked to write poetry and both came from middle-class families. Erdrich is an enrolled member of the Turtle Mountain Band of Chippewa Indians. Dorris claimed Modoc heritage, though David McNab says this was a construct invented by female relatives in Kentucky to cover up his black lineage, a factor not known by him until the late 1990s ("Of Beads" 111–12, 119). After their marriage in 1981 they produced several short stories under the single pseudonym of Milou North—a combination of their first names and the region (the Northeast) from which they were writing. These stories were romantic pieces, not at all about American Indians, but centered on domestic crises and written mostly for economic survival. This is a different couple from the one we now picture, that is, two writers who became major voices for Native Americans in general. So in stage 1 they met, got married, and wrote as one person to have enough money to live and raise their children—three that Dorris had adopted as a single parent. Along with their interest in teaching, in each other, and in children, creative writing (poetry, but, increasingly, prose) was a major force in both their lives.

The second stage of their collaboration begins in the early 1980s with the development of Erdrich's story "The World's Greatest Fishermen." One might ask, why is this period different? In 1982 Dorris prompts Erdrich to revise the story and enter it in the Nelson Algren fiction competition. Then, along with other stories Erdrich had published, the couple made the story part of what eventually became her first novel, *Love Medicine* (1984). Here she is the primary writer, he the motivator—the one who makes suggestions about theme, language, characterization, and the like. Shelby Grantham says, "Dorris may have his fingers in a good many pies, but Erdrich is the writer" (47). In the opening section of the novel, for instance, Albertine meets Lipsha and grabs his arm at the bottom of the hill; she then looks up at the sky—the "northern lights"—which becomes a "dance hall," with June looking down on her sons (37). This is pure poetry, where Erdrich is at her best, and there is nothing like it in Dorris's writing. James Ruppert says Erdrich "merges the Native sense of multiple levels of meaning for each physical act with a powerful belief in the mystery of events" ("Celebrating" 71). At this point it is important to emphasize that many of the details that critics note about their literary collaboration come from interviews, and given the facts that have emerged about their relationship since Dorris's death, much of this material is difficult to trust. Elizabeth Cook-Lynn goes so far as to say Dorris mastered the art of "self-deception and duplicity and fakery" (*Anti-Indianism* 86). No doubt, the material from interviews must be weighed against other evidence from their working relationship, such as the various texts they have published. But as Suzann Harjo, a longtime friend of Dorris's, says, "When you commit suicide, you give up the right to truth and cloud everyone else's" (Covert A12).

At any rate, collaboration from this couple's point of view means they talk, read scripts out loud, and discuss details regarding choice of language. For the most part, however, it is Louise who writes; Michael says, I am "Louise's student" (Trueheart 116); that he began to publish novels much later than she is proof of his claim. At the same time, he is responsible for inspiring the creation of such characters as Sister Leopolda in the "Saint Marie" story in *Love Medicine*. Though the confrontation between Marie and Leopolda may be "a ritual tale incorporating both Chippewa and European elements" (Jaskowski 28), the old nun is reminiscent of Dorris's early schooling, not hers (Erdrich and Dorris, Interview [Wong] 41). From Erdrich's viewpoint, Dorris also "had ideas for the whole structure of *Love Medicine*" (Bruchac, "Whatever" 103), a novel that is often criticized as a collection of stories rather than a unified work. Erdrich makes the point that there is no central figure or consciousness in the book, "no real theory behind the form" (Grantham 46), but the novel still functions well as a whole—thanks to Dorris. What we do know is that in stage 2 as a team they move beyond sentimental stories into serious literature, for there is nothing sentimental about *Love Medicine*. The balance between their respective contributions, however, remains in question. The poetic elements of the text, like the "northern lights," belong to Erdrich, as does the Ojibwe mythology underpinning stories like "Crown of Thorns," where the deer Gordie kills (and thinks is his wife) suggests the presence of the Ojibwe deer woman come back to prick his conscience. Also Erdrich's are stories like "A Bridge," set in the old Roundup Bar in Fargo—a landmark not far from where she grew up. This does not mean that Dorris is not there, adding details, as in "Saint Marie," or helping to arrange the stories into a workable whole.

Actually, Erdrich's first three novels are a part of this second stage, for Dorris did not begin to publish fiction until well into the 1980s. She was working with *Tracks* (1988) even before *Love Medicine* (1984), though it was published as her third novel. The second was *The Beet Queen* (1986), another work in which Dorris has a significant, though supporting, part. Later, he will say that in working out the dynamics of their collaboration, it was while writing these early works, especially *Love Medicine* and *The Beet Queen*, that they had to make major decisions about whether to use one name or two; finally they decided to move toward single authorship because, says Dorris, "Separate bylines work" (Cryer 84). In *Beet Queen*, however, the seeds of their full-fledged collaborative relationship took root. Here, if we can trust what they say about themselves, they both read the manuscript, often aloud, and talked about it; both made suggestions and rewrote, always reaching consensus on a word-by-word basis. Dorris says:

Nothing goes out of the house without the other person concurring that this is the best way to say it and the best way of presenting it. One of the beauties of the collaboration is that you bring two sets of experience to an issue or an idea, and it results in something that is entirely new. (Berkley 59)

But collaboration here involves more than editing. Dorris tells us that after *Beet Queen* was sent out to the publisher, the two of them rewrote the last third, so that it is substantially different from the first draft (Wong, "Interview" 35–36). This is important, for *Beet Queen* is a novel about a family's demise, but in the new draft the ending is filled with hope—the unruly Dot returns to her part-Ojibwe mother. This idea belongs to Dorris, who we know is more given to happy endings, as his two novels testify—*Yellow Raft* culminates in the second of three parts with the reunion of three women, and *Cloud Chamber* ends in a grand reunion of three generations and three distinct races. Moreover, A. LaVonne Ruoff, an early friend of Erdrich's, suggested that Louise abandon the linear plot of the early "Tracks" she wrote in college and adopt a more disjointed narrative (Afterword 182). Years later, Erdrich, depressed about the three hundred pages of "memories, stories, bits of conversation," compressed every bit of this material into "one story." But it was Dorris who told her, "Go back . . . and see what you can do with it" (Schumacher 176–77). In a larger sense, the North Dakota mythology for which Erdrich is now famous, one that includes key characters like Dot and Fleur, was developing organically to the point that Dorris and Erdrich were trying to figure out "who characters are" (Huey 126). Critics now compare her North Dakota literary world with that of Faulkner's Yoknapatawpha County, though students of the writing process need to be aware that this overall mythic universe came to be only through a highly complex, organic process.

The third stage involves the collaboration between two accomplished writers. Now Dorris has begun to publish different kinds of works—essays and short stories; his first novel, *Yellow Raft in Blue Water* (1987); and his popular explanation of fetal alcoholic syndrome, *The Broken Cord* (1989). It is this new Dorris who characterizes stage 3. It is also in the mid-1980s stretching into the 1990s that Dorris and Erdrich are interviewed by a host of people on their backgrounds, their writing, and also on what they think about Native Americans. In an interview with Bill Moyers they talk about Native spirituality after the Indian Religious Reformation Act of 1978, the difficulty of writing about Indians as a whole rather than as separate nations, and problems connected to writing as mixed-blood Americans. Speaking in this authoritative way represents an expanded version of their combined role as authors, though Dorris had written about Indians long before he met Erdrich. Moreover, their oral collaboration in such interviews involves their going back and forth, often interrupting each other on major issues, so that even in the process of being interviewed their working together—talking about writing as well as writing itself—has matured.

In these interviews—now collected in a single volume edited by Allan Chavkin and Nancy Feyl Chavkin—both began to talk extensively about what they do practically as well as psychologically. Such exchanges resulted in major revisions in both their works, revisions that involve significant personal sacrifice on the part of the original writer. Dorris says, "You have to let your ego fall back and let the work come first" (Trueheart 115). If he was instrumental in changing the point of view of Erdrich's story "Saint Marie" in *Love Medicine*, now Erdrich is talking to Dorris, suggesting he make the protagonist of *Yellow Raft* a girl—which he does, and it works (Wong, "Interview" 36). While he has always been Erdrich's editor, her characterization of him goes far beyond that: "Michael is a spiritual guide, a therapist, someone who allows you to go down in where you just exist and where you are in contact with those powerful feelings that you had in your childhood" (Trueheart 116).

Such statements illustrate the couple's tendency to bring out the best in each other. Still, these two are individual writers, and their styles are not the same. Vince Passaro notes that Dorris tends to be more realistic and to work in the context of contemporary social issues. *Yellow Raft* depends on the context of MIAs and the Vietnam War. Erdrich's novels, in contrast, are set in the past and have a magical quality, as well as a spiritual vibrancy. She is also more direct about violence, death, and sexuality (161). In *Love Medicine* Albertine in "A Bridge" recounts "the bones of her pelvis cracked wide" (179)—lovemaking that William Gleason calls "nearly brutal" (121); immediately following this chapter is "The Red Convertible," in which Henry commits suicide—"and there is only the water" (154). At the same time, Erdrich and Dorris are producing major works, and (according to them) both are at ease with collaborating, both making comments on the other's work without loss of one's individual stature. Truly, they seem to trust each other, claiming they are "equally committed to one another's fiction" (Caldwell 66). For them, giving voice to a people (Native Americans) "out of sight and out of mind in the 80s" (Cryer 80), while endeavoring "to become those characters" (G. Stokes 59) is their fortification against competition with each other. Now Erdrich has evolved into a major writer with an amazing confidence, one who writes, "not to please readers, but out of a sense of necessity." But she always gives Dorris credit for the roots of her success, as when she says, "*Love Medicine* would not have become a novel if Michael hadn't pointed out that it was a novel and I should finish it" (Chavkin and Chavkin 253, 258). So moving into the 1990s, both tell us they are ready to accept "each other's suggestions completely" (Croft 90).

Then, in 1991, Dorris and Erdrich enter a fourth stage with the publication of *The Crown of Columbus*. Is this a new mode of collaboration? One difference is that it is published under both their names. Perhaps it is the least artistic of any of their novels; some see it as "a distinctly commercial novel" (Kakutani), since the writers were given an advance of $1.5 million. Still, it does tell us something about the way they write. The two claim the work was in their minds for ten years and finally came to fruition while they were on a trip through Saskatchewan and discovered a translation of Columbus's diary in an old library. In developing this novel, they say, one did one chapter and then turned the next over to the other (Schumacher 181); if this is what they did, it is a different procedure from before. Chapter 10, for instance, is obviously Dorris's, for it is speculative and prosy; Roger is concerned with "meat" for the trip to the Bahamas, the importance of a "plan" to get there, certain problems with Vivian—"all impulse, all exterior signal" (176), coupled with his reliance on her: "She led, I endeavored to follow, to anticipate her forward step with a backward feint of my own" (179). By contrast, chapter 11 is more Erdrich. It is rooted in violent action, complete with tough language, as when Vivian meets Cobb—the man who holds part of the mysterious diary of Columbus. Now there is imagery—it is Cobb's "heart of darkness"—strong dialogue, excerpts from the diary. There is also speculation on Vivian's part, but it is more intense than Roger's and focused on her end. "My obsession to know matched his (Cobb's) to possess," Vivian says (200). The chapters complement one another, but they are different in tone as the two academicians struggle to discover something significant—for themselves, but also for the country's history. Vivian says, "Cobb wanted only a crown. I wanted America back" (199).

No doubt the overall style of *Crown of Columbus* is closer to Dorris's than Erdrich's, though the subject more befits her, for the protagonist is a woman on a wild journey to the Caribbean, followed by a tentative, questioning husband. The protagonists, of course, are not the authors, but the theme and structure of the work involves two people struggling in different ways to come up with something significant. Erdrich says at one time, "We shared in one book the creation of ourselves" (Chavkin and Chavkin 226). And though some see it in the context of "Raiders of the Lost Ark" (Kakutani), others claim it is "an important literary achievement" in which the authors' "passion for history and poetry brings a texture to the novel that catapults it far beyond the thriller's realm" (Wood E3). Here both are writers searching for a subject, and they frame the process in the context of Christopher Columbus setting out for a new world treasure. Central to the book is the process of discovery, and I think we can trust that it is "the power of curiosity" (Chavkin and Chavkin 211) that drives the writers, as it did Columbus, to their goal.

At this point (stage 5) one might note that, after the publication of *The Crown of Columbus* in 1991, our perception of the collaboration between Erdrich and Dorris is largely limited to textual analysis, for the two have stopped giving interviews. Despite considerable tension in their lives, it is still a highly productive time for both writers, though the kind of writing each is pursuing now appears to be more individual than communal. For his part, Dorris is dealing with the aftereffects of *The Broken Cord*, whose subject had little to do with Erdrich. No doubt, both as a writer and as a father, he was disturbed at the response to the book, for he found it necessary to answer the Sioux writer-critic Elizabeth Cook-Lynn when she called his approach irresponsible and demeaning to Native mothers (see her "*Why I Can't Read*" 11–16). It is also revealing that in "The Benchmark," the lead short story in *Working Men*, the protagonist mourns the physical and psychic loss of his family, first his favorite son—Dorris had lost an adopted son—and finally his wife, while trying to keep his mind on something stable. The straightforward style of writing is not one that reflects Erdrich's input in any obvious way. Consider this reflection of the progatonist after learning of his wife's terminal cancer:

> We made a weir of habit that lasted almost a year, and gave the idea of death the time to settle, buried it from conscious thought. . . . [A]fter that it got so we could talk in cautious ways, disagreements, agree on plans. Martha took the lead and I listened, became the sounding board for her.   (13–14)

Here the relationship of the couple parallels that of Roger and Vivian in *Crown of Columbus*. Indeed, Dorris dedicates the book to Erdrich, "the sifter, the sander, the ear, the eye, the careful heart." But given the tragic circumstances within their family at the time—Dorris's son died when hit by a car—the dedication and the story itself are reminiscent of past (rather than present) experiences of the author. Dorris also published other works, like *Rooms in the House of Stone*, a collection of essays that challenge the reader to confront large human problems, like poverty in Zimbabwe, which he had visited. Such reflective pieces have little connection to Erdrich as his collaborator.

Even more to the point are the works published by Erdrich around this time. In 1993 she published a revision of *Love Medicine*, adding four new chapters and making small changes in others. Then in the next two years she wrote two novels—*The Bingo Palace* and *Tales of Burning Love*. Here she is more concerned with championing traditional Ojibwe values—values that Allan Chavkin sees as the source of her "greatest originality" (Introduction 2). Lipsha, as a young medicine man on a vision quest, and his trickster father Gerry escaping from prison, return from the pages of *Love Medicine* to come together once again as family in *Bingo Palace*. Likewise, Fleur returns from the shores of Matchimanito Lake in *Tracks* to win back the land lost in that novel. In these works more emphasis is put on "Indi'n humor" as a survival technique (Peterson). Gambling seems to be a more open-ended possibility (as exemplified in the development of Lyman Lamartine) for saving Indian land and thereby enabling Natives to flourish in the future (Purdy). Metaphors related to hunting are used to perpetuate ancient values associated with the forest as a means of capturing traditional ways while transforming them to fit contemporary contexts (Gish). The new Erdrich also surfaces more overtly as a feminist; witness the development of Fleur, Marie, Lulu, and even Zelda— female characters who more aggressively further Native concerns (Van Dyke). In short, recent critics see this author as connected to the old, while becoming highly involved in the politics of the new. This is a different Erdrich from the one Dorris helped to put together her first three novels, and here the two are mute about any mutual support.

It is also possible to look at the themes of her 1990s works in a new way. Both *Bingo Palace* and its successor, *Tales of Burning Love*, are about frustrated romantic love—a subject of growing interest to Erdrich, but hardly present in Dorris's works. In *Bingo Palace*, Lipsha, who had come of age through discovering his parents in *Love Medicine*, has dissipated his life in Fargo and must return to the reservation once again to find himself, this time through romance. In the end he loses his loved one, Shawnee Ray (though she is still thinking of him). Here the author employs such techniques as the trickster motif (Lipsha), magic realism (Lipsha's parents fly away together in a mythical car), and Indian humor (a skunk capping off Lipsha's vision quest). Foreign to Dorris's writing, these techniques help emphasize the importance of family and tribal support (J. R. Smith, *Writing Tricksters* 86), subjects emerging as more crucial for its author. Similarly, *Tales* is about lost love, or five women frustrated in love. Here the male protagonist (another Erdrich trickster) needs these women desperately and pursues them relentlessly, though he never seems to appreciate who they are as individuals. The book is set in Fargo, a town Erdrich more than Dorris knew something about, and it is here she works out the longing of her characters for passionate love, though they are scarcely satisfied. Lee Siegel notes, however, that Erdrich is different from other contemporary women authors of erotic novels in that she seeks to "re-educate" her protagonist rather than indict him (100).

The sixth and last stage embodies the final years surrounding Dorris's death, in the spring of 1997, when collaboration between the two had apparently ended, for Louise moved out of their home in 1995 (Covert A12). Dorris's second novel, *Cloud Chamber*, was soon to be published, and it was during the years following their separation that Erdrich wrote *Antelope Wife*, though it was not published until after Dorris's death. The theme and style of *Cloud Chamber* are very different from those in any of Louise's earlier novels, though in one curious way Erdrich's influence is quite evident. The book includes characters from *Yellow Raft*, and the author develops the plot of that novel, thus creating a mythic universe not unlike the one that Erdrich developed around an Ojibwe reservation in North Dakota. Again, Dorris dedicates the book to Erdrich, who "found the song and gave me voice," yet that voice is not the same as the voice in *Yellow Raft*, where the contemporary theme (the Vietman War) and three-part, cyclic structure (vs. the linear plot of *Cloud Chamber*) are far more original. At that time, when Dorris was writing *Yellow Raft*, Erdrich was also involved in the creation of characters. *Cloud Chamber* is simply chronological and in many ways autobiographical; it is rooted in Dorris's Irish background, his having been raised by three women in Louisville, and his attachment to a Montana reservation where he worked as a young man. But the novel contains nothing like the poetic prose and old Ojibwe traditions in Erdrich's novels. And unlike the endings in her books, which are often ambiguous and open-ended, his is a kind of roundup, indeed apocalyptic. A Native girl (Rayona) celebrates her naming ceremony in the presence of her black father (Elgin) and her aunts, who present her with a vase belonging to her Irish great-grandmother, Rose, after whom she is named. Still, *Cloud Chamber* lacks the social, historical, and religious power of *Yellow Raft*. Thematically and stylistically the novel is his, not a combined effort, even though Dorris in the mid 1990s continued to call Erdrich his "sifter and sander," his "ears, eyes, and heart" (*Working Men*) and never hesitated to attribute his "voice" to her, as in the dedication of *Cloud Chamber*.

Antelope Wife, by contrast, is a curious novel when considered in the context of collaboration or the lack of it. Many things about it suggest a radical separation from Erdrich's past writing and consequently from her traditional editor. It is not about North Dakota, her usual mythic background, which she developed in concert with Dorris. Rather, it is set in Minneapolis—"The city. Where we are scattered like beads," says the author (220)—where the couple had been living until their separation. In the prologue to the novel, Erdrich thanks different people but then takes the blame on herself for any errors. It is as if she is conscious that her main editor is gone. Some things about the novel remain consistent with her past. There is again no central focus or character. As far back as *Love Medicine* she speaks of a "community voice" (Coltelli, "Erdrich" 22) rather than a single protagonist. It is a perspective symbolized in the earlier novel by a spider's web, one of her favorite images— in *Beet Queen* Celestine sees "a tiny white spider making its nest" (176), the image seeming to tie together the desperate members of an extended family (see Owens 211). In *Antelope Wife* Erdrich returns to that style which made her famous and evolved when Dorris was near. There are also newer facets of this book that suggest a consciousness of Dorris. In *Cloud Chamber* Dorris traces his roots in a semiautobiographical way from Ireland to Louisville to Montana; Erdrich parallels that journey in *Antelope Wife* with a historical structure, beginning with the Ojibwe past (which is her history) and traces it through two family trees, German and Ojibwe (her ancestors) to the present. Moreover—and this is most revealing—she includes not only Ojibwe mythology but also classical mythology. Here Ceres is a key character, as is Diana, reminding us of independent women for whom feminine relationships were crucial to survival. Classical mythology was Dorris's major in college, not

Erdrich's, and in this curious way her collaborator remains in the background. Still, the voice is her own, and thematically she treats violence, death (including suicide), marital rejection, and various kinds of grief far more directly than her husband does. And though her protagonists transcend loss, for her there is no grand reunion in the end. Ultimately, the novel is hers, not his.

So what does all this say to the student of Erdrich and Dorris's unique style of collaboration? It evolved out of their lives as two creative writers, both of whom claimed to be of mixed blood, coming together at a particular time and place. Erdrich grew up in a strong family whose father paid her nickels to write stories (Bruchac, "Whatever" 97). Storytelling became her passion. Dorris, first her teacher, became her husband, then her coauthor, then her primary editor. When Erdrich writes a story about an Ojibwe reservation in North Dakota, Dorris pushes her to submit it for a $5,000 prize—a prize that she won and that sets them off on her, if not his, more serious career. Now a new kind of collaboration begins; her early novels find him in the background while she becomes known worldwide. Then he starts to write on his own, and collaboration becomes mutual. "Ego be damned" (Trueheart 121), Erdrich says, and Dorris agrees: "We've evolved a way of collaborating that works for us and we've come to depend on and enjoy and find challenging and stretching" (Foster 172). In *Crown of Columbus* they experimented, some say for the money, with coauthorship, and if nothing else the book became a testimony to their penchant for research.

After this their careers peaked, though ironically their collaboration waned. Dorris published different kinds of writing—essays theorizing on Indians as well as challenging readers morally on world poverty, short stories mostly about middle-class whites, and then *The Broken Cord*. These works came out of his study and life experiences, but they show little evidence of Erdrich's presence, except indirectly, as in "The Benchmark," which speaks of a family dissipated by loss. Meanwhile, Erdrich is evolving as a writer in new ways. With the revision of *Love Medicine* and the publication of *Bingo Palace* and *Tales of Burning Love*, she surfaces as a writer more focused on her Ojibwe roots, a connection more genuine than Dorris's, whose Indian concerns have always been more intellectual than experiential. In these mid-1990s novels, her characters are hunters and the hunted, gambling evolves as an issue related to Native survival, and Indian humor permeates the texture of her prose. Certain female characters are changed or evolve as unambiguously strong characters, and though the meaning of "love medicine" will always be her trademark, adult love relations became even more important in these later novels leading up to—and including—*Antelope Wife*.

Dorris's final novel, *Cloud Chamber*, is just that, a "clouded chamber," that is, a story at best misleading. Some, including Dorris's friend Mark Anthony Rolo, say that the image Dorris created was often a "façade" (see Covert A11). Truly, if *Cloud Chamber* is semiautobiographical, many of the details, like the death of Elgin's father in Europe after World War II and the grand reunion of the extended family at the end, mask events in Dorris's life. His father took his own life in Europe, and at the time the novel was written, Dorris's immediate family was in disarray. Early on, Passaro in interviewing Dorris and Erdrich said that the "talk of their collaboration fades almost without distinction into talk of their marriage" (167). That kind of collaboration ended with their separation from each other. *Antelope Wife* is a story about loss, anybody's loss, in situations involving great personal ties. Unlike Dorris's *Cloud Chamber*, Erdrich's novel deals directly with personal loss, betrayal, even suicide. Although their early collaboration seemed idealistic, a "literary marriage," in a letter to the *Minneapolis Star Tribune* written after Dorris's death, Erdrich speaks of "the dark and helpless side" of married and family life that is "mixed with love." Even so, she still speaks of Dorris as her "creative partner" (Covert A13). No doubt, this has a different meaning now than it did when they were editing each other's manuscripts. Still, their past together cannot but continue in some way to influence her future writings. In an earlier interview, Erdrich said, "Life is about loss and survival. And the search for tenderness" (Frenkiel 78). Or at another time, "[T]hat the characters are on a reservation is important . . . but not as important as the linked themes of survival and the healing power of love" (Grantham 45). In general, this is what she writes about, and that is what *Antelope Wife* is about, and in this sense it flows naturally from years of collaboration with Dorris, her husband and "soul" editor.

Doubling the Last Survivor: *Tracks* and American Narratives of Lost Wilderness

John McWilliams

The Surrounded—They called that place *Sniél-emen*
(Mountains of the Surrounded) because there they had
been set upon and destroyed.
> —D'Arcy McNickle, epigraph to
> *The Surrounded* (1936)

In a 1985 interview, Louise Erdrich remarked, "I don't think American Indian literature should be distinguished from mainstream literature. Setting it apart and saying that people with special interest might read this literature sets Indians apart too" (Coltelli, "Erdrich" 25). Three years later, during the year *Tracks* was published, she reaffirmed this belief, giving an additional reason to support it: "I would rather that Native American writing be seen as American writing, that all of the best writing of any ethnic group here would be included in American writing. These are university-inspired divisions so that people can have courses and concentrate on certain areas" (Chavkin and Chavkin 111). My essay seeks to honor Erdrich's preference by exploring the meanings that emerge from contextualizing *Tracks*, not within Erdrich's novels or within Native American writing but within "mainstream literature."[1] More specifically, I argue that a crucial measure of the power of *Tracks* lies in its reconfiguration of mainstream literary representations of the dilemma of the last survivor, symbolic of his or her race and occupation, who acquires heroic qualities in the moment of dispossession.

For purposes of comparison, I have chosen three well-known novels of different eras, regions, and fictional traditions: Howard Frank Mosher's *Where the Rivers Flow North* (1978), William Faulkner's *Go Down, Moses* (1942), and James Fenimore Cooper's *The Pioneers* (1823). Considered collectively, these four texts suggest that the power of fictional scenes of dispossession has even more to do with a long-standing transracial cultural condition—apprehensive regret at the loss of everything that the wilderness represents—than with the very real wrong done by the dispossession of particular Native American peoples. My essay is thus intended as a challenge, though not an affront, to those who, like me, teach courses based on the "university-inspired division" of literature into so hypothetical and separatist an entity as "Native American literature."

First, two paradigms. As long as dispossession was seen in predominately racial terms as the relentless combined force of white land speculators, cavalry, railroaders, and homesteaders taking over the red man's tribal lands, the controlling image of dispossession remained the plight of the aged male chief whose isolated dignity evoked the loss of ancestral lands, tribal customs, and a natural life attuned to circular rhythms of earth and sun. The tone of elegiac despair could range from rueful acceptance of the white man's superior technology to rage over genocide, but the keynote of this solitary patriarchal voice—as recorded by whites—was the inevitability of Indian demise. From Senachwine's "The time is near at hand, when the red men of the forest will have to leave the land of their nativity, and find a home toward the setting sun" to Chief Seattle's (alleged) "The Red Man has ever fled the approach of the White Man, as the morning mist flees before the morning sun" (Turner 250, 252) to Chief Joseph's "From where the sun now stands I will fight no more forever," this prevalent image of dying native cultures has provoked guilt over past wrongs while relieving the white man of any responsibility for future restoration (Brown, *Bury* 128). It is not surprising that the apogee of pictorial representations of this image occurred in the turn-of-the-century photographs by Edward Curtis and in the paintings by Frederic Remington, images that were created shortly after the close of the Indian Wars and after Frederick Jackson Turner proclaimed the closing of the American frontier.[2] Its literary prototype can be traced back at least to the famous closing words of the aged Tamenund in Cooper's *The Last of the Mohicans* (1826):

> The pale faces are masters of the earth and the time of the red men has not yet come again. My day has been too long. In the morning I saw the sons of Unamis happy and strong; and yet, before the night has come, have I lived to see the last warrior of the wise race of the Mohicans. (394)

This long-standing convention of quasi-epic melancholy was to acquire new life during the Native American Renaissance of the late 1960s and 1970s through the immense popularity of two books: the republication of John G. Neihardt's *Black Elk Speaks* (1932, 1961) and Dee Brown's *Bury My Heart at Wounded Knee* (1971). Indian women do not even seem to exist in Dee Brown's panorama of the wronged nobility of the West's last, doomed Indian warriors. Similarly, Neihardt renders Black Elk, whose vision quest had once allowed him to see the sacred hoop, as a reluctant warrior who lost his blood people at Wounded Knee, but not the spiritual values he shared with them. Black Elk's last words, lamenting that "a people's dream died there," declare an absolute closure for a "nation" that is seen as exclusively Sioux: "the nation's hoop is broken and scattered. There is no center any longer, and the sacred tree is dead" (230).

The second paradigm uncovers a common pattern in the shaping of the narrative climax of all four of the novels. As white economic forces of commercial development take over tribal lands, a courageous Indian, who is sometimes a survivor, sometimes a holdout, and usually a full-blood, demonstrates contempt for his or her bodily displacement at the hands of "progress." All four of the fictions symbolize the primacy and priority of tribal ways of life through the survivor's commitment to preserve a particular sacred place, sacred because it has remained undefaced by white civilization and has long been cherished by its first inhabitants. All these sacred places combine three life elements into one visualization of an ecologically balanced way of living: a stand of first-growth trees, a body of water, and a cabin or hut that remains, ironically, as the sign of a right of prior land possession, whether that right be individual, familial, or tribal. Leatherstocking's hut by the shores of Lake Otsego, the hunting camp at the Big Bottom of the Tallahatchie, Noel Lord's cabin near the headwaters of the Kingdom River, and Fleur Pillager's cabin near Lake Matchimanito must all, at the end of their respective novels, yield to the combined powers of written statute law and moneyed commercial development (farmers in *The Pioneers*, an electric power company in Mosher's novella, a lumber company in the novels of Faulkner and Erdrich). Indeed, the cutting down of a patch of first-growth forest, in all four fictions, is the culminating sign of natural decline, cultural change, and the need for departure. The counterweapons employed by the resisting survivor are limited to physical defiance (usually by the rifle), to trickery, to calling on the aid of natural forces, and to the spoken word. Although physical resistance and trickery prove effective only momentarily, the power of the words spoken by the dispossessed, especially in the novels of Cooper and Erdrich, remains in the reader's mind long after the survivor has become half resigned to leave the sacred place and to abandon or destroy the symbolic dwelling built upon it.

What sets the paradigm of the four novels clearly apart from the doomed melancholy of the dispossessed patriarch chief is the interracial, and sometimes bigendered, doubling of the last survivor. *The Pioneers*, prototype for all historical fiction about the American West, is the novel in which Cooper first establishes the bond between his two heroes, Leatherstocking and Indian John, the first a white frontiersman who dresses, looks, and often acts as an Indian and the second a dispossessed sachem whose powers of survival and protest have only recently been corrupted by Christianity and alcohol. Cooper became aware of the heroic possibilities of the two men's blood brotherhood, as D. H. Lawrence described it,[3] only when he imagined them living together, as squatter and dispossessed chief, in the hut that was the first dwelling on the shores of Lake Otsego. For Faulkner, similarly, the almost wordless hunters' bond formed between young Isaac McCaslin, white heir to the McCaslin plantation, and Sam Fathers, a triracial patriarch who lives a marginal life on the plantation and an integrated life in the big woods, is the deepest human bond formed in the entire history of the remarkably self-destructive McCaslin family. It is so deep a bond that Ike's developing view of primal wilderness and farmed land as originally and forever unownable will lead him to repudiate his plantation inheritance forever. Mosher provides for interracial doubling in a different way; he binds his defiant, aged logger, Noel Lord, to a housekeeper-mistress named Bangor, a Penobscot full-blood whose commitment to their cabin life along the Kingdom River, beside one hundred first-growth oak trees, is almost as strong as her devotion to Noel Lord himself.

Why this need, among the three "mainstream" white novelists, to link Euro-Americans and Native Americans within the already surrounded spaces of the last survivor? Historical arguments can provide a partial explanation. Whether legally or not, white frontiersmen and seeming squatters like Natty Bumppo were in fact driven off the very lands that their scouting skills had opened for settlement. In the North and in the South, lumber companies have for decades clear-cut seemingly inexhaustible forests that once provided initiations into manhood through the rituals of the hunt. Rivers long used for logging have repeatedly been dammed to serve the interests, corporate and consumer, of "cheap" electric power. In sum, many a white man, who was both competent in and respectful of the wilderness, has been callously dispossessed along with the Indian. But such historical explanations cannot by themselves account for the intensity that these interracial fictional relationships acquire within their novels. In part the explanation may be that such doubling provides the white author, through the white survivor, a vicarious way of participating in the Indian experience of dispossession from which he, because he does not know Indians intimately, feels excluded. A different or additional explanation may be sought in long-standing traditions of literary romanticism that link intuition into the divinity of nature with the viewpoint of primal peoples—a tradition that extends back beyond Thoreau or Wordsworth at least to such once-famous works as Scott's "The Lay of the Last Minstrel" and Macpherson's *Ossian*. The intensity with which Leatherstocking speaks of God in the forest, Ike McCaslin elegizes the once unpossessed land, and Noel Lord recalls his logging years in the Maine wilderness is empowered, even authenticated, by close character associations with the Indian.

Erdrich's way of doubling the last survivor alters this traditional, almost stereotypical, pattern of the last survivor in multiple ways. To begin with, her last survivor is a young woman rather than an old man. Although Fleur Pillager has all the courage, wilderness skills, and defiant determination that characterized her patriarchal literary predecessors, she is also a fully sexual being possessed of all the powers needed to call up tornadoes, to best men at the poker table, and to unite her body with a lake monster. Neither a flower nor a pillager, Fleur has remarkable abilities that are focused on preservation of sacred places and traditional ways, not simply for their own sakes, but because they might be handed down, together with her personal powers, to her daughter, Lulu. By contrast, Leatherstocking, Indian John, Sam Fathers, Ike McCaslin, Noel Lord, and Bangor had all remained insistently childless. Their dying without issue is mentioned so often that it seems to define their entire future. To Cooper, Faulkner, and Mosher, the ironic dilemma of the childless patriarch, his race dying out together with his natural purity, has to be treated with a gravity due to the signifying of a major, troubling shift in American culture. Perhaps because Erdrich is no longer primarily interested in the Lockean change from "the state of nature" to "the state of civilization" (Locke 18, 20–21), she has no interest in eliciting melancholy from the racial doubling of the barren traditionalist. In fact, Erdrich's novels develop in the opposite direction. As readers of *Love Medicine* well know, the life force that Fleur passes on to Lulu will in later years virtually mother the reservation as Lulu gives birth to nine children by many different men.

Although Fleur allows Eli Kashpaw to spend lover's time with her, she inhabits her cabin alone. Fleur's stature as lone survivor is, however, complicated by the presence of two persistent visitors who alternate and divide the novel's narrative. The fascination that Nanapush and Pauline Puyat have for Fleur's character and way of life, their attempts to support or thwart her, associate them forever with her, making them not only narrators but alternative models for ways of surviving the impending loss of Ojibwe lands. Nanapush inherits the trickster identity of Nanabozho, as Erdrich tells us,[4] but Nanapush is also a comically subversive variant of the aging childless patriarch familiar to readers of Cooper and Faulkner. Contemptuous of the Turcot Land Company, committed to the old ways, Nanapush nonetheless will make the accommodations necessary to best serve his people. His claim to father Lulu is neither sentimentality nor wish fulfillment; it is a seriocomic way of linking Ojibwe bloodlines and providing for the future. His constant sexual banter (and activity?) with Margaret Rushes Bear, his teasing of Pauline for her sexual repression, and his delight in outwitting the paper bureaucracy of the BIA demonstrate what Erdrich calls "survival humor" (Moyers 144)—a kind of humor, often about not surviving, that enables one to survive and that therefore could have no place in characterizations of the aged Indian patriarch from Cooper to Neihardt.[5]

Pauline Puyat, a mixed-blood Ojibwe, wishes to see herself as victimized survivor turned virtuous reformer. Because she presumes that the Ojibwe are a vanishing race and an inferior culture, she obsessively longs to supplant Fleur Pillager and all she represents. Her jealousy of Fleur's sexuality assumes the most perverted forms: fantasizing that Fleur is sexually insatiable, dwelling on Fleur's "rape" in the Argot butcher shop, imagining that she (Pauline) is seduced by the Devil, putting love potions in Fleur's lover's lunchbox, and, finally, stripping herself naked in order to combat Fleur's lake monster, with the ironic result that she apparently rapes and then kills her own former lover who is attempting to rescue her. Pauline's notions of worthy conduct during her people's crisis include leaving her family during the outbreak of tuberculosis, trying to kill her newborn child, and mumbling condemnatory Latin prayers over the Pillagers to show her purity before God. As narrator and would-be savior for her people, Pauline is Nanapush's exact opposite; readers of *Tracks* have repeatedly been struck by the fact that its two narrators agree on little or nothing.

The ways in which the characterization of Pauline transforms the literary tradition of racial doubling reveal Erdrich's subversive, comic purpose. Pauline fantasizes that her greatest moment of self-vindication occurred when God told her she was white, entitled to become Sister Leopolda, bride of Christ. Instead of the doubled white survivor sharing vicariously in Indian values, Erdrich's "white" survivor thus prides herself on trying to disavow and eliminate Indian traditions entirely. To Erdrich, the hidden face of the last survivor is violent conversion to the white Christian missionary tradition. The sado-masochistic fantasies that prompt Pauline's mad violence could have caused deadly ruin, were they not controllable through the comic power that Nanapush's tricks and Nanapush's narrative voice finally exert over them. One cannot imagine so grotesque a character as Pauline Puyat being introduced among the Indian survivors of the "mainstream" literary tradition. Because Sister Leopolda is in fact a mixed-blood Ojibwe, her characterization tempts the reader of *Tracks* to conclude that, whenever Pauline is speaking, a temporary plague seems to have descended, in perversely comic ways, on both racial houses.

In all four fictions, the doubling of the last Indian survivor is accompanied by a divided response to the disappearing frontier. As a symbol of wilderness, the first-growth forest, with its static associations of age, dignity, splendor, and the impress of the Deity, is contrasted with the last survivor's hunting of a particularly feral, violent, almost protean beast. In Cooper's novel, it is the thoughtlessly strong Billy Kirby who axes down the forest and whose presence before Leatherstocking's cabin, search warrant in hand, leads Leatherstocking to resist arrest with a rifle. But the wrongs done by Billy Kirby to both the forest and its admirable frontiersman are balanced against our contrasting concern over the instinctive glee with which Leatherstocking slits a deer's throat to defy a conservation law and over his real need to instantly shoot a panther that is about to attack Elizabeth Temple.

Faulkner's beast sometimes seems to be an emanation of the forest. Old Ben and the Big Woods from which he emerges share essential traits ("an anachronism indomitable and invincible out of an old dead time, a phantom, epitome and apotheosis of the old wild life, which the little puny humans swarmed and hacked at in a fury of abhorrence and fear" [193]). However, Old Ben not only leaves a path of wreckage, blood, and destruction behind him; he also "has broken the rules" (214) in a way that requires his death, along with the deaths of Sam Fathers and the vicious killer dog named Wolf. Mosher's novella continues the pattern. During the days in which Noel Lord struggles to harvest "his" ancestral oak trees, hoping to preserve them from becoming a tourist attraction and hoping to earn the money to move to

Oregon, he is drawn away from his logging into futile pursuit of a beast said to be Vermont's last panther.

Because the lake monster Misshepeshu, an Ojibwe spirit force dwelling in Lake Matchimanito, derives from tribal legend rather than authorial invention, its identity as a beast must remain unverifiable. Misshepeshu may be a real natural power, a fantasy for arousing sexuality and violence, or a legend invoked to scare away possible intruders and unify the Ojibwe survivors—or perhaps all three, depending on the uses of the occasion.[6] We can be sure only that the feral, uncontrollable, violent qualities ascribed to Misshepeshu correspond to, perhaps strengthen, the same qualities in Fleur herself. This evasive association, however, confirms the troubling insight all four fictions offer into the juxtaposition of first-growth forest with murderous beast. Nature's sacred grandeur may be symbolized by a stand of first-growth forest,[7] but within that forest is a beast that represents the primordial ferocity of nature from which human beings have become at least partially—and perhaps thankfully—separated.

Despite the remarkable similarities of situation at novel's end, the survivors' attitudes toward their dispossession range tellingly along a spectrum from resignation to defiance. To use Faulknerian terms, the last survivors must find the right balance between the necessity to relinquish, the urge to renounce, and the consequences of repudiation. For Cooper's Indian John, the balance is comparatively easy to find. Because Indian John dies in the fire that consumes Mount Vision, his end is a highly staged speech of racial denunciation, ostensibly addressed to Elizabeth Temple, but in reality intended for Cooper's reader. During his last hours, John reverts to his Mohican allegiance, denouncing whites for practicing the worst atrocity charged against the Indian, namely, "burying their tomahawks in each other's brains, for this very land" and tearing land from the Indian "as a scalp is torn from an enemy" (401). By Faulkner's time, such arguing against the wrong of Indian dispossession seemed unfortunately to have become a futile anachronism. Sam Fathers's role is primarily to serve as Ike's surrogate father, a wilderness mentor who enables Ike's initiation into manhood. The integral reverence for the wild that seems to pass away as Sam dies is sometimes implied by Sam's few terse words in Chickasaw ("Oleh, Chief, Grandfather" or "Let me go home"), but it is more often conveyed by gesture and picture. Sam Fathers's body "lying motionless on his face in the trampled mud" as Old Ben dies and Sam's wordless death on his cot ("He just quit") remain the silent scenes by which Faulkner's mixed-blood chief will be remembered (184, 245, 248).[8]

The narrative resolutions for the surviving Indian in the two late-twentieth-century novels are as different from each other as they are from Cooper and Faulkner. Instead of the memorable death of an aged chief, Mosher and Erdrich conclude their plots with scenes of dispossessed Indian women enacting ritualistic departures. Bangor mourns Noel Lord's death by providing him with a biracial burial: she places Lord's rifle and horse in his grave but also fashions a Christian gravestone on which is scratched the single word "Oregon" (205). Although Bangor had scorned the steam-crane operator of the power company, whom she had named "New York Money" (166), Mosher at the novella's end is not interested in developing the possibilities of Bangor's bearing witness against the forces of corporate development. Because Bangor's stature is rather traditionally linked to her devotion to her man and their way of life together, she must depart into a placeless and undefinable future.

Bangor would have had no desire to meet Noel Lord's continuing lease payments even if she had had the opportunity. Fleur Pillager, by contrast, does everything she can to meet the yearly fees due on the Pillager land allotment, only to be foiled by trusting her fellow Ojibwe, Nector Kashpaw, to make the payment at the land agent's office.[9] When the Turcot Company, "leveler of a whole forest" (219), moves in to surround "the square mile of towering oaks, a circle around Fleur's cabin" (220), Fleur at first summons the kind of strength needed to commit suicide in the lake rather than yield up the Pillager land and trees. Rescued by Eli and Nanapush, she then summons a quite different kind of strength. After secretly axing the oaks nearly through the trunk, she awaits the tornado that will level the trees and crush the lumber company's machines and men, including paid Ojibwe day laborers, beneath the weight of the tree fall. Fleur anticipates her triumph in a gesture that combines animal revenge with trickster calculation. As the tornado gathers strength, the Turcot Company's laborers "bit their lips, glanced over their shoulders at Fleur, who bared her teeth in a wide smile that frightened even those who did not understand the smiles of Pillagers" (223). The climactic felling of the Pillager oaks thus associates the power of a full-blooded Indian woman's will with a sweeping natural force capable of subduing, if only momentarily, the forces of corporate legality and male strength.[10] But Erdrich's climactic scene also reminds us, as Cooper, Faulkner, and Mosher never do, that those "progressive" Indians (Morrisseys and Lazarres mainly), who have eagerly bought up land allotments and labored profitably for white corporations, have contributed significantly to their people's collective dispossession.

Indian John, Sam Fathers, and Bangor all brought one life, one way of living, to complete closure. The reader's last image of Fleur is utterly different in kind. Out of the Pillager oaks she fashions the green cart whose wheels will make the tracks of her ongoing life. Instead of burying her old way of life, as Bangor does, Fleur literally takes her ancestors' grave markers with her, fastened to her cart as witness to her belief in generational continuity, her faith in a future that will contain her past. Although the occasion for the telling of the novel is Nanapush's need to inform Lulu of the admirable truth about her mother's strength, it is also true that the indomitable Fleur, and not Lulu of the many children, is the only character who appears in the four novels. The closing scene of *The Bingo Palace* leaves the reader with a virtual dream vision of Fleur returning to the shores of Matchimanito as its presiding spirit, dragging Pillager bones back to repossess the lakeshore, no matter how many times the land may have been sold, rebought, gambled away.

The responses of the doubled white character to final dispossession again show Erdrich's divergence from the pattern of literary tradition. Leatherstocking chooses to leave his hut and the lake, not only because he has been hounded by the law and because of the encroachments of Judge Temple's town, but also because Indian John's death has released him from his human tie to the sanctity of that particular place. After defiantly burning his hut in front of the law's minions, Leatherstocking chooses to depart into the receding western wilderness, exposing the pretense of civilization's progress by a final, barbed anticipation of "the great day when the whites shall meet the red-skins in judgment, and justice shall be the law, and not power" (455). Ike McCaslin's decisive repudiation of his patrimony, after his hunting experiences and after Ike fully understands the wrong of his family's denial of miscegenation, proves costly in the extreme. Although Leatherstocking never felt that a paper deed could legitimate land possession, he (and Cooper as well) clearly believed that the Indians had been "the original owners of the soil" (83). For Ike the experience of the primordial purity of the big woods has been so overpowering that he even condemns the "Indian ruthless enough to pretend that any fragment of it [the big woods] had been his to convey" (101). Because the wilderness available to Leatherstocking is gone by the 1880s and because Ike is not a frontier hunter, no matter how intense his hunting experiences may have been, the absolutism of Ike's ethical purity reduces him to the marginality of a rented room, to societal as well as sexual barrenness and ultimately to an inability to love. Leatherstocking's repeated departures may represent a loss to the civilization that follows him, but Ike's repudiation of possession in any form must deprive his spiritual virtue of any power and can end only, as Cass Edmonds reminds him, in severest cost to self. By Faulkner's time, preserving natural innocence through repudiating the social compact seemed to have become far more complex, if not impossible.

Instead of departing in a burst of high-minded renunciatory rhetoric, Noel Lord dies as a logger attempting to thwart the power company. His end, however, is every bit as dramatic and symbolic as Leatherstocking's or Ike's. The most memorable single image of Mosher's novella is of Noel Lord, hanging above the rushing waters, trying to save himself by driving his hand hook into his wooden dam's crosspiece. This aged lumberman, half Canuck and half Anglo, unmarried to his Penobscot mistress, but a would-be "owner" of his pines and his logging flume, has at the last become, literally, hoist with his own petard. From the outset, Noel Lord would rather cut down his first-growth pines for sale than have them preserved for tourists to gawk at. Releasing the immense pines down the flume may smash the power company's dam, but it also causes his own death. Stuck on his own hand hook, Mosher's ironically named Lord is in fact wilderness logging's last holdout, an unmetaphysical Ahab who cannot possibly survive because he has always preferred, in Bangor's taunting refrain, to "cut off him nose to spite him face" (87).

The drive to closure evident in the way these doubled white characters face dispossession has no equivalent in *Tracks*. Pauline's mad fantasy that she is the "white" bride of Christ is her way of entirely renouncing a woods life and her Ojibwe heritage. The character in *Tracks* who, in age, endurance, skills, courage, and decency, is most closely linked to the Leatherstocking tradition is Nanapush. But instead of publicly defying dispossession as Leatherstocking and Indian John had done, Nanapush refuses to sell his allotment to the lumber company, but then uses the benefits of his Jesuit education to retain and regain whatever he can, by craft and language, for his people. A year before the lumber company closes in on Fleur's square mile of first-growth oaks, Nanapush has a dream:

> I stood in a birch forest of tall straight trees. I was one among many in a shelter of strength and beauty. Suddenly, a loud report, thunder, and they toppled down like matchsticks, all flattened around me in an instant. I was the only one left standing. And now, as I weakened, I swayed and bent nearer to the earth.   (127)

Nanapush's dream is prophetic of the novel's resolution in more than the obvious way. Fleur's oaks may be flattened like matchsticks, but Nanapush will remain, weakened but standing, because he knows how to bend to the ground while remaining rooted. Is it any wonder that the simile in the last sentence of the novel describes Nanapush and Margaret holding on "like creaking oaks" against the rush of Lulu, returning from government Indian school to confront them in her smoldering orange dress (226)?

A last measure of the ways *Tracks* reconfigures its fictional tradition is the crucial moment of Lulu's birth. Nanapush recalls, "You were born on the day we shot the last bear, drunk, on the reservation" (58). True to his grammar, Nanapush reminds Lulu that it was indeed the bear, not Fleur or Nanapush himself, who was drunk. After consuming Nanapush's jug of wine, the bear "then lost her mind and stumbled into the beaten grass of Fleur's yard" (58). Because there has continued to be much talk among the Ojibwe about this legendary moment, Nanapaush is not quite certain that the intruder was not "a spirit bear," but he remains sure of one thing: "So I know that when Fleur saw the bear in the house she was filled with such fear and power that she raised herself on the mound of blankets and gave birth" (60). Given Erdrich's often proclaimed admiration for Faulkner's novels, it is hard not to read this moment as her playful recasting of "The Bear," as well as a reference to the

Pillagers' belonging to the Bear Clan. The sacramental gravity with which Faulkner had rendered the hunting of the decidedly male Old Ben is here replaced by comedy of accident as the she-bear stumbles drunkenly into the moment of Lulu's birth. The "fear and power" with which Fleur confronts the she-bear and brings Lulu into the world provide a model of counterheroism to Faulkner's ultimately barren male hunt. For Louise Erdrich, the ongoing force of sheer human vitality, embodied in such different ways in Fleur and in Nanapush, compensates for, even overwhelms, the rage or melancholy long associated with being the last survivor. Fleur's dispossession will prove to be a beginning, not an end.

NOTES

[1]If Erdrich continues to write interconnected fictions in series, the form of the entire work is likely to resemble, even more closely than it currently does, Faulkner's Yoknapatawpha novels or Balzac's *Comédie humaine*.

[2]Notable examples are Frederic Remington's *When His Heart Went Bad* (1908) and *The Outline* (1909) and the following Curtis portrait-photographs: *Slow Bull-Oglala Sioux*, *Chief Joseph Nez Percé*, *Black Eagle-Assiniboin*, *Raven Blanket-Nez Percé*, and *The Scout-Apache*.

[3]Lawrence dwelt on "this perpetual blood-brother theme of the Leatherstocking novels" in order to insist on its presumably still hidden importance: "At present it is a sheer myth" (36, 37).

[4]Nanapush tells Lulu that his father gave him his name "[b]ecause it's got to do with trickery and living in the bush" (*Tracks* 33). On Nanapush as Nanabozho, see J. Smith, *Writing* 90–103.

[5]An equal degree of difference separates Nanapush and Fleur from such seemingly similar last-survivor full-bloods as grandmother Aho in Scott Momaday's *The Way to Rainy Mountain* (1969) and Old Betonie in Leslie Silko's *Ceremony* (1977). For Momaday and Silko, the aged, solitary patriarch or matriarch serves primarily as a means by which a young man of mixed blood can recover the knowledge and power of tribal traditions he has too long neglected. Fleur and Nanapush, however, are powerful as people rather than agents; their ability to do is finally more important than their ability to advise.

[6]On Erdrich's references to Misshepeshu and their relation to ethnographers' versions of Ojibwe tales of the male water monster Micipiju, see Brehm.

[7]William Cullen Bryant, the first American poet whose voice attained broad cultural reach, often wrote as if nature's sacrality could be fixed forever if a solitary observer would only enter with true humility into a cathedral grove of trees. See, for example, Bryant's 1817 "Inscription for the Entrance to a Wood" and his 1825 "A Forest Hymn" (McQuade et al. 1016, 1019).

[8]Sam Fathers's dying plea spoken to no one and everyone, "Let me out. Let me out. . . . Let me out, master. . . . Let me go home" (245), seems clearly meant to provide a Chickasaw version of the refrain from the Negro spiritual: "Go Down, Moses, way down in Egypt land / Tell old Pharaoh, let my people go."

[9]Erdrich's description of the ways in which the provisions of the infamous Dawes Severalty Act of 1887 (also called the Allotment Act) eventually deprived Native Americans of much of the best land within their reservations is persuasive. William T. Hagen concluded, "Between 1887 and 1934 the Indians were separated from an estimated 86,000,000 of a total of 138,000,000 acres. Most of that remaining was desert or semi-desert: worthless to the white population." For the Ojibwe, the process had started even earlier: "Of 1,735 Chippewas granted allotments about 1871, five-sixths of them had sold their lands or been defrauded of them by unscrupulous whites by 1878" (Hagen 147, 141).

[10]Annette Van Dyke has rightly linked Erdrich's characterization of Fleur Pillager to the celebration of the hitherto suppressed powers of Native American women voiced in Paula Gunn Allen's influential *The Scared Hoop*. The repulsive attitudes and sporadic violence of Pauline Puyat, however, must complicate any claim that Erdrich's fictions uniformly affirm Indian women's presumably "natural" powers.

Identity Indexes in *Love Medicine* and "Jacklight"

James Ruppert

In a 1990 interview with Bill Moyers, Erdrich speaks of seeing herself and Michael Dorris as a "citizen of two nations" (Moyers 469), and doubtless that perception is carried over into her literary work. As such a citizen, Erdrich is positioned to move fluidly between the two nations and to help subtly enhance the one that has been "left in the wake of catastrophe" ("Where" 23). She strives to celebrate her Native heritage and to protect it, while creating engaging narratives that illuminate and challenge members of both nations. For Erdrich, the two nations have different histories, perspectives, and worldviews, some of which she shares with Moyers in the interview. As a writer trying to satisfy both nations, she must try to create characters who are as complex and mediational as she is herself. These characters must inhabit a realm of two nations whose definitions of identity are not always the same, and yet the characters must have an identity comprehensible by members of both nations. Later in the interview, Dorris remarks how he and Erdrich always try to give readers a choice in the interpretation of the actions of a character, a choice between a mystical reason and a psychological one. Such dual, mediational characters, who are not rigid or locked into one symbolic meaning but open to a variety of interpretations, eventually lead readers to larger questions about values, assumptions, worldview, and identity.

Many students are tempted to look at Erdrich's characters as humorous, exaggerated, or, as they say to me, "not real," often because the characters seem to be talking about many things at once. There is almost a magic realist element to them that distances readers from personal identification while directing them to larger cultural concerns. Students need to understand that Erdrich is not interested in realist representation. Her characters are intended to lead us to what Barre Toelken calls "culturally moral subjects" (86)—those discourses about values, community, continuance, history, meaning, health, and love that affect members of both nations, but affect them differently. The character constructs are intended to mediate among different epistemological frameworks with the goal of using them to illuminate and enrich one another. To do this, the constructed identities of characters must lead to the important cultural discourses in both nations, discourses that will determine the fate of individuals and nations.

To get at this view of identity, I digress for a moment to ask you to recall the work of C. S. Peirce, an influential figure in the history of linguistics. In his discussion of signs, Peirce identifies three categories of signs found in language: the icon, the index, and the symbol. The icon, according to Peirce, is a sign that represents its object mainly by its similarity to it; the relation is not arbitrary but is one of resemblance or likeness. Thus, for instance, the portrait of a man resembles him. An index is a sign by virtue of an existential bond between itself and its object. Examples of this might be footprints in the sand, weathercocks, or medical symptoms. Lastly, a symbol is an arbitrary sign that requires no resemblance or existential bond; it is a matter of convention, like the meaning assigned the American flag or specific words (101–15).

As a sign, the index is the most fluid, most dynamic, since it is given its nature by the context or referent. It points to subjects and creates meaning through its pointing, but then moves on and points elsewhere. As the wind blows, the weather vane moves. We could express this textual position as dialogic discourse that mediates Native or Western perspectives expressed through characters constructed as indexical signs ready to direct listeners and readers to other cultural meanings, to culturally moral subjects.

Perhaps we could look at one of Erdrich's better-known and often republished poems, "Jacklight," to tease out her use of indexical representation so as to engage multiple discourses through a fluid sense of identity. The work is structured around a *we/them* dichotomy sustained throughout the poem. As a persona poem, it immediately draws the reader's attention to the speaker. Who is the *we*? Who is the *them*? The reference to jacklight suggests that this is a hunting scene with the *we* being animals, perhaps deer, and the *them* being hunters. The *we* are drawn out of the woods by the jacklight. Frozen, they smell the hunters using this unethical hunting technique and consider their brutal lives and the obdurate and unyielding nature of their relationships. However, as the *we* retreat, they now draw the *them* into the dark of the forest, a darkness unknown to the *them* but one they enter with a transfixed gaze, similar to the jacklighted stare of the *we*. In the poem, then, the tables are turned, and the hunters are lured into the forest by the prey. Perhaps Erdrich suggests that the natural world has hidden enticements to pull us out of brutal lives often considered civilized and rational. The more we are willing to use unethical means of subduing the world around us, the more we are placing ourselves in a position to be drawn into it, but with no clue to its depth. The 1980s discourse in Native and non-Native communities on ecological destruction and Native worldviews might provide the cultural conversations referenced here. One might say that Erdrich uses the idea position of the *we* to engage a discourse about the natural world versus civilization and the animal nature that is on occasion hidden within us. Both of these may sometimes jacklight us.

However, the poem's epigraph suggests a second direction the index of the *we* may take us. The epigraph reads, "The same Chippewa word is used both for flirting and hunting game, while another Chippewa word connotes both using force in intercourse and also killing a bear with one's bare hands." It suggests that the encounter depicted might be addressing a discourse about men and women since flirting and sex are equated with the violence of hunting. If the *we* points to women, then readers can see the women in seclusion from the dominant violence of the men. They are drawn out of the protecting natural shelter of the forest, perhaps even from the enfolding community of women, by the power of men, but it is a power used unethically. They are jacklighted straight to their hearts by love, sex, or even the sensuality of the faceless men. Yet their knowledge of the continuation of this uneven relationship empowers them to draw the men into the forest (the realm inhabited by women), where the men, having no tools and no knowledge, are at a disadvantage. It seems the men are hypnotized too, perhaps even jacklighted.

When followed in this direction, the *we* leads to a series of idea positions on love, sex, violence, power, and dominance. Certainly one can see these positions in terms of the dominant society's 1980s cultural discussion regarding feminism, domestic violence, and women's empowerment. However, such a discourse was current and continues in many Native communities and organizations. Indeed, Erdrich's reference to the Ojibwe suggests a Native context for the poem. Erdrich's epigraph might suggest that the difficulties of male-female relationships and the discourse about these difficulties is age-old, old enough to have been incorporated into the language itself. Such an idea position surely responds to other positions of the day that postulated changed cultural roles as the source of difficulties between Native men and women.

Returning to the epigraph, the reader may now be ready to think about why Erdrich's reference is to Ojibwe language and custom. The *we* may be seen as engaging discourses about animals and women, but Erdrich places it in a Native context. The identity of the *we* can be seen to have a major Indian component not readily apparent to the non-Native reader. It is with no little irony that Native communities have watched and discussed Americans and Europeans trying to become Indians, from the hippies of the 1960s to the German Indian clubs to the New Age movement. Indeed, in "Harold of Orange" Gerald Vizenor has Harold joke about luring the Anglos onto the reservations and confining them there, while the Natives escape. Seen from this angle, the *we* identifies the reality of victimization and oppression. The Native *we* knows completely the identity of those who have hunted them for centuries and knows the deep fascination with the hidden qualities of Native experience. Such discourse often works on ways to turn the tables. The *we* knows that it may be able to jacklight the non-Native world as much of Native experience has been jacklighted by the dominant society. Though this discourse field is one more readily available to those engaged in the Native discourses of the early 1980s, Erdrich fuses it with the others.

The identity of the *we* is accessible only when one understands the discourses engaged. The *we* is an index that leads to identity questions; however, those questions have meaning only in terms of the positions taken in a discourse field. Some of those discourses continue today; some are centuries old; others are quiet now like lulls in conversations.

When students have looked at a poem like "Jacklight," they can move back to *Love Medicine* with a much greater understanding of the characters and the discourses they engage. First of all, there's the character of Lipsha Morrissey. A major thread holding the novel together is Lipsha's attempt to define an identity for himself. As an abandoned child, Lipsha deals with competing stories that surface in his mind as paths to an understanding of who he is, where he comes from, who his father is, and what his place is in the world of Erdrich's imaginary North Dakota reservation.

This quest for identity is expressed by his engagement in a number of fields of discourse. Erdrich wants us to see him as an orphan with no clear parentage; however, he also assumes responsibility for the care of the older members of his adopted family. Lipsha sees himself as defining his identity in terms of a social discussion of how he acts toward others and the role of love and loyalty to family. He also sees himself as an innocent, someone driven by the need to know his background, for he believes that he will know himself better if he knows with certainty who his parents were. These discussions of identity lead readers into differing lines of thought and conversation. Caregivers and orphans, innocents and identity quests are identifiable components of modern American discourses. They are well outlined in psychological and sociological discussions of selfhood, though Erdrich may stake out new positions through them.

Less immediate is the way Lipsha engages discussions of a more communal sense of self. He knows that his touch can help heal people. These actions give him an identity and a role. Only when he realizes that he comes from a long line of Native healers can he place himself in a communal identity. As he does this, Erdrich engages the reader in a discourse about healing and spirit power that might be a bit disconcerting for non-Native readers. But it is a discourse that gives Lipsha a position and advances the discussion of efficacy and agency in spiritual and physical interactions.

When Lispha understands himself to be the son of Gerry Nanapush, he completes his construction of identity by engaging a discourse about the relationship between myth and reality. As the son of a trickster, Lipsha comes to understand his own nature as an extension of his trickster heritage. Rather than separate myth from reality, Erdrich uses Lipsha's sense of identity to posit the eternal expression of myth in the world around us. As she takes this position, she moves readers into accepting the legitimacy of the discourse fields engaged. Each sense of identity functions like an index. No one sense is fixed, superior, essential. Identity is existential and contingent. Or, as Lipsha says, "Belonging is a matter of deciding to" (348). Through Lipsha's senses of identity, Erdrich is able to converse with what she sees as the culturally moral subjects of *Love Medicine*. Lipsha is just the convenient weather vane.

Something similar could be said for Gerry Nanapush. Erdrich uses the character of Nanapush to direct the reader to a number of discourses. A convict turned political hero, he explores the discourse surrounding the American Indian Movement type of political activism, yet he is a reluctant activist. He sees himself, and is seen by others, as a social symbol. They project their hopes and fears on him. Through the indexical nature of his identity, they are able to discuss resistance and survival, to give it a face and form. Yet Erdrich humanizes this symbol by making Nanapush a loving husband and tender father. Personal and political passions are interwoven, as is true for all charismatic leaders. Nanapush assumes the identity of a warrior against modern America, but it is a role consistent with his communal heritage as son of Old Man Pillager. Nanapush's style of confrontation and evasion echoes the actions of his namesake Nanabozho, the trickster. Every one of his magical escapes reinforces an Ojibwe cultural identity and defines him as a physical representation of the trickster. However, his presence is felt only by his absence, his escapes. He is the perfect cipher. It is through the discourse that surrounds him that Erdrich addresses a reality greater than Nanapush's indexical identity.

One could look at all the characters in *Love Medicine* or in many poems besides "Jacklight" with an eye toward the discourses to which Erdrich's characters lead the readers. Clearly Henry Lamartine introduces much of the discourse surrounding the Vietnam War, such as the disproportionally large number of minority veterans, and the Native American experience of the war. Suicide and the conflict between leaving and returning to the reservation give context to Henry's personal life. Lulu Lamartine introduces the effects of economic development on the reservation but also engages a discourse about the freedom of intimate affections. Marie Lazarre introduces the question of adoption, and Nector Kashpaw presents the ideas of media stereotyping and of the intricacies of tribal government. All this is not to say that Erdrich is uninterested in character formation. Rather, all character formation leads readers to the discourse about important cultural issues. Once the readers move down that path, they are pulled into a web of discourse about culturally moral subjects at the bedrock of meaning creation. Old Nanapush in *Tracks* explains that the stories of people pull listeners and tellers into that web of narrative because "[t]hey're attached, and once I start there is no end to telling because they're hooked from one side to the other, mouth to tail" (46).

Reading *The Beet Queen* from a Feminist Perspective

Vanessa Holford Diana

This essay suggests some of the ways that a feminist approach to Louise Erdrich's *The Beet Queen* might be implemented in the classroom. A revolutionary feminist pedagogy aims, according to bell hooks,

> to teach us an oppositional world view . . . that would enable us to see ourselves not through the lens of racism or racist stereotypes but one that would enable us to . . . look at ourselves, at the world around us, critically—analytically—to see ourselves first and foremost as striving for wholeness, for unity of heart, mind, body, and spirit. (79)

Hooks's comment suggests that achieving this "wholeness" depends on "see[ing] ourselves" in ways that critique the influences of sexism, racism, homophobia, or other oppressive constructs on self-perception. While a feminist analysis might traditionally consider only issues related to gender, critics such as Gloria Anzaldúa and Cherríe Moraga argue that gender, race, and sexuality are inextricably related and must be considered together. Similarly, while a feminist reading typically "emphasizes the destructive results of . . . gender teachings on those who are biologically female" (Baym 245), Erdrich's novel demands that readers consider the results of harmful gender teachings on both women and men.

To consider gender apart from other locations of oppression is to oversimplify Erdrich's vision in *The Beet Queen*. Although, according to Susan Meisenhelder, critics have noted an "apparent silence on the issue of race" in the novel, in fact the novel presents an "examination of the relationship between . . . race and gender," exploring not only gender issues but also the complexities of defining a Native American identity (45). In addition, Erdrich's critique of the matrixes of oppression in America shows that homophobia operates much as sexism and racism do. A feminist reading of *The Beet Queen*, then, might invite students to consider ways that Erdrich presents her characters from an "oppositional world view," a perspective that critiques the ways stereotypes of gender, race, or sexuality inhibit individuals from forming healthy identity definitions that unite "heart, mind, body, and spirit."

Public Representations of Gender Ideals

One way to begin a discussion of gender construction is to ask students to consider the public representations (visual and written) they associate with conventional definitions of masculinity and femininity. Magazines, such as *Sports Illustrated* and *Cosmopolitan*; children's toys, such as G.I. Joe and Barbie; and film genres, such as military action or romance, all present a matrix of gender images predicated on the binary concept of male-female biological difference. At the same time, pop culture contains examples that subvert—though often only superficially—these conventional categories. Female action heroes, for example, often still have the exaggerated physical attributes that mark them as sex objects. The relation between race and gender stereotypes can also be introduced through reference to such popular images. Eurocentric standards of beauty evident in fashion magazines or mass media representations of athletes of color offer students an opportunity to look "critically—analytically"—as hooks suggests—at some of the familiar images they encounter daily. By beginning a discussion of Erdrich's use of characterization in *The Beet Queen* in the context of such stereotypical representations, an instructor can then ask students to consider ways that Erdrich dramatizes her characters' responses to these social messages. A logical grouping would be to contrast Erdrich's characterization of those who apparently buy into conventional gender roles—Sita, Russell, and Adelaide—with her characterization of those who resist (to varying degrees) those roles—Mary, Celestine, Karl, Wallace, and Dot.

Erdrich, it can be argued, created Sita and Russell to "represent the extreme constructions of femininity and masculinity" (L. Flavin, "Gender Construction" 20). By considering the parallels Erdrich constructs between Russell's and Sita's stories, students have an opportunity to analyze Erdrich's critique of the unquestioning acceptance of externally imposed gender, sexual, and racial identity. As Meisenhelder explains:

> Erdrich . . . reserves the direst fate for two characters in the book who come closest to fulfilling social definitions of ideal male and female. In her treatment of the white woman, Sita, who bases her identity on physical beauty and marriage, and Russell, the Native American male who strives for success through football and military exploits, Erdrich both critiques white America's ideals of masculinity and femininity and suggests underlying similarities between racial and gender oppression in American society. (46)

Erdrich dramatizes the risk of Sita's fantasies of womanly success, encapsulated in her dream of modeling in Fargo and marrying a successful businessman whom Sita meets while working at a department store, by emphasizing the emptiness of a dream taken straight from a fashion magazine. Russell's "success" in the eyes of mainstream society can be summarized by a series of public representations Erdrich includes over the course of the novel: newspaper photos of Russell as a high school football star, his uniform on display in the museum, Russell mounted on the veterans' float in the Beet Festival parade.

Erdrich undercuts her representations of Sita and Russell, both of whom have attained the gender ideals they have emulated, by describing them in deathlike terms. That Sita's attempts to maintain physical perfection end up leaving her looking "stuffed and preserved" (112) communicates the danger of such mainstream public images of femininity (evident, for example, in the high rates of eating disorders among white adolescent girls). Similarly, through Russell's deathlike appearance in the parade Erdrich deconstructs not only definitions of masculinity that equate manliness with military prowess but also stereotypically romanticized representations of Native Americans as a dying race fit for museum display. Meisenhelder notes that in the parade scene "both characters [Sita and Russell]—mute and completely immobilized—receive unqualified approval. . . . Russell is amused that 'the town he'd lived in and the members of the American Legion were solemnly saluting a dead Indian' (300)" (51). Instructors can help students appreciate the irony of Russell's comment by offering a brief reference to *Love Medicine*, in which Nector observes that in the movies, "The only good Indian is a dead Indian" (124). Commenting on the parallels between Erdrich's portrayal of gender and racial stereotypes, Meisenhelder continues, "Russell's presence in the parade starkly demonstrates the dependency and spiritual death American society offers as success to Native Americans. . . . Erdrich develops this idea about racial oppression further to suggest that in white American culture, the only 'good woman' is also lifeless" (51).

Just as Erdrich illustrates how public media representations of gender identity inform Sita's and Russell's self-definition, so too she shows that gendered fiction genres, such as popular romances or adventure stories, are reference points for Adelaide's, Celestine's, and Karl's self-perception. To encourage students to analyze the assumptions on which popular representations of romance, gender, and marriage tend to rely, instructors might raise questions about popular fiction, films, television programs, or advertisements: for example, How do those media portray courtship and marriage? What do the principals in such representations look like, act like, care about? Are the couples always heterosexual? If not, what have students noticed about representations of same-sex couples in mainstream media?

Erdrich borrows from these popular genres in describing Adelaide's elopement with Omar, a flight into romantic fantasy that ultimately offers her no happiness. Similarly, in describing Karl's first sexual relationship with Giles Saint Ambrose in the freight car, Erdrich emphasizes Karl's belief in the promise of romantic adventure. Karl tries to reenact the elopement of his mother, Sita, fantasizing about a future with Ambrose:

He planned how he and Giles would travel in the boxcar, occasionally jumping off in a town they liked the look of, stealing food, maybe finding an abandoned house to live in. He pictured them together, in danger from dogs or police, outrunning farmers and store clerks. He saw them roasting chickens and sleeping together, curled tight in a jolting boxcar, like they were now.   (24–25)

Erdrich makes clear that Karl's fantasies are as much a product of popular adventure fiction as his mother's and Celestine's fantasies are the product of popular romance novels. In Karl's case, Erdrich shows that sexuality is, like race and gender, another location of oppression in the United States; Karl's homosexuality in a homophobic culture, like Sita's and Celestine's femaleness in a misogynist culture, prevents him from achieving the desired freedom and human connection represented in his fantasy. By helping students consider the parallels between Karl's and Sita's experiences, teachers can emphasize Erdrich's repeated questioning of mainstream social scripts: in Sita's case, that social script promises her reward for enacting a deathlike femininity; in Karl's case, there is no available social script in popular representations that he might follow to achieve romantic fulfillment.

An emphasis on parallels among sexism, racism, and homophobia allows instructors to present the complexity of Erdrich's social critique. Throughout the novel, Erdrich juxtaposes characters whose varying degrees of success in healthy self-definition form—by way of contrasts among them—a critique of external influences on that process of self-definition. In *The Beet Queen*, survival depends on resisting the social script. For example, unlike Sita and Adelaide, Celestine manages to resist externally imposed definitions of womanly behavior. She has learned in romance novels that "female passivity is part of experience as scripted" (L. Flavin, *"Love Medicine"* 53), but she quickly tires of that role and instead forges an identity independent of scripted femininity. The following sections discuss ways in which Erdrich's use of physical descriptions and portrayals of family and sexual relationships function to deconstruct restrictive gender definitions.

Physical Descriptions and Gender Deconstruction

To carry out feminist literary analysis, students are often encouraged to investigate "images of the female body as presented in a text" (Bressler 190). In *The Beet Queen*, however, Erdrich relies heavily on physical descriptions of both female *and* male bodies to complicate binary conceptions of gender difference. Louise Flavin notes the important contrasts in the gendered physical descriptions of Mary, Celestine, and Karl. The two women "become increasingly masculine in appearance and habits. Mary takes over her Uncle Pete's meat shop, and Celestine and she work like men. Celestine says of Mary, 'If you didn't know she was a woman you would never know it' (214), and Celestine is described as 'handsome like a man' (67)." In contrast, "Karl is described by his sister Mary as 'delicate,' with full red lips" ("Gender Construction" 19, 20). Repeatedly, Erdrich describes Celestine and Mary as physically "strong and imposing" (*Beet Queen* 125) presences, while Karl's beauty is the personal quality he seems to value most (125). The characters' ambiguous gender identities parallel their ambiguous sexual orientations as well. For each, it seems that existing models of conventional gendered behavior are inadequate.

Most striking in Erdrich's physical descriptions of her female characters is how unbeautiful the beautiful Sita seems and how attractive the "not pretty" Celestine and Mary seem (125). Erdrich's analysis of gender perceptions critiques Eurocentric definitions of beauty in ways similar to other contemporary Native American women writers'. For example, Paula Gunn Allen argues:

> If American society judiciously modeled the traditions of the various Native Nations, the place of women in society would become central, . . . [and] the ideals of physical beauty would be enlarged (to include "fat," strong-featured women, gray-haired, and wrinkled individuals, and others who in contemporary American culture are viewed as "ugly").
>
> ("Who Is" 211)

In *Yellow Woman and a Beauty of the Spirit*, Leslie Marmon Silko similarly presents a Pueblo cultural perspective on the narrow Western definitions of femininity and beauty evident in American mass media and popular culture.

Students might be asked to trace the progression of one character's physical descriptions over the course of the novel to consider the ways that gender definitions do or do not prevent that character from achieving "unity of heart, mind, body, and spirit." For example, as noted above, Erdrich's physical descriptions of Sita and Russell become increasingly deathlike as the novel progresses. Meisenhelder explores the relationship between physical and mental deterioration for Sita and Russell, both of whom end up "physical wreck[s]" as a result of their gendered behavior. At the same time, the "debilitating 'nervous' disorders both endure—Sita's drug dependency and mental breakdown, Russell's alcoholism and stroke—reflect the spiritual deaths preceding their literal ones at the end of the novel" (Meisenhelder 48, 49). In a similar depiction, Erdrich charts Wallace's physical deterioration during preparations for the Beet Festival. In his suffering can be seen the effects of rigid adherence to societal norms. In hopes of fitting into Argus society, Wallace maintains the pretense of heterosexuality, a decision by which he ironically sentences himself to a life of isolation. His relationships with others are stunted by his adherence to rigid definitions of gender and sexual orientation. His understanding of how to give his figurative daughter Dot happiness—by crowning

her the Beet Queen—is as much defined by restrictive mainstream conceptions of gender as are Sita's fantasies of life as a fashion model. As a result,
Wallace's attempt to bring Dot closer to him instead drives her away. By
contrast, the evolving physical descriptions of other characters seem to illustrate those characters' progress toward achieving "unity of heart, mind, body,
and spirit." Mary, for example, becomes first masculine, then genderless, then
completely independent in her eccentric costumes and turbans, costumes by
which she announces—albeit as a somewhat comic figure—her determination
to unhampered self-definition. The contrast between these two characters'
responses to socially defined gender roles and norms of sexuality illustrates
Erdrich's implicit argument that resisting those rigid norms is essential to the
unity hooks defines.

Sexual and Family Relationships

Another way of considering the sexual politics of *The Beet Queen* is through
an analysis of family and sexual relationships in the novel. *Sexual politics*, a
term coined by Kate Millet, "refers to the political character of gender relations, which are based on the unequal distribution of power between men
and women," so that politics are seen to "structur[e] the personal realm, every-
day life at home, as well as public institutions" (*Columbia Dictionary* 276). If
patriarchy can be represented on the microcosmic level by the conventional
nuclear family, with the father as head of the household, then the very unconventional family structures in *The Beet Queen* can be seen as ways through
which Erdrich imagines alternative, nonhierarchical familial relations between
the sexes.

As a dramatization of oppressive patriarchal sexual politics, Erdrich's
description of Sita's traditional marriage relies on images of entrapment and
death. To consider the ways that Sita's story illustrates the sexual politics of
conventionally defined family structures, students might be asked to analyze
the courtship of and wedding scenes between Sita and Jimmy. Meisenhelder
comments that the kidnapping scene at Sita's wedding implies that "marriage
represents, for Sita, not self-fulfillment but loss of autonomy" (47). While most
of the heterosexual relationships in the novel are doomed, Erdrich includes
the seemingly egalitarian and loving marriage of Pete and Fritzie as the one
exception. It is this partnership that Mary and Celestine seem to model in
their relationship. Although Erdrich never describes sexual intimacy between
Celestine and Mary, she does describe their relationship in homoerotic overtones, and theirs is a lifetime partnership. Erdrich seems to suggest that in
comparison with the two women, gay and bisexual men have a harder time
achieving the freedom to love members of their sex openly. The bisexual Karl,

in stark contrast to Mary and Celestine, is unable to maintain meaningful relationships with men (or with women, for that matter, which is, perhaps, a result of his mother's abandonment). Karl and Wallace seem unable to maintain a relationship because the social structures of Argus offer no place for them; in fact, Wallace feels compelled to preserve among Argus residents the fictional story of his dead (female) sweetheart. Erdrich shows through her depictions of both successful and unsuccessful family units the sexual politics of mainstream conservative family values. In *The Beet Queen*, she critiques the conventional, monolithic definition of heterosexual family structure for excluding alternative family units that offer the potential for love and nurturing.

Through the unconventional family made up of Celestine, Karl, Mary, Wallace, and Dot, Erdrich offers an "oppositional world view" of family roles in relation to gender and sexuality. Louise Flavin explains, "With the breakdown of conventional family structures, gender construction becomes increasingly ambiguous. . . . [T]he dissolution of the family unit necessitates the redefinition of familial roles" ("Gender Construction" 18). Erdrich creates Wallace as arguably the most conventionally maternal figure in Dot's life: he acts as midwife on the night of her birth, becomes her confidante, and imagines her triumph as a beauty queen. Mary's role in Dot's life, by contrast, seems that of a hot-tempered father, as is evidenced when she physically abuses Dot's first-grade teacher or encourages the childhood Dot to be a bully. To consider more closely Erdrich's rewriting of gendered family roles, students could be asked to note contrasts between various twinned characters in terms of their relationships to others. For example, an instructor might ask students to contrast depictions of the mother-daughter relationships between Adelaide and Mary and between Celestine and Dot. Or students might contrast the parenting styles of Wallace, Mary, Karl, and Celestine toward Dot. Literal or figurative sibling pairs also offer fruitful contrasts in terms of gender construction and family relationships: consider Adelaide versus Fritzie, Mary versus Karl, Mary versus Sita, or Mary versus Celestine.

The title of *The Beet Queen* suggests that Dot be considered the central figure in the narrative. Concluding descriptions of Dot offer students an opportunity to synthesize the various thematic approaches to feminist analysis described above. The coronation of the Beet Queen as Wallace has planned it would perform a public representation of traditional femininity. The physical descriptions of the Beet princesses and of Dot's dress, hair, and demeanor during the coronation ceremony also offer excellent material for appreciating Erdrich's use of humor to critique stifling female gender definitions. Becoming the Beet Queen would mean for Dot resigning herself to unequal relationships to men. Students could reread closely the description of Adelaide's flight and then consider Dot's escape from the coronation, for in that action, Dot frees herself by repeating—but with important differences—Adelaide's flight. Unlike Adelaide, who wants to escape reality by flying into a romantic fantasy of female dependency on a man, Dot, 'vault[ing] in [to the plane] without a hand up, or permission' (327), embarks not on an unproductive escape but on a journey of independent self-definition.

(Meisenhelder 55)

Erdrich emphasizes that Dot's self-definition encompasses a healed relationship with her mother and a connection with her relatives on the reservation.

Some students might feel resistant to the positions implied by a feminist reading of Erdrich's novel. The homoeroticism not only between Karl and Wallace or Karl and Giles but also between Celestine and Mary is an important part of Erdrich's deconstruction of restrictive gender definitions. Just as teachers should expect of their students a respectful form of civil discourse about issues of race or gender, so too should they expect civility in discussions of sexuality. In exploring Erdrich's presentation of homosexuality, instructors can encourage students to think critically about the assumptions surrounding family, gender, and sexuality that underlie such realities as bans on gay marriage or the obstacles same-sex couples face in adopting children. Because students tend to feel particularly knowledgeable about popular culture in the form of television, film, and music, I have emphasized strategies that instructors can use to draw on that knowledge during introductory or prereading discussion. Instructors might begin an analysis of homosexuality in Erdrich's novel by pointing to current, student-generated examples from popular media to introduce a discussion about mainstream representations (or lack thereof) of gay and lesbian characters.

Students may also feel resistant toward Erdrich's critique of conventional gender roles through the fates of Sita and Russell; they may want to defend traditional marriage roles, patriotism, even success in sports. In this case, students could be asked to consider Sita's experiences with marriage in contrast to Fritzie's, for Erdrich would not have included her depiction of Fritzie and Pete's nurturing relationship if her aim were to offer a blanket condemnation of the marriage institution.

As hooks warns instructors who engage a revolutionary feminist pedagogy, "courses that work to shift paradigms, to change consciousness, cannot necessarily be experienced immediately as fun or positive or safe" (83). But by asking students to consider the harmful ways that conventional gender, racial, and sexual definitions are often enforced and by challenging students to see the relevance of externally imposed identity definitions in their own experiences, an instructor can offer students access to an "oppositional world view" in *The Beet Queen* from which they can question their own processes of self-definition.

Gender as a Drag in *The Beet Queen*

Kari J. Winter

Louise Erdrich is best known for complex narratives that powerfully dramatize the devastating effects of colonialism and race. However, her second novel, *The Beet Queen*, like her 2001 novel *The Last Report on the Miracles at Little No Horse*, is centrally an exploration of gender as a social construct that shapes identity in conjunction with race, class, and place. Unlike Erdrich's Ojibwe or mixed-blood characters who have access, in varying degrees, to traditional Ojibwe definitions of identity, most of the characters in *The Beet Queen* are white and are embedded in Western definitions of gender. The word "queen" in the title introduces the motif of gender as a drag in the multiple definitions of *drag*: (1) a lingering, painful tedium; (2) a costume; and (3) a performance. To elaborate, Erdrich represents the Western system of gender as a long-standing, deep-rooted set of social practices that inflict great pain on women and men. Meditating on how people who are socially constituted as women or men display, prove, practice, and perform their gender, Erdrich creates bountiful images suggesting that ordinary people enact, in familiar ways that are naturalized by patriarchal ideology, a sort of drag-queen show in their daily lives. First, they don the external markers of femininity or masculinity through clothes, jewelry, hairdos, and so on. Second, they perform gendered rituals that are assumed to constitute their identity. By repeatedly directing narrative gaze to her characters' gendered appearances and performances, Erdrich represents gender as both a comedy and a tragedy that profoundly damages people, whether they embrace and succeed at performing gender (e.g., Sita and Russell) or reject or fail at it (e.g., Celestine, Mary, Dot, Karl, Wallace).[1]

To introduce the concept of gender as a drag, I begin class discussion of *The Beet Queen* by analyzing a photograph of Erdrich taken at the moment she was crowned homecoming queen of her high school in Wahpeton, North Dakota. Reproduced at the beginning of Erdrich's autobiographical essay "Conversions," the photograph offers an illuminating spectacle of Erdrich's own bewildered, self-alienating participation in the dominant system of gender as deployed in a high school beauty pageant. Erdrich wonders in the essay what induced her to participate in a ritual for which she feels, in retrospect, fundamentally ill-suited. As a teenager, she saw the coronation as "proof" that "[i]f I tried hard enough I could garner things I craved, but I wouldn't be the same once I got them" (26). The essay provides a provocative segue into *The Beet Queen*'s representation of how society entices, rewards, and punishes people for participating in gendered self-constructions. To encourage students to consider gender complexly, I then introduce a series of study topics that approach issues of gender from multiple angles. The rest of this essay summarizes seven of these topics.

The Social Construction of Gender

After explaining the basic theoretical concept that gender is socially constructed,[2] I ask students to describe the social forces (ideologies, economics, threats of violence) that entrap and stifle various characters. What choices do characters make that reinforce their own oppression? Do they rebel? If so, how? What options do they appear to have, in Erdrich's representation? I encourage students to understand that freedom from long-standing social scripts is achieved through social processes and collective movements, not through solitary effort. Focusing primarily on white immigrants, *The Beet Queen* meditates on the problem of identity for people who are abandoned, uprooted, displaced, and alienated. Louise Flavin's and Susan Meisenhelder's essays on gender in *The Beet Queen* provide helpful pointers for exploring how Erdrich "chronicles the toll that defiance of gender norms" takes on characters, while she reserves "the direst fate for two characters [Sita and Russell] who come closest to fulfilling social definitions of ideal male and female" (Meisenhelder 46).

Motherhood

The Beet Queen opens with startling violations of conventions of motherhood. Adelaide is trapped in a prison house of economic oppression, sexual illegitimacy, and gender. Her children witness her affecting the drag of a regal paramour when her married lover, Mr. Ober, comes to visit. Adelaide pins "her dark red braid into a crown" (7) and dons a blue silk dress and a sparkling necklace. (The necklace recurs in the novel as a signifier of false wealth, femininity, deceit, and death.) After learning of Mr. Ober's death, Adelaide "shudder[s] like a broken doll" (7). Aside from the emotional cost, Mr. Ober's death spells financial ruin. With two children and a baby on the way, Adelaide is bereft of means to support her family. Forced to shed the accoutrements of femininity when the baby is born, Adelaide must "cut her petticoats up for diapers" (9). Ironically, devotion to femininity precludes maternal competence and vice versa. After cutting up all her "ordinary things" for the baby, Adelaide has nothing left to wear but "her fine things, lace and silk, good cashmere . . . a black coat, a black dress trimmed in cream lace, and delicate string gloves"— items that are useless for a mother (9). Desperate, she abandons her children during a bazaar at the city fairground when she flies off with a pilot who calls himself "The Great Omar" (12). All image, Omar with his fancy scarf and plane is a fraud in masculine drag.

As Hertha Wong notes, "Erdrich's novels are filled with orphans, thrown-away children, adoptive (by choice or circumstance rather than by law) mothers, and quests for or denials of one's mother" ("Adoptive Mothers" 180). She continues, "Mothering, and its inherent interconnectedness, is central to female identity in [*The Beet Queen*]" (189). I ask students to contemplate the reasons for and the consequences of Adelaide's abandonment of her children. In what ways does *The Beet Queen* represent a quest to discover mothers' true stories?[3] If Adelaide is a failed mother, does Erdrich represent any models of successful motherhood (biological or surrogate)? To what extent are mothers' voices heard? What insights are achieved or what work is accomplished in the relations between mothers and children over the course of the novel?

Clothes as a Signifier

Erdrich attends throughout *The Beet Queen* to clothes, jewelry, perfume, and other physical signs of gender conformity or transgression. This gendered cultural coding is easy for students to identify with and important for them to reflect on. One of the most insightful essays I received in my graduate seminar on Erdrich was an analysis of clothes as a signifier. Enlightened by femininity manuals from the 1920s through the 1960s (e.g., Helen Andelin's *Fascinating Womanhood*) as well as work by theorists like Judith Butler, the student, Robin Rapoport, traces the significance of clothes worn by Erdrich's characters from Adelaide to Dot. A brief summary of Rapoport's analysis of Sita demonstrates how fruitful students can find this line of investigation. After a close reading of Adelaide's devotion to the accoutrements of femininity, Rapoport notes that "Adelaide's brand of femininity is continued and refined by Sita Kozka, her niece" (2). Emotionally disconnected from herself and other women, Sita is infatuated with Adelaide's "style," which she believes will lead to affirmation from men. Obsessed with cultivating white feminine beauty, disguising her bodily odors, and maintaining an anorexic figure (like Vivien Leigh), Sita "relies on the display of her female body to win her attention, allegiance and power" (Rapoport 3). Both sad and comical in the reader's eyes, Sita is "sabotaged by her dress" as well as by men on her wedding night when the men who objectify her as a symbol of femininity kidnap her and dump her in front of a bar. The wind opens her dress, turns it inside out like an umbrella, and blows her in the door. A bystander aptly exclaims, "It's a fucking queen." "Shut your mouth," another woman exclaims. "It's a bride" (*Beet Queen* 100). Whether a queen or a bride (both roles are a performance, a drag), Sita has become an "it."

The (Gendered) Politics of Food

In *Tracks* and other novels, Erdrich shows how colonialism deprived Indians of resources and produced widespread starvation. At the same time, Erdrich pays sensuous attention to food in a manner that reclaims the body from patriarchal discourses that belittle women's bodies and women's labor. In her historicized representation, the advance of capitalism in the twentieth century causes the politics of food to shift in various ways. Kozka's Meats, which was a site of exploitation, gratuitous violence, and rape in *Tracks*, becomes a woman-dominated but not necessarily nurturing small business in *The Beet Queen*. Mary Adare, a German American, inherits the butcher shop from her Aunt Fritzie and Uncle Pete in the 1940s. From a traditional Ojibwe perspective, Kozka's Meats is an alien site of disconnection between human beings and animals. From Mary Adare's perspective, it is "my perfect home" (67), a warm, light place where customers chat with the butchers, who work dialogically by both making and taking recommendations about meat cuts and preparation. Juxtaposed to emerging corporate factories that slaughter animals by the thousands and package the meat for huge grocery chains, the butcher shop is a site of (meager, constrained) human community. The mode of meat production in Kozka's Meats sustains a relationship, albeit distant, between human beings and animals. Stopping in the Kozka kitchen, customers simultaneously view the living animals and consume the meat products. Mary reflects, "Across Fritzie's garden and the wide yard, [customers] could watch cows and sheep moving in the darkness of the stockpens, half visible between the heavy rail ties" (67). Fritzie, Pete, and Mary make sausages from their own recipes and give samples to customers. Although the customers are described as "heavy people, Germans and Poles or Scandinavians, rough handed and full of opinions" whose "light eyes did not shift nor their conversation falter when they happened to look up, on slaughtering day perhaps, to see a pig penned in the killing chute, having its throat cut" (68), Erdrich suggests that the butcher shop is less atomized, alienated, and anesthetized than the supermarket culture that will replace it in the 1960s and 1970s and will eliminate the last shreds of relationality between animals and human beings. Customers will buy meat so neatly packaged that its relation to actual animals and to the people who slaughter them is imperceptible.

Cultural alienation, bourgeois affectation, and detachment from the processes of creation that produce food lead to food poisoning, hunger, and comic disaster when Sita Kozka opens a French restaurant with the name "Chez Sita, Home of the Flambeed Shrimp." Large crowds turn out for her heavily publicized opening night and wait hungrily in "ghostly" candlelight for food that Sita is incapable of providing. Her chefs have been poisoned by their own food. By the novel's conclusion, we see that Sita is her own greatest victim, but the food-poisoning episode suggests that devotion to feminine appearance over substance endangers the whole community. By directing the reader's gaze to the ways characters relate to food, Erdrich balances the post-structuralist concept that identity is constructed through language with reminders that human beings are embodied and form their identities in material conditions.

The Role of Place in Shaping Identity

In "Where I Ought to Be: A Writer's Sense of Place," Erdrich asserts, "In a tribal view of the world, . . . [p]eople and place are inseparable" (1). She wonders what "provides a cultural identity" to people who do not feel connected to the land and who do not share a sense of place with other people. In *The Beet Queen*, Adelaide literally escapes her physical and social landscape by taking flight into the air. Her disconnection from the land and her refusal or inability to return to her place are a consequence of the alienation engendered by her embracing of femininity. Similarly, the way other characters relate to places—to the landscape—reveals a great deal about their identity or lack of identity. On one end of the spectrum, Karl, who is permanently injured by his mother's flight, becomes a chronic wanderer who lands for fleeting moments in the arms and in the homes of more rooted characters like Wallace and Celestine but who is unable to form lasting attachments to either places or people. Although he biologically fathers Dot, he is never around long enough to parent her. Adrift and devoid of meaning in his life, he does not have a strong enough sense of self to pass on a sense of self to his daughter. At the other end of the spectrum, his sister Mary roots herself in her aunt's house in Argus, North Dakota, with an immovable determination never to leave, never to take flight. Though she is dependable and stolid, her identity lacks the flexibility and fluidity that constitute true strength and enable balanced relationships. She adheres to her niece, Dot, with bonds of love tight enough to strangle her. In the middle of the spectrum are Ojibwe characters like Fleur Pillager and mixed-blood characters like Celestine, who, though uprooted by colonialism, maintain intimate relations with the land and nurturing relationships with other people. Instead of being fixed in one place, Fleur and Celestine move fluidly through a myriad of places that they nourish and are nourished by, in a way that reflects traditional Ojibwe patterns of seasonal homemaking rooted in a regional landscape. At home with the land, Fleur and Celestine are able to form strong, flexible connections with other people.

Intersections of Gender, Sexuality, and Race

In *The Beet Queen*'s final chapter, "The Grandstand," Erdrich creates a carnivalesque explosion of dominant American culture's intertwined but contradictory systems of gender, sexuality, and race. Dressed as the town's Beet Queen, Dot is crowned as the result of a fraud perpetrated by Wallace Pfef, her surrogate father. Habitually dishonest (a homosexual who is in the closet because of homophobia), Wallace loves Dot's courage and honesty. He says, "True, her lack of fear had become quite tedious and rude. Her utter honesty turned teachers and classmates to stone. But she was what I was not. She was not afraid to be different, and this awed me" (302). His determination to make Dot the Beet Queen is a sign of his love, but it is also a betrayal of her honesty. Suffering from the unpopularity that attends nonconformity, Dot indulges in clichéd fantasies about being "discovered" and "suddenly I'm gorgeous" (304). Wallace makes the mistake of thinking it would help Dot's self-esteem to have "a fantasy come true for once" (304). He works himself to the bone to make Dot queen, but Dot in drag is a monstrous drag for everyone involved.

In the parade over which Dot reigns as queen, two other characters are celebrated by townspeople for their gendered costumes. Sita, the novel's reigning image of white femininity, oversees the parade. More precisely, after her untimely death, Sita's cadaver, "imperial and stern" in a gleaming necklace formerly worn by Adelaide, is propped up by Celestine, who waves Sita's dead hand at the crowd while Mary Adare drives them slowly through the parade. Meanwhile, Russell, an Ojibwe man severely wounded in the Vietnam War and close to death in a nursing home, finds himself dressed up in military uniform to be exhibited in the parade as the town's "most decorated hero." Propped up like a mannikin in a wheelchair with medals over his heart and a rifle across his lap, "Russell waited for his hat to be set on at an angle, the way it was in his portrait-studio pictures" (298). In a comic twist characteristic of what Erdrich calls "survival humor," the contradiction between Russell's performance of idealized masculinity, which is implicitly white, and his Indian identity prevents him from dying in the parade. As he is imagining himself dead, "[i]t struck him as so funny that the town he'd lived in and the members of the American Legion were solemnly saluting a dead Indian, that he started to shake with laughter" (300). He laughs so hard that he falls off the old-time Chippewa road of death. By juxtaposing Sita's death with Russell's near-death, Erdrich illuminates how racial constructions intersect with and disrupt gender constructions. As a wealthy white woman, Sita can read herself as, and can become, the dead image of idealized femininity, whereas the incongruity between his Indian identity and the white image of heroic masculinity rescues Russell from premature death. He recognizes the ironic appropriateness of white people, who have long been obsessed with the idea that "the only good

Indian is a dead Indian," saluting an Indian in white military drag. Laughter revives and restores Russell by negating the official culture's construction of reality.

Identity Politics in Criticism on The Beet Queen

A discussion of *The Beet Queen* seems incomplete without mentioning the well-known review in which Leslie Marmon Silko accuses Erdrich of minimizing racial issues and selling out to white American culture ("Odd Artifact"). Silko has repeated this accusation on subsequent occasions.[4] Responses to Silko have unduly preoccupied criticism of *The Beet Queen*, and the controversy may be one reason many teachers hesitate to teach it. Committed to "teaching the conflicts" (Graff), I juxtapose Silko's attack with a review by Angela Carter, the British postcolonial feminist writer, who praises *The Beet Queen* for "impart[ing] its freshness of vision like an electric shock." Observing that Erdrich writes from the triply marginalized position of a woman, an ethnic minority, and a progeny of the farm belt, Carter argues that Erdrich "is part of a wedge being driven deep into WASP fiction from new contenders for their share of the Great Tradition" (151). Citing examples of Erdrich's "exquisitely precise" social history, Carter contends that Erdrich is "thoroughly in tune with the surreal poetry of America" (154). Whereas Silko is disgusted by the "rarified" places and the uncertain racial identities of characters in *The Beet Queen*, Carter reads Erdrich's landscape as richly imaginative and her characters as "variously cracked, and crazed, and barking mad: but never, for all the elements of the fantastic, less than true to life" (153). With these contrasting views in mind, students can develop their own analyses of the social landscapes of and gendered identities in *The Beet Queen*.

NOTES

A preliminary version of this essay was presented at "Feminism(s) and Rhetoric(s): An International Conference" at the University of Minnesota in October 1999. I would like to thank Lillian Bridwell-Bowles for organizing an extraordinary conference.

[1] Erdrich's novels *The Antelope Wife* and *The Last Report on the Miracles at Little No Horse* elaborate the concept of performing gender. In *The Antelope Wife*, a white male character who has committed horrific masculinist acts of violence against Indians (symbolic rape and matricide) finds himself restored to humanity by a hungry baby whose desperate suckling literally transforms his body: "Pity scorched him, she sucked so blindly, so forcefully"(7). His breasts begin to produce milk. In *The Last Report* we learn that the Catholic priest of *Tracks*, Father Damien, is actually a woman who spends most of her adult life in drag on Erdrich's fictional reservation, Little No Horse.

[2] As Simone de Beauvoir explains in *The Second Sex*, one isn't born a woman, one

becomes one. In other words, "femininity" and "masculinity" are not innate qualities that stem from femaleness or maleness but rather notions constructed by society. Traditional American Indian cultures organized gender in a myriad of different ways, many of which were egalitarian in their valuing of women and men. In contrast, European and other cultures organized gender in a patriarchal hierarchy in keeping with the ancient Greek and Roman systems of gender. Aristotle articulates the fundamental move whereby patriarchy naturalizes and validates itself: "as regards the relationship between male and female, the former is naturally superior, the latter naturally inferior, the former rules and the latter is subject" (Wiedemann 18).

[3]Elaine Tuttle Hansen argues persuasively that Erdrich's novels "cohere around the quest to know mothers' true stories" (123).

[4]See, for example, her interview in the *Native American Novelists* series. For an illuminating reading of the Silko-Erdrich controversy, see Castillo, "Postmodernism."

A Postcolonial Reading of *Tracks*

Dee Horne

Louise Erdrich's *Tracks* is a text that invites students and teachers to engage in dialogue; to think about the assumptions each person makes when reading; and, through reading and discussing *Tracks*, to learn from the text and from one another. Postcolonial theories are tools that teachers and students can use to open up discussion and generate dialogue. They might well begin with a discussion of the term itself. Literally, the term *postcolonialism* implies that colonialism is over, and, in this sense, the terminology is misleading because First Nations are still being colonized. Seen in a broader context, postcolonial theories offer ways to examine colonial relationships and the power imbalance between colonizers and colonized. Ania Loomba observes, "It has been suggested that it is more helpful to think of post-colonialism not just as coming literally after colonialism and signifying its demise, but more flexibly as the contestation of colonial domination and the legacies of colonialism" (12). Teachers and students might identify some of the legacies of colonialism that they see in the texts they read and in the world in which they live. In reviewing the limitations of the term *postcolonialism*, students may also consider who defines terms and how definitions and other attempts to classify or organize knowledge reveal colonial assumptions and power relationships. Loomba is right to point out that this definition is also fraught with limitations and reminds us that postcolonialism "is useful only if we use it with caution and qualification" (18).

In *Tracks*, Erdrich enters into a dialogue with colonial discourse, without perpetuating its rules of recognition, by creating a multivoiced discourse that illustrates the "complex relationalities" of power (Shohat and Stam 343). She alludes to Ojibwe, or Anishinaabeg, oral traditions while also recontextualizing oral stories in a contemporary written narrative.[1] In addition, Erdrich unsettles colonial stereotypes and discourse. Drawing on Ojibwe oral traditions while challenging the hierarchical imbalances of power underlying the colonial relationship, Erdrich takes issue with the ways in which the settler society has attempted to define First Nations, specifically within Eurocentric epistemologies. By articulating cultural differences through a discourse written in English, the language of the colonizers, Erdrich creates a hybrid narrative. Instead of replicating the colonial relationship, she deconstructs and subverts colonial discourse from within. Erdrich's subversive narrative offers readers an alternative perspective in which colonizers may see images of themselves through the eyes of the colonized. For instance, readers who choose to identify with Pauline and her narrative may find that they (like Pauline) become the butt of Nanapush's jokes. Moreover, through Nanapush's and Pauline's narratives and the multiple narratives woven throughout, Erdrich encourages readers to question their affiliations and to reassess and shift them in the light of ever-changing information. In this respect, *Tracks* signifies "the historical movement of hybridity as camouflage . . . a space in-between the rules of engagement" (Bhabha 193).

In *Tracks*, narratives elude definition and classifications, as different stories unfold through the alternating voices of Nanapush and Pauline.[2] Telling stories is, as Nanapush notes, a way to resist cultural genocide:

> They're [stories] all attached, and once I start there is no end to telling because they're hooked from one side to the other, mouth to tail. During the year of sickness, when I was the last one left, I saved myself by starting a story. . . . I got well by talking. Death could not get a word in edgewise, grew discouraged, and traveled on.   (46)

Erdrich suggests multiple connotations for tracks while using them as a pervasive image of survival. For instance, the title alludes to the need for communities to survive, to continue to leave tracks. Tracks can be signs in the snow as well as signs on a blank page. One can follow tracks in a hunt. A person can step into tracks, circle tracks, backtrack, or even become sidetracked. An understanding of context, cultural and environmental, is helpful for those who attempt to decipher tracks, and this understanding is based on one's experience.

Just as it is necessary to learn how to decipher tracks when hunting, so readers decipher the tracks, or words, on the printed page. This process of interpretation is not passive. Rather, not unlike oral stories, *Tracks* invites readers to interact with the stories. Readers relate to the stories by considering their own experiences. In so doing, they identify their positions and frames of reference and consider how they read a text, what assumptions they make when they read, and what their assumptions reveal about their cultural biases and, for some readers, their colonial stereotypes. In reading *Tracks*, some students become frustrated when they try to pin the narrative down and ask, What is this book about? What is the story? What is Erdrich doing? The text, like Ojibwe oral stories, resists any single interpretation and does not offer one story or one meaning or one narrative; rather, there are many stories. In this way, Erdrich challenges readers to reexamine their assumptions but also to pay attention to their frustration and think through their questions, often by posing further questions. The text encourages readers, teachers and students alike, to step out of familiar patterns of reading, to identify what they do not understand (and often why, or the assumptions and patterns they have learned that limit their ability to expand their frames of reference).

A class discussion about reading and interpretation might branch off into a conversation about oral and written stories and the ways in which oral stories differ from print.[3] Erdrich is careful to point to the dangers of the printed word and validates oral stories over the written word that government agents use to break promises and treaties. Consider Margaret Kashpaw's response when she brushes against Nanapush's newspaper:

> She swiped at the sheets with her hand, grazed the print, but never quite dared to flip it aside. . . . She didn't want the tracks rubbing off on her skin. She never learned to read, and the mystery troubled her.
>
> (47)

Similarly, Nanapush does not want to write his name, because "Nanapush is a name that loses power every time that it is written and stored in a government file. That is why, [he explains, he] only gave it out once in all those years" (32). It is only later, when Nanapush is endeavoring to bring Lulu, his "granddaughter," back from the residential school, that he reluctantly takes on the role of a bureaucrat. He tells Lulu:

> To become a bureaucrat myself was the only way that I could wade through the letters, the reports, the only place where I could find a ledge to kneel on, to reach through the loophole and draw you home.
>
> (225)

It is Nanapush who sees the tracks of Eli's snowshoes and guides Eli on his hunt. Eli's vision clears, and he is able to track the moose. Nanapush's song and drumming help Eli reserve his strength so he can come home (101–04). Similarly, Fleur's tracks attest to her powers.

Pauline observes how "we followed the tracks of her bare feet and saw where they changed, where the claws sprang out, the pad broadened and pressed into the dirt. By night we heard her chuffing cough, the bear cough" (12).[4] Later, when Pauline stays with Fleur and Eli, she compares them to wild animals whose "fingers left tracks like snails, glistening and wet" (72). Lack of tracks often signify the spirit world and spiritual empowerment. In her vision of a visit to the spirit world, Pauline observes, "There were no fences, no poles, no lines, no tracks" (159).

Near the end of the novel, when Fleur laments her powers diminishing and feels the loss of her child, her land, and her community, she is, according to some stories in the community, said to "walk now without leaving tracks" (215). This image suggests death and loss of power as well as Fleur's ability to gain power on a different plane; her spirit is untrackable. Here, teachers and students can return to a discussion of how colonizers, through their civilizing mission and legislation, have often attempted to define First Nations according to their own worldview and epistemology in order to force First Nations to assimilate.[5] Given her untrackable spirit, Fleur exemplifies the hybrid moment of camouflage, of being there but not being perceived as there. This camouflage, when viewed as a metaphor for the effects of assimilation, signifies the loss of life and the loss of culture that Fleur's family and community have experienced. At the same time, camouflage is a survival strategy; Fleur escapes settlers who attempt to track her; she eludes capture. Fleur has the ability not to leave tracks and not to be hunted or tracked.

Similarly, Erdrich's text often eludes those readers who attempt to track it down, to define it according to Eurocentric literary conventions and traditions. Readers who try to track or interpret this text without questioning their own assumptions and reading strategies perpetuate colonial readings.

Camouflage is also a subversive strategy. Erdrich writes in English, the language of the colonizers, yet does not perpetuate colonial discourse. In teaching *Tracks*, instructors can discuss how readers who attempt to decipher Erdrich's tracks through a colonial lens will now feel displaced, made aware of cultural traditions that challenge colonial definitions. That displacement and alienation may give readers insight into the effects of assimilation. The narrative subverts colonial discourse by delineating effects of colonialism and assimilation in haunting images of cultural genocide. In the first chapter, Nanapush describes Fleur's transformation and sense of her diminishing powers. Fleur's change is most noticeable after she loses her second child. The loss of her child is compounded by the loss of her land. Nanapush tells Lulu that there are many forms of loss. While some lose their children to death, others lose their children or themselves through assimilation, in which they can become alienated from their cultures and from themselves:

> But Fleur [Nanapush explains] was dangerous. We lose our children in different ways. They turn their faces to the white towns, like Nector as he grew, or they become so full of what they see in the mirror there is no reasoning with them anymore, like you. Worst of all is the true loss, unbearable, and yet it must be borne. Fleur heard her vanished child in every breath of wind, every tick of dried leaves, every scratch of blowing snow. (170)

In her characterization of Pauline, Erdrich alludes to the dangers of assimilation and the deleterious effects of the colonizers' civilizing mission. Coming from a family of "mixed-bloods, skinners in the clan for which the name was lost" (14), Pauline is a colonial mimic who attempts to deny her identity.[6] At an early age, she asks her father to send her to "the white town" so she can learn lace making from the nuns, and she tries to be like her grandfather, whom she describes as "pure Canadian" (14). In denying part of her heritage and becoming a martyr, Pauline participates in her self-annihilation. After she goes to the convent, she decides to reject her identity.

Converted to Christianity, Pauline takes part in the civilizing mission. To justify her cause, she identifies with settlers. However, colonial mimics who

endeavor to emulate colonizers can only partially mimic them and are ultimately disavowed.[7] In an effort to affiliate with settlers, Pauline denies her
identity. She differentiates herself from "Indians" and refers to "Indians" as
"them" instead of as "us" (138). Internalizing the lens of the colonizer, Pauline
perpetuates the colonial discourse and participates in her self-effacement.
Further, she attempts to re-create her identity and to justify her transformation as the will of God:

> He said that I was not whom I had supposed. I was an orphan and my
> parents had died in grace, and also, despite my deceptive features, I was
> not one speck of Indian but wholly white. . . . He pressed the tears away
> and told me I was chosen to serve. . . . He had an important plan for
> me, for which I must prepare, that I should find out the habits and
> hiding places of His enemy. . . . I should not turn my back on Indians.
> I should go out among them, be still, and listen.   (137)

Near the end of the novel, Pauline continues to re-create herself when she
renames herself Leopolda (205), an allusion to King Leopold II (1835–1909)
of Belgium, who organized "development" in central Africa and financed an
expedition to the Congo River (1879–84). Leopold is known for his exploitation of the Congo; hence, his name is suitable for Pauline, who attempts to
"civilize" her community.

While Erdrich critiques settler society and its attempts to dispossess First
Nations, she also provides readers with a portrait of Nanapush, Margaret
(Rushes Bear), Fleur, and other memorable characters who resist assimilation.
Thus *Tracks* is a testimony to the struggle and survival of First Nations.
Erdrich adapts oral storytelling techniques to print and infuses the multiple
stories with humor. She illustrates the importance of community—of family
relations and of ancestors—while also demonstrating how settler society fos-
ters and preys on internal divisions in its attempts to divide and diminish First
Nations and their communities and cultures.[8]

In these respects, the narratives affirm cultural differences and unsettle the
colonial discourse that positions settlers as dominant and First Nations as
subordinate. In telling Lulu the story of the Ojibwe community and her
mother, Nanapush's narrative is itself a process of commemorating and "re-
memorating" Ojibwe oral stories and traditions.[9] Erdrich's novel opens with
Nanapush telling Lulu, "We started dying before the snow, and like the snow,
we continued to fall." Nanapush goes on to tell of the ways in which settler
society has attempted to eradicate this community. He tells of the "spotted
sickness" and the treaty and "exile in a storm of government papers." He tells
his granddaughter that she is "the child of the invisible, the ones who disap-
peared" (1), and he tells her about the "new sickness" (2), consumption, which
led to the further dwindling of the clans. The images of death and cultural

genocide are tragic and signify imbalance. Armand Ruffo has elaborated on this idea:

> For the Anishnawbe the significance of this cannot be overstated. Imbalance means destruction and death—which itself has many implications, for to kill without considering the spirit of that which is dying is akin to destroying one's own spirit. It is a view of creation as one complete whole; the world of objects and the spiritual world, the conscious and the unconscious, thought and feeling, are the embodiment of one great and powerful essence. Thus the ability to commune with the spirits is premised upon the inherent belief in a highly ordered and moral universe in which the earth, planets, animals, men and women all function in harmony and in accordance with the vision of Kitche Manitou (the Great Spirit or Great Unknown) [9].   (164)

Erdrich illustrates how the changes that settlers have imposed are devastating First Nations even further when Nanapush tells his granddaughter, "I saw the passing of times you will never know. I guided the last buffalo hunt. I saw the last bear shot. . . . I axed the last birch that was older than I, and I saved the last Pillager" (2). Teachers and students can review how their cultures have displaced First Nations or, for those who have experienced colonization, how settlers have displaced their cultures. Together they can discuss the implications of cultural dispossession and the need for alternative approaches to writing and reading. In considering how Erdrich's text encourages readers to be aware of cultural dispossession (society has dispossessed First Nations of their land, destroyed the animals and resources, and attempted to destroy their cultures), teachers and students can consider how Erdrich's text offers alternatives. Nanapush's stories as well as Erdrich's hybrid narrative strategies illustrate how First Nations can combat cultural dispossession through self-determination, through telling their stories in their own ways. In telling of the disasters their community has experienced over the years, Nanapush describes how he saved the last Pillager in a story to Fleur's daughter. Lulu represents the next generation, which can survive and resist cultural genocide through practicing its culture.

Despite the bleak picture that Nanapush's story presents, the telling of the story is affirming because it is part of the process of resistance and survival. Nanapush tells Lulu:

> [F]or it was through Fleur Pillager that the name Nanapush was carried on and won't die with me, won't rot in a case of bones and leather. There is a story to it the way there is a story to all, never visible while it is happening. Only after, when an old man sits dreaming and talking in his chair, the design springs clear.   (34)

He tells his granddaughter the story so that she may learn why her mother decided to send her to residential school. In addition, he tells her the stories of her community and family so that she may understand how the community came to be internally divided and so that she may reconsider her plan to marry a "no-good Morrissey" (218).

Nanapush's stories give Lulu the context and history of her family and community. The elaborate genealogy in *Tracks* illustrates how members of the community need to remember their ancestors and respect their relations. Power, as Pauline points out, lies in relations and relationships, in community: "Power travels in the bloodlines, handed out before birth. . . .The blood draws us back, as if it runs through a vein of earth" (31). By telling Lulu the story of her past, Nanapush helps ensure that the story and the family will not be forgotten. Distrustful of colonizers and the ways they exploit the written word, Nanapush tells Lulu, "Land is the only thing that lasts life to life. Money burns like tinder, flows off like water. And as for government promises, the wind is steadier" (33). Erdrich partially represents this power imbalance in the colonial relationship while at the same time refuting, and refusing to perpetuate, the very binary assumptions that underpin it. In this way, Erdrich alludes to the legacies of colonialism and depicts some of the effects the colonial relationship has had on the Ojibwe people. Through the stories the characters tell, she alludes to and affirms Ojibwe oral traditions.

Adapting strategies from oral storytelling traditions to print, Erdrich offers readers a written conversation that operates on multiple levels simultaneously.[10] There is the conversation between Nanapush and Lulu as well as the implied dialogue between Nanapush and readers; the dialogue between Pauline and her implied audience and readers; the implied dialogue between settlers and this fictional First Nations community to which Nanapush's and Pauline's narratives allude, and the dialogue between Nanapush and Pauline that the reader gleans from reading their alternating narratives. These are but a few of the dialogues that students and teachers might discern in Erdrich's text. In identifying and responding to these dialogues, readers also interact with the text as they look at how context and history influence what each speaker chooses to tell (or not tell) and how the relationships among characters influences how and what they tell. Through dialogues, Erdrich encourages readers to engage in a dialogue with the text, with their own history and culture, and with one another. The multiple narratives illustrate some of the challenges of cross-cultural communication and miscommunication.[11] Students who become frustrated with *Tracks* can use this frustration as a starting point to identify what is blocking their understanding and to be receptive to new ways of reading and thinking. The text models ways of opening up dialogues and working toward new, decolonized relationships.

Through the interplay of diverse voices, Erdrich calls into question the notion of a single, authoritative truth. Nanapush's words often influence our perceptions of Pauline, while Pauline's story encourages readers to revisit Nanapush's words in the context of his trickster discourse. Through Nanapush, Erdrich also exposes and challenges the cultural binarism and colonial stereotypes underlying much of settler thinking and language. His name alludes to the trickster Nanabush and, like trickster, Nanapush is "a healer and comic liberator in narratives, not an artifact or a real victim in historical summaries" but "a communal sign in imagination, a comic holotrope and a discourse that endures in modern literature" (Vizenor, *Narrative Chance* 205). By affirming his culture, Nanapush subverts colonizers and colonial discourse. Through his narrative, Nanapush foregrounds the importance of his community's traditions, and he lives according to the customs and traditions of his ancestors. He is a powerful figure and is well versed in traditional medicine. It is Nanapush who takes in Fleur when others are afraid to go near her. It is Nanapush who instructs Eli in ways to approach Fleur initially and in ways to return to her when Fleur later shuns Eli. And it is Nanapush who sets the snare to trap the Morrisseys, using Father Damien's piano wire.

Unlike colonial discourse and the civilizing, often-didactic mission of colonizers, Nanapush's criticisms are never overt. In trickster fashion, he tempers his examples with humor, allowing Pauline, and readers, opportunities to review the colonial assumptions underlying her actions. Throughout the book, Nanapush's narrative functions like a subversive mirror that reflects and refracts Pauline's peculiar internalization of colonial "rules of recognition" (Bhabha 114). The humorous scene in which Nanapush tests Pauline's resolve to do penance begins by illustrating the miscommunication that arises from Pauline's and Nanapush's different cultural frames of reference. Speaking in the "old language," Nanapush observes, "You never have to answer the call." Pauline insists that she "must answer His every word," only to discover that Nanapush is referring to profane, bodily functions, not sacred sacrifices. As a reminder of Christ's sufferings, Pauline imposes unusual forms of penance on herself. Having discovered Pauline's practice of withholding her bladder, Nanapush comments, "I have noticed . . . that you sit here all day and never visit the outhouse" (147). He laces her sassafras with sugar and then tells her a story about a rainstorm that leads to a flood. Cursing "all the talk of water" (149), Pauline sees Nanapush's tea and story as a "plan" to "test" her "resolve" (150). Ultimately, she is unable to hold out. Thanks to Nanapush's story, Pauline visits the outhouse and ceases her self-inflicted punishments (148–51).[12]

Nanapush's stories offer those who listen opportunities to learn from examples. Teachers and students can discuss how different cultural frames of reference can collide as well as color how we read and listen. Those who have a cultural frame of reference that is unfamiliar with the traditions to which Nanapush alludes may miss some of the context for the stories. Readers who, like Pauline, are familiar with these traditions but hold colonial assumptions may find that their assumptions, having been challenged and reconfigured through Nanapush's stories, no longer hold true.

Teachers and students might also reflect on the value of humor and the way that laughter is a tonic that helps defray some of the painful effects of colonization. Laughter is essential for survival, and, in reviewing the scene just mentioned and other humorous scenes in *Tracks*, students and teachers can discuss the diverse functions of humor in oral and written stories. Nanapush tempers lessons with humor, but instruction is not didactic. Rather, the stories offer opportunities for those who listen to learn in their own time and way.

Similarly, *Tracks* offers a nondidactic, innovative approach to reading and to teaching practices. Just as there is not one narrative or one story but many, so there is not just one approach to reading or to teaching. There are as many approaches to teaching and to learning as there are learners, each with different learning styles and each with his or her own cultural frame of reference. Erdrich does not advocate one frame of reference over another or suggest that one narrative is superior to another (as colonizers have done in their civilizing mission). Rather, she creates a text in which diverse narratives and voices coexist; the different narratives in the text and in the minds of diverse readers sometimes collide and challenge, but they also inform one another. Erdrich's subversive narrative eludes colonial binary definitions and those attempting to track it down. At the same time, the narrative offers an alternative pedagogical approach to reading; readers have to watch the tracks— the words on the page and the implied words and meanings between the lines, the allusions to Ojibwe oral traditions.

Through multiple narratives, Erdrich encourages readers to deconstruct their reading practices. She draws attention to colonial binary oppositions between print and oral traditions, settler and First Nations, individual and community but does not participate in or perpetuate these colonial constructs. Through diverse voices and stories, her hybrid text tracks colonial assumptions without replicating colonial power structures. By using camouflage and subversive humor, Erdrich ambushes those who hold colonial assumptions. In an effort to decipher *Tracks*, readers circle back over their tracks and may deconstruct their reading practices and sometimes their colonial assumptions. Thus reading becomes a process of transformation in which readers collaborate in the decolonization process, and those with colonial assumptions help to undo the very colonial and imperial structures of which they are a part.[13]

NOTES

[1]Anishinaabeg is the name for people of the woodland whom colonizers later renamed Ojibway and Chippewa. Gerald Vizenor explains, "The word Anishinaabeg, the singular is Anishinaabe, is a phonetic transcription from the oral tradition" (*People* 13).

There are many variations on the spelling. Armand Ruffo, for instance, spells the word "Anishnawbe" (64), while Basil Johnston spells it "Anishnabeg" (*Ojibway Heritage* 21).

[2]Here, I am taking issue with readers who interpret *Tracks* as a dual narrative that sets up a binary division, a discourse and a counterdiscourse: Pauline versus Nanapush; outsider versus insider; nontraditional versus traditional; colonial versus noncolonial. Such a reading misses the mark and is colonial because the aforementioned binary divisions operate within, and perpetuate, the colonial discourse. Rather, I am suggesting that Erdrich partially references the colonial discourse to deconstruct and subvert it. She does not replicate the colonial terms. In this respect, I agree with Gloria Bird, who writes, "Nanapush and Pauline are playing upon the dichotomous relationships inherent in colonialism by providing the reader with an insider/outsider perspective into the communal landscape of *Tracks*" (44). Erdrich plays on these binary terms but does not replicate them.

[3]Nanapush, for example, is telling his story to Lulu so that she may understand Fleur and the context and history that informs the stories.

[4]Here, and throughout *Tracks*, readers question Pauline's words since she is an unreliable narrator.

[5]The term "civilizing mission" refers to the process wherein settlers attempted to "civilize" those they colonized.

[6]Pauline's name may also be an allusion to Paulinism, the teachings of those who follow the doctrine of Saint Paul. In viewing Pauline as a colonial mimic, I am alluding to V. S. Naipaul's work *The Mimic Men* (1967). In this novel, Naipaul depicts the colonial mimic in his characterization of Ralph Singh.

[7]In their desire to fix identity and to define themselves against reformed others who are encouraged to emulate, to become like, colonizers but are never quite the same, colonizers create a "discourse of mimicry" that is "constructed around an ambivalence": "mimicry emerges as the representation of a difference that is itself a process of disavowal" (Bhabha 86).

[8]Pauline's plan to "snare" Eli (80) by making him desire Sophie and incur Fleur's anger is, as Nanapush later tells Lulu, a key factor in dividing the community against itself by instigating family feuds.

[9]Toni Morrison coined the term "rememory" in *Beloved* (36). Here, I am using the term to mean the act of remembering from the position of having been silenced.

[10]Ruffo also discusses how the narrative is like a conversation and approximates oral stories because "the process of reading implicates the listener into becoming an active participant in the experience of the story" (164).

[11]For more on transcultural and personal readings of Erdrich's work, see Rainwater ("Ethnic Signs," "Reading"); Sarris (*Keeping*).

[12]Another example of how Nanapush, through his stories, reflects and refracts colonial "rules of recognition" occurs when he tells the story to Father Damien of the new lawgiver in town who "makes love with himself" (216).

[13]I have discussed creative hybridity in other contexts in *Contemporary American Indian Writing: Unsettling Literature*.

"This Ain't Real Estate":
A Bakhtinian Approach to *The Bingo Palace*

Patrick E. Houlihan

Although *The Bingo Palace* is arguably Louise Erdrich's most humorous novel,[1] beneath the veneer of laughs and love story lie deeply relevant social and political struggles concerning Indian gaming and sovereignty issues. Many of the initial critical responses to *The Bingo Palace* passed up the opportunity to investigate the rhetorical and political significance of the work.[2] It is the first Native American novel to juxtapose long-standing sovereignty conflicts between indigenous peoples and the United States government and the economic and legal battles currently being fought between numerous Indian tribes and federal and state gambling commissions. Grounded in oral storytelling traditions, *The Bingo Palace* weaves a complex tale that invites readers to join in its communal dialogue. Whether or not students bring a prior position on Indian gaming rights to their reading of the novel, Erdrich will no doubt complicate their thinking about past, present, and future problems surrounding Native nations' rights.

The ensuing discussion shows how the Russian literary critic Mikhail Bakhtin's language theories can be used to construct meaning. Used as an interpretive model in a reading of *The Bingo Palace*, Bakhtinian dialogism can help teachers and readers become more aware of cross-cultural perspectives and of the important roles that social and historical contexts play in understanding any text's potential meaning. In a nutshell, the theory of dialogism suggests that meaning is derived through negotiation, through "dialogues" created within a text and "dialogues" between readers' worldviews and the worldviews represented in a given text. Bakhtin insists that context plays as important a role as text in making meaning from any utterance, whether a word, a sentence, or a complete novel.[3]

To heighten students' awareness of the novel's historical contexts even before they begin reading it, teachers can assign a little background research on Indian gaming, United States treaties with the Ojibwe, or some of the devastating effects of the Indian Removal Act of 1830 and the General Allotment Act (Dawes Act) of 1887.[4] Students should then be asked, as they begin reading, to identify how cultural tensions propel the novel and its characters.

A year before the release of *The Bingo Palace*, the Ojibwe writer Gerald Vizenor, in a brief article entitled "Casino Coups," explicitly urged politically concerned readers to become aware of the connection between sovereignty issues and Indian gaming.[5] Not only does Erdrich's novel take place in and around a reservation bingo palace, but one of the central tensions in the story is the potential expansion of the gaming operation onto the main character

Lipsha Morrissey's ancestral burial grounds. To enhance students' appreciation of the novel, teachers should identify some of the key characteristics of Native American writing, specifically, the recurring theme of mixed-blood identity.[6] Resolving rhetorical arguments for and against the gambling enterprise is as important to the hero's evolving sense of personal identity as it is to tribal identities and political sovereignty in Native America today.

Bakhtinian Analysis

Bakhtin's concepts of novelistic "orchestration" and "polyphony" help uncover an overall unity in Erdrich's complex dialogic design despite its apparent fragmentation.[7] Polyphony refers to a multivoiced narrative consciously orchestrated by an author to create intratextual dialogues within and between characters and to create extratextual dialogues within and between writers and readers (Faulkner's *As I Lay Dying* is a clear example of Bakhtin's concept in action).

The entire mixed-blood Ojibwe community can be considered the functional center of the novel. As William Faulkner does in "A Rose for Emily," Erdrich employs a communal first-person-plural narrator to draw the reader into the storytelling act, placing the reader in the community of the novel before placing the reader in any individual's shoes. The central protagonist, Lipsha Morrissey, provides first-person-singular narrations in ten chapters. But these chapters, as well as the community's first-person-plural chapters and the supposedly omniscient third-person narratives, are all constantly interspersed with various individuals' stories, anonymous voices, remembrances, and occasional imperatives directed to the reader. Greg Sarris, in his discussion of critical theory and American Indian oral literatures, suggests that "culture-specific theories and presuppositions are at work in any encounter between peoples or between peoples and texts, regardless of the way interlocutors . . . are conscious of those theories and presuppositions, which shape both the encounter and any understanding of it" ("Encountering" 127–28). Mimicking in written form the interactive nature of oral storytelling, Erdrich's polyphony of narratives bounces the reader between community identity and individual identity, effectively forcing the reader to negotiate the same struggle the protagonist is experiencing.[8]

To better understand Lipsha's dilemma, students should be asked to ponder some of the ethical questions raised by Lipsha's continual vacillation between traditional Ojibwe cultural values (embodied by Fleur Pillager, Gerry Nanapush, Shawnee Ray, and sometimes Lyman) and modern American cultural values (embodied by the bingo palace). The problem of identity that Lipsha faces cannot easily be resolved. Erdrich builds her characters of two conflicting Ojibwe family histories: Lispha is a descendant of both Pillager and Kashpaw lineage. In Ojibwe tribal history "Cashpaw was the chief of the Indians and was quite friendly to the white men" (Libbey 119), whereas the matriarch of the novels, Lipsha's great-grandmother, Fleur Pillager, is identified with a historically rebellious faction, "known to belong to the band of Pilleurs (Pillagers), also called rogues" (Agee Horr 235). With this subtle dialogic naming, Erdrich's Lipsha vacillates between adherence to his traditional rogue heritage and his attempts to adapt to white society. And in keeping with Bakhtin's dialogic model, in which no final resolution is possible (or the dialogue would cease), Erdrich leaves Lipsha (as well as the other key younger generation characters, Shawnee Ray and Albertine) nascent, emerging, in the process of becoming whole, suspended in "those anxious hours when we call our lives into question" (274).

The dialogic structure of *The Bingo Palace* is exhibited in the polyphonic play of voices throughout the text. Erdrich's oral acuity in the novel amplifies the language beyond the usual visual range of the written word, invoking aural qualities more commonly associated with the medium of music. Bakhtin's notion of novelistic orchestration aptly applies the musical metaphor to the form of the novel.

Combining the techniques of traditional American Indian storytelling and orchestral conducting, Erdrich employs a symphonic theme-and-variations structure to create polyphony in the progression of voices in *The Bingo Palace*. In orchestral compositions the melodic theme forms the principal subject from which harmonic variations are developed. In the manner of orchestral overtures that introduce the major theme and hint at a number of variations, Erdrich introduces in the opening chapter the central theme of Native American mixed-blood identity through the choric voice of the Ojibwe community speaking as one. It is helpful to point out to students as they begin to interact with the text that they should "hear" this story rather than see it. Like many oral cultures' stories, it begins with the elders—in this case, Lipsha's grandmother, Lulu Lamartine. As she awakens, the reader is drawn into the eavesdropping community that Erdrich creates with the first-person-plural voice striking up the chorus:

> We know her routine—many of us even shared it—so when she was sighted before her normal get-up time approaching her car door in the unsheltered cold of the parking lot, we called on others to look. (1)

The choric voice serves a multiplicity of rhetorical functions in the novel, not the least of which is to engage readers in dialogic negotiations. Erdrich joins reader and text from the start when she writes, "*We* don't know how it will work out, come to pass, which is why *we* watch so hard, *all of us alike, one arguing voice*" (6, emphasis added). After sounding the names of characters like notes of various instruments to come (including Lulu, Marie Kashpaw,

Gerry Nanapush, Lyman Lamartine, June Morrissey, Albertine Kashpaw/Johnson, Shawnee Ray Toose, Zelda Kashpaw, and Fleur Pillager), the chorus introduces the melodic theme. Lipsha Morrissey provides what Bakhtin calls the "horizontal" message with which the vertical countervoices harmonize. The "we" voice concurrently establishes a central tension as Lipsha returns to his reservation home attempting to find a niche, a place for the "I" within the social matrix of the "we."

Louis Owens has pointed out that "at the center of the American Indian tribal community . . . individualism and egotism are shunned and 'we' takes precedence over the 'I' celebrated in the Euramerican tradition" (197). So Lipsha has a dual conflict: trying to develop an individual sense of self, he must simultaneously subjugate that self. Lipsha's difficulties are compounded by the fact that his mother tried to drown him, and both his mother and father abandoned him as an infant, so as he struggles to discover his dissociated personal identity, he must also try to define his dislocated tribal identity.

The chorus announces that "immediately we had to notice that there was no place the boy could fit." Adding to the weight of Lipsha's burden, the chorus runs through a long list of tribal roles that he does not fill, concluding, "He was not our grandfather . . . not a traditional . . . not one of us" (9). This choral contextualization of Lipsha as a marginal figure solidifies his tribal and familial role. Students can benefit from an understanding of the trickster figure familiar to most Native American cultures. C. W. Spinks illuminates the trickster construct: "Trickster, in his rawest form, is pure ambivalence; he is always the border creature who plays at the margins of self, symbol, and culture" (177). A spiritual descendant of Old Nanapush, the tribal elder and trickster figure, Lipsha inherits his life on the edges.

After chapter 1's overture introduces the theme of chance in the form of the trickster and hints at variations to come, chapter 2 launches Lipsha's first-person narration, the controlling voice that appears in ten of the twenty-seven chapters. With rhythmic regularity, Erdrich returns to Lipsha, alternating various other voices for a chapter or two in between, enhancing the resonance of Lipsha's solo voice with countermelodies, harmonies, dissonance, and resolve. The "eavesdropping" reader soon becomes part of the communal "we," hearing stories and opinions about Lipsha that he may or may not be privy to. All the voices presaged in the overture are heard either individually or in various combinations, always commingling with one another and with the constant interpolations of Lipsha's narratives until the choric voice resounds in three of the final four chapters, signaling the novel's coda. The shifting voices propel readers through disorienting struggles that mimic Lipsha's, but as readers continue, Erdrich's prose persists in urging them to become community members charged with accepting or rejecting Lipsha's liabilities as well as his potential contributions. While the surface text seems to emanate from members of the Ojibwe community on the reservation, the subtext repeatedly pulls the reader into Erdrich's writing process:

> Some of us tried to resist, yet were pulled in just the same. We were curious to know more, even though we'd never grasp the whole of it. The story comes around, pushing at our brains, and soon we are trying to ravel back to the beginning, trying to put families into order and make sense of things. But we start with one person, and soon another and another follows, and still another, until we are lost in the connections.　　　　　　　　　　　　　　　　　　　　　　(5)

The tangled histories of mixed-blood characters, often impossible to decode, lie at the heart of mixed-blood narratives and Native American political struggles.

Designed more like a web of indigenous oral narratives than a typical linear literate construction, *The Bingo Palace* possesses an orality that gives it a sense of simultaneity, wherein author, character, and reader are equally unsure of what will transpire. In a 1993 interview, when asked about her creative process for the novels, Erdrich explained:

> I never know the basic plot, it becomes more evident during the writing as the images evoke questions and explanations must be concocted. . . . The novel comes to light as it is written. It gathers its own material and acquires life, substance. I've got everything and nothing to do with it.
> (Chavkin and Chavkin 239, 243)

Teachers should remind students that this novel requires active participation.

Noting the challenge implied by her form, Erdrich, through Lipsha, flatly states, "Beginnings are lost in time and the ends of things are unpronounceable" (129). This statement reflects a key feature of Bakhtin's dialogism. In maintaining her oral dialogic stance, Erdrich cannot pronounce an end to her tale. She cannot even suggest what is to become of Lipsha, because to do so would suggest a closure that might prevent readers from actively composing their own dialogues and that would require a means of divining the future:

> Yet no matter how *we* strain to decipher the sound it never quite makes sense, never relieves *our* certainty or *our* suspicion that there is more to be told, more than *we* know, more than can be caught in the sieve of *our* thinking.　　　　　　　　　　　(274, emphasis added)

Again, she invokes the ambiguous communal narrator, which by this point readers should realize includes them.[9]

That Erdrich ends her story at an apparently random impasse will no doubt disturb readers who long for resolute endings, but to remain true to her oral rhetorical purpose, the author sneaks away like trickster, laughing beside the tempest she has conjured. Lipsha's final scene finds him once again abandoned by his parents, stuck in a blizzard in a field "out in the middle of nothing" off the main road. Erdrich circles back to Lipsha's original state of abandonment, but this time he is not completely alone. Faced with a twisted version of his father and mother's problem, he doesn't abandon the baby he has accidentally kidnapped in the back seat of his stolen getaway car:

> My father taught me his last lesson in those hours, in that night. He and my mother, June, have always been inside of me, dark and shining, their absence about the size of a coin, something I have touched against and slipped. . . . Come what might when we are found, I stay curled around this baby.   (259)

This final image Lipsha gives of himself completes a healing cycle for his childhood abandonment. In one of Erdrich's most effective decrescendos, Lipsha is left metaphorically pregnant: "But at least I can say, as I drift, as the cold begins to take me, as I pull the baby closer to me, zipping him inside of my jacket, here is one child who was never left behind" (259).

The healing becomes evident in Lipsha's shift from the first-person-singular voice, in which he has spoken throughout the novel, to his parting words, spoken in the plural, which harmonize with the choral voice of the following three chapters' coda, the communal voice of his tribe:

> As I fall away into my sleep, I'm almost happy things have turned out this way. I am not afraid. An unknown path opens up before *us*, an empty trail shuts behind. Snow closes over *our* tracks, and then keeps moving like the tide. There is no trace where *we* were. Nor any arrows pointing to the place *we're* headed. *We* are the trackless beat, the invisible light, the thought without a word to speak.
>
> (259, emphasis added)

In terms of Bakhtinian orchestration, Lipsha's individual voice, the novel's melodic theme, resolves into a communal voice, one of the novel's harmonized variations on that theme. In a deft dialogic trick, readers finally become part of Erdrich's fictional community, as gossip blends with an authoritative radio voice to bring the harmonized variations to a thematic resolution. We hear no more about Lipsha, but two chapters later, Shawnee Ray hears an anonymous radio voice reporting "a hostage found in good condition" (268). The child has been returned to his home, and, perhaps metaphorically, Lipsha rejoins his community, even as his trickster antics force him inexorably toward its fringe.

The Bingo Theme

Bakhtinian dialogism posits that a novel's meaning is generated when readers interact and "dialogue" with its various voices, creating a meaningful "conversation" grounded in multiple social and historical contexts. Though Erdrich avoids a tidy conclusion to her tale, she does not avoid the gambling issue central to current Native American sovereignty battles. Erdrich's Ojibwe ancestors suffered immeasurably because of the government land grab during the nineteenth century. Historical accounts show that the Ojibwe lost nearly ten million acres of territory in the treaty of 2 October 1863. As we enter the twenty-first century, individual states and tribes are fighting with each other and with the federal government to establish financial boundaries in unresolved conflicts that prolong the treaty tribulations and territorial wars fought in North America over the past centuries.

A little knowledge of the author's tribal past makes the words of Lipsha's comic vision-quest visitor, the talking skunk, resonate beyond the comic moment in the novel. When the skunk first says, "This ain't real estate" (200), a profoundly simple declaration of Native American beliefs regarding ownership of the earth, Lipsha is too chagrined to realize the impact of the skunk's statement. But Erdrich doesn't move on from this side-splitting scene without hinting at the deeper dialogue with which Lipsha must come to grips: "This ain't real estate, I think, and then I am surrounded and inhabited by a thing so powerful I don't even recognize it as a smell" (200–01). While readers are still laughing at our hero's misfortune, the author has cleverly lit the fuse on the dialogic bomb. The ambiguous pronouncement spoken by the skunk heralds the larger dialogue in the novel: the proposed development of a gambling casino on Pillager land would reduce sacred tribal burial grounds to commercial real estate. Erdrich plays out the pros and cons of Indian gaming, the dialectical crux of current Native American sovereignty debates, entreating readers to join the dialogue, to negotiate its meaning.

Erdrich extends Lipsha's internal debate over three pages of text, dialogizing the gambling question, inviting readers to question themselves as Lipsha worries about repeating the mistakes of the past:

> The thing is, I already know the outcome, and it's more or less a grey area of tense negotiations. It's not completely one way or another, traditional against the bingo. . . . And yet I can't help wonder, now that I know the high and the low of bingo life, if we're going in the wrong direction, arms flung wide, too eager.   (221)

Lipsha hasn't resolved his position on the bingo development yet, but an interesting transformation has taken place since his return to the reservation. After struggling through most of the novel trying to establish his individual identity, Lipsha evolves toward a maturing moral and social consciousness, as evidenced by the shift from the first-person-singular to the first-person-plural voice. Still, the storyteller leaves some of the story up to readers to dialogically construct, to interpret from the communal story that now includes them.

The resonances that Ojibwe tribal history and current Native nations' sovereignty struggles add to a reading of *The Bingo Palace* show how Bakhtinian dialogism can enhance the meaning-making process. This is not to suggest that every reader must read about every Native American writer's tribal history before beginning a given work, but the richness of the reading, the dialogue, grows in direct proportion to the number of pertinent contexts that each reader brings to a text's discourse.

Teachers should challenge students to negotiate, in the context of *The Bingo Palace*, the values of individual versus social consciousness, not just to ponder what "I" would do in Lipsha's place but to ponder what "we" should do. Active readers can dialogize the story's issues beyond the surface text, extending the contexts to include themselves and those who may not have considered their relations to Indian gaming and to Native American sovereignty.

NOTES

[1]Erdrich often uses various forms of humor in her novels, but in *The Bingo Palace* her serious political theme is consistently juxtaposed with slapstick humor. The opening scene's clumsy postal employee, the "pie-in-the-face" donnybrook that spreads from Lipsha and Lyman to the whole crowd of customers in the Dairy Queen scene, the racially charged joking between Lipsha and the convenience store clerk when Lipsha goes to buy condoms, the hilarious vision quest scene (from which I draw my title) in which Lipsha encounters his "power animal" (a skunk that sprays him for not listening to his message the first time), the ludicrous escape scene in which Lipsha impulsively decides to shoplift a giant stuffed bird—all these scenes exhibit Erdrich's most sustained use of humor.

[2]Writers who reviewed the novel in 1994 in *World Literature Today, World and I,* the *Antioch Review,* as well as mass market periodicals such as *Time, People,* and *Cosmopolitan,* focused on a variety of themes, but none emphasized the gambling and sovereignty issues central to the novel's discourse.

[3]In his translation of *The Dialogic Imagination,* Michael Holquist sums up Bakhtin's concept of dialogism by explaining that in any use of language, "[e]verything means, is understood, as a part of a greater whole—there is a constant interaction between meanings, all of which have the potential of conditioning others" (426).

[4]An excellent starting place for background on Indian gaming, www.indiangaming .org provides information on the history of gaming, myths, proceeds, regulation, sovereignty, states, statistics, and links to other resources. For more on the Ojibwe, see David Agee Horr's and O. G. Libbey's works or *Treaties and Agreements of the Chippewa Indians.* The Indian Removal Act was the legislation by which the government moved numerous tribes west of the Mississippi. Tales of the concentration camps and

removal marches that resulted in thousands of deaths for Native Americans can be found in histories of the Cherokee and in historical references to the "Trail of Tears." According to Louis Owens, in the name of allotting "real estate" to tribal members, the General Allotment Act had the net effect of "[taking] land away from Indians so effectively that in the forty-five years following the Dawes Act's passage 90 million acres passed from Indian ownership" (30).

⁵Coincidentally, Vizenor and Erdrich are both members of the Ojibwe tribe though descendants of different bands.

⁶For full-length discussions of this theme, see Owens's *Other Destinies* and Vizenor's *Narrative Chance*.

⁷Michael Holquist's glossary of Bakhtinian terminology provides a useful working definition of orchestration: "Bakhtin's most famous borrowing from musical terminology is the 'polyphonic' novel, but orchestration is the means for achieving it. Music is the metaphor for moving from seeing (such as in 'the novel is the encyclopedia of the life of the era') to hearing (as Bakhtin prefers to recast the definition, 'the novel is the maximally complete register of all social voices of the era'). For Bakhtin this is a crucial shift. In oral/aural arts, the 'overtones' of a communication act individualize it. Within a novel perceived as a musical score, a single 'horizontal' message (melody) can be harmonized vertically in a number of ways, and each of these scores with its fixed pitches can be further altered by giving the notes to different instruments. The possibilities of orchestration make any segment of text almost infinitely variable" (Bakhtin 430).

⁸Owens's description of the role that stories play in defining self in the oral tradition helps contextualize Erdrich's shifting voices: "In the oral tradition a people define themselves and their place within an imagined order, a definition necessarily dynamic and requiring constantly changing stories"(238).

⁹Gary Saul Morson suggests that certain fictions attempt to achieve the immediacy of improvisation: "Is it possible to bring the reader even closer to the author? Could the two be not just in a similar kind of time but in the same time—literally simultaneous in the usual sense of the word? That is, could the author actually be composing while the reader is reading? In oral performances, such simultaneity is of course possible . . ." (104).

Appendix A: Genealogical Charts

Nancy L. Chick

ADARE

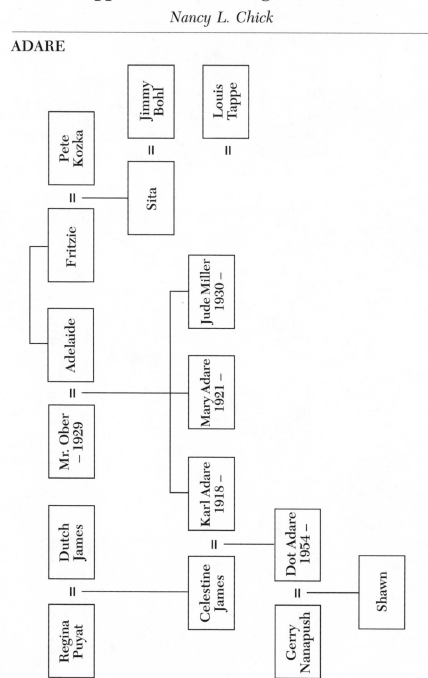

KASHPAW

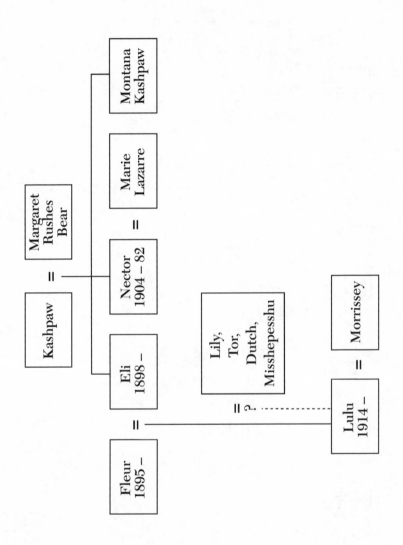

LAMARTINE

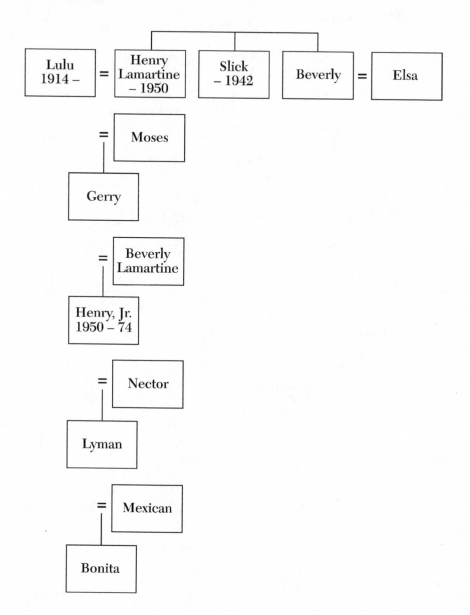

LAZARRE

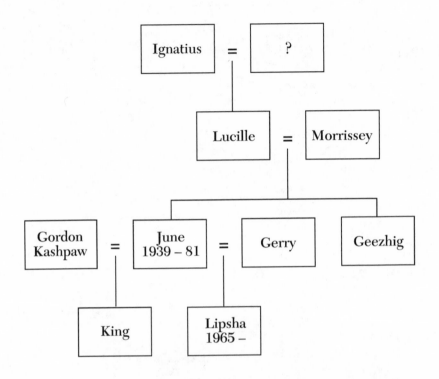

MORRISSEY

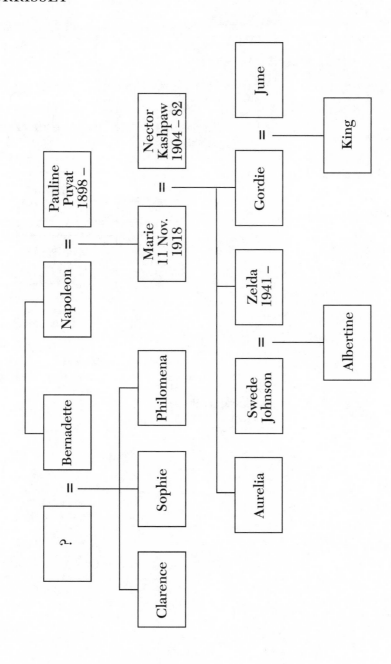

NANAPUSH

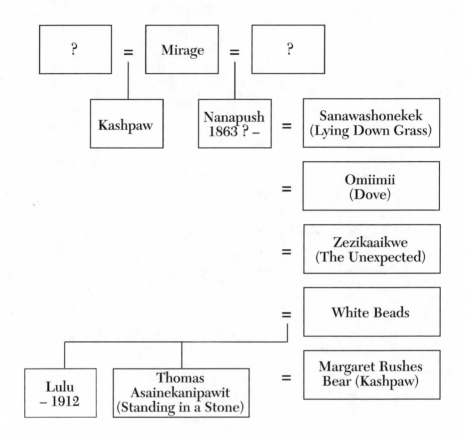

PILLAGER

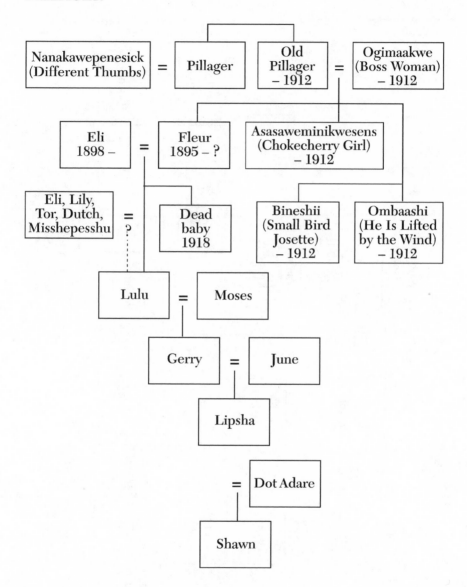

PUYAT

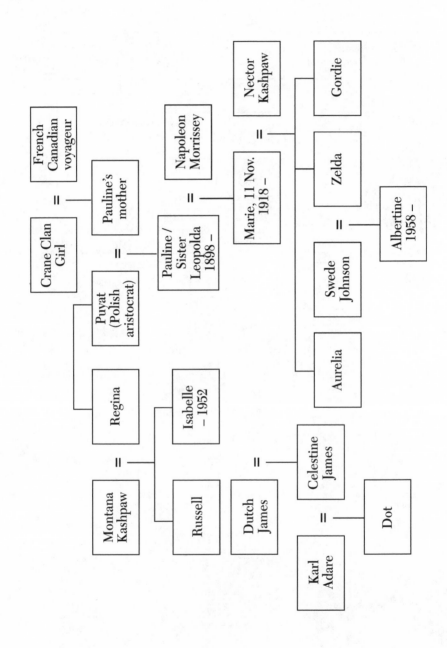

ROY

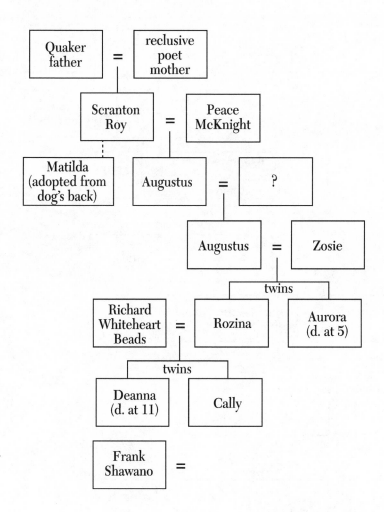

SHAWANO

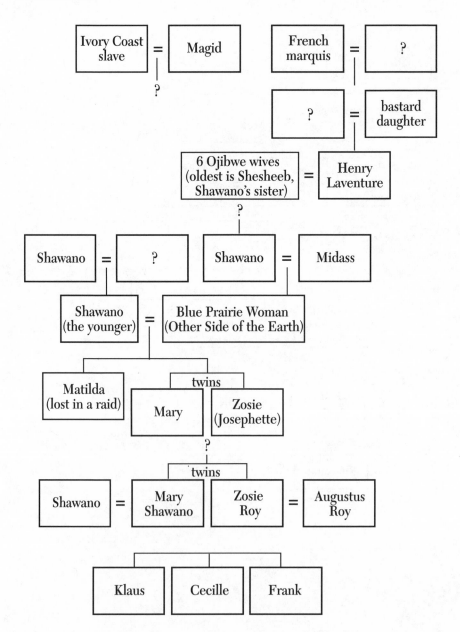

TOOSE

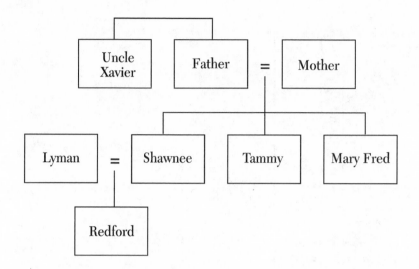

WHITEHEART BEADS

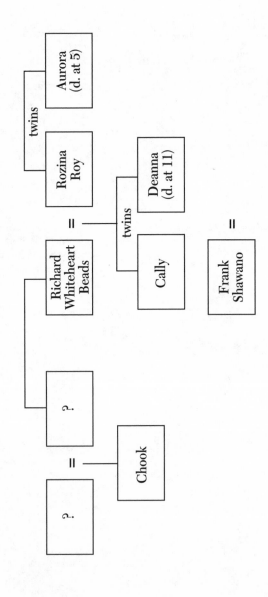

Appendix B: Maps

Connie A. Jacobs

Ojibwe Boundaries, Late 1800s

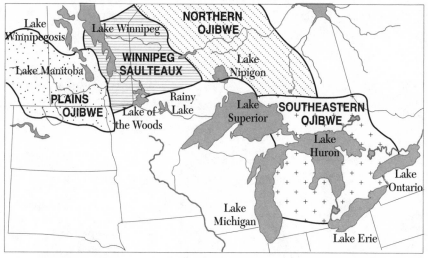

Map by Connie A. Jacobs and Lisa Snider Atchison

The Historical and Current Turtle Mountain Homeland

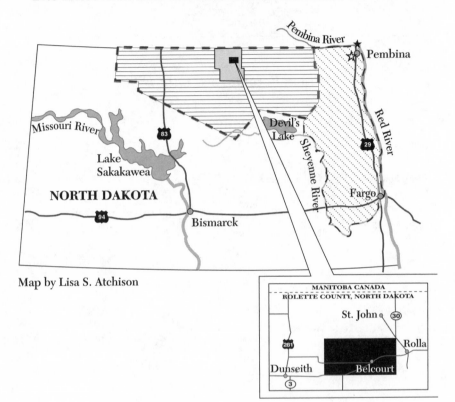

Map by Lisa S. Atchison

KEY

--- The original lands claimed by the Turtle Mountain Chippewa constituted about one-fifth of the state of North Dakota.

★ 1797: Northwest Company of Montreal establishes a trading post.

☆ 1843: Norman Kittson establishes the Pembina trading post.

▨ 1863: Little Shell, leader of the Turtle Mountain Band of Chippewa, cedes eleven million acres of the Red River Valley. Red Lake and White Earth Reservations are created in Minnesota for the Chippewa. White farmers increase; buffalo herds decrease.

▤ 1882, October: Without the consent of the Turtle Mountain Chippewa and without any payment made as compensation, the General Land Office opens up for Anglo settlement between nine and eleven millions acres of land claimed by the tribe.

▢ 1882, December: President Chester Arthur signs an executive order creating a 24-by-32-mile reservation in Rolette County, which contains excellent farmland. The reservation is intended for three hundred to four hundred full-bloods; it does not account for one thousand Métis.

■ 1884: The reservation is again reduced in size. The government opens up to European settlers twenty of the twenty-two townships of the best farmland set aside for the Turtle Mountain Chippewa in 1882. The government claims it is acting in deference to the full-bloods, who did not want their lands in severalty, and tells the Métis to take their allotment on public lands.

1904: The McCumber Agreement originally made in 1892 is finally ratified, and the tribe officially cedes the nine to ten million acres it still claims. Now known as the "ten-cent treaty," it compensated the tribe ten cents an acre.

The government allots 160-acre tracts to 326 families. Seven hundred male tribal members are forced to take off-reservation land in Rolette County near Devil's Lake, on public lands, and in Montana, and the tribe is thus effectively dispersed.

Twentieth-Century United States Plains-Ojibwe Reservations and Reserves

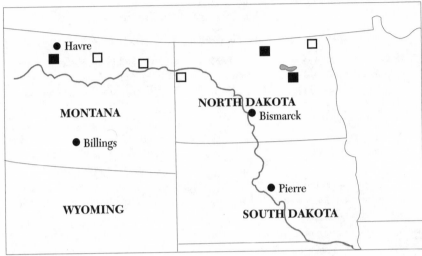

Map by Lisa Snider Atchison

KEY

■ Full-blood reservation

☐ Métis communities

● Major cities

Appendix C: Important Dates in the History of the Turtle Mountain Band of Chippewa Indians

Connie A. Jacobs

1780–82	A smallpox epidemic decimates the Ojibwe.
1780–90	Ojibwe from Leech Lake and Red Lake (Minnesota) and Northern Ojibwe from the Rainy River country (Minnesota) begin moving into the North Dakota area and successfully adapt to Plains life.
1797	The Northwest Company of Montreal builds a large trading post near Pembina (North Dakota) in the Red River Valley.
1800	The Ojibwe are hunting buffalo with the Cree.
1818	The United States-Canadian border is established.
1848	Father Anthony Belcourt establishes a mission at Pembina.
1850	The Métis population stands at around five thousand people, making them the largest group on the northern Plains. Cree becomes the lingua franca on the northern Plains.
1861	The Territory of North Dakota is created.
1863	The Plains Ojibwe surrender the Red River Valley.
1870	The Métis merge with the Pembina Ojibwe and the Ojibwe-Cree in the Turtle Mountain area.
1871	The Northern Pacific Railroad and the Pacific Railroad from the East reach the Red River Valley, accelerating the flow of settlers into the area.
1876	The Turtle Mountain Band petitions Congress for three thousand square miles of reservation land.
1880s	The great buffalo herds roaming the Plains, once numbering sixty million, have been nearly exterminated by white buffalo hunters. Saint Ann's Catholic Church erected in Belcourt, where today it remains the center of most religious life for tribal members.
1882	President Arthur creates the first reservation for three hundred full-bloods; the land includes excellent farmland. The Métis settle on public lands next to the reserve. Little Shell, chief of the Turtle Mountain Band, posts a warning to whites not to encroach on Indian lands.
1884	The reservation is reduced from twenty-two townships to two, based on an erroneous assumption that only the three hundred or so full-bloods were entitled to land. The best land is returned to the public domain. The Sisters of Mercy and Father John Malo

	open a school; the children enrolled are Métis, not Ojibwe. The sending of children from the reservation to boarding schools begins.
1886–87	On the reservation 150 people starve to death during a harsh winter.
1887	The Dawes, or General Allotment, Act allows reservation lands to be parceled into individual allotments.
1890	Little Shell and his group of Ojibwe-Métis move to Montana seeking a reservation area where they could live a traditional lifestyle.
1891	The band petitions the secretary of the interior, asking that 446,670 acres be removed from adjoining public lands and annexed to the reservation.
1892	The McCumber Agreement restores nine million acres to the public domain without the consent of the tribe, who are paid $1 million, earning the agreement the name the "ten-cent treaty." The United States government now owns all the Plains-Ojibwe land in North Dakota with the exception of two townships that are unsuitable for dry farming. This land is divided into allotments, and those not receiving land are allowed to settle on available public lands to which they believed they had legal title and consequently did not file for titles. Many mixed-bloods are dropped unfairly from tribal rolls.
1893–96	A national depression occurs.
1895	Game, fish, and fur-bearing animals are nearly depleted on the overcrowded reservation. Many full-bloods move off the reservation and squat on public lands near Dunseith. Believing that they already legally own the land, many full-bloods do not apply for their rightful titles.
1890–1910	Smallpox and tuberculosis epidemics strike the Turtle Mountain Reservation.
1900	Little Shell dies; he has been the leading spokesman against the McCumber Agreement. Kakenowash succeeds him as tribal leader.
1904	The "ten-cent treaty" is ratified by Congress. The tribe continues to disperse as land is allotted to its members in surrounding areas in North Dakota and in Montana.
1911	Tribal members who were issued off-reservation allotment land still have not received trust patents for their land. When they do, most of the mixed-bloods sell them within a year.
1920	Nearly ninety percent of tribal members receiving a patent have lost their land, increasing their government dependence.

1930	Many tribal businesses are operating in Belcourt.
1932	An eight-person tribal council is established.
1941	The government purchases thirty-three thousand acres for landless tribal members.
1950	The termination policy is enacted by the government, which no longer feels obligated to help support reservation tribes.
1952	The Indian Relocation Act seeks to move Indians into the cities.
1960s–70s	The Vietnam War is waged; the Civil Rights Act is passed.
1966	The American Indian Movement (AIM) is formed by Dennis Banks, a mixed-blood Ojibwe from the Leech Lake Reservation, and Clyde Bellecourt, a mixed-blood Lakota from the Pine Ridge Reservation. They seek to force the government to recognize Indian rights.
1971	Turtle Mountain Community College opens.
1979	The Indian Claims Commission awards $52,527,338 to the tribe in recognition of the unfairness of the McCumber Agreement.
1980s	The tribe establishes a shopping mall, a heritage center, a buffalo park, and a bingo palace.
1982	The government establishes "Chippewayan Authentics" to mass-produce native crafts. The venture fails because there is no market for the machine-made goods.
1988	President Ronald Reagan signs legislation establishing a commission to regulate gambling on reservation lands. The United States Court of Claims, in accordance with P.L. 97–403, issues the first partial payment to tribal members as compensation for the "ten-cent treaty." "This award was made from the 1905 value of a large aboriginal tract of over eight million acres of land in North Central North Dakota" (*BIA Bulletin*, Turtle Mountain Agency).
1994	The United States Court of Claims, in accordance with P.L. 97–403, issues the final partial payment of $1,232.97 for each tribal member.
2000	There are 28,703 tribal members on the roll, with 15,000 of them living on or near the reservation.

Appendix D: Study Guides to Eight Erdrich Novels

Peter G. Beidler

First-time readers of Louise Erdrich's novels almost invariably find them both fascinating and difficult. To help students get a handle on the novels, I have found it useful to distribute one-page study guides at the class meeting before we start discussion of a given novel and to go over them orally as a way of previewing things to watch for. The opening paragraph of each guide summarizes the contents of the novel and mentions the names of most of the important characters. After that I list and outline five areas that form the basis for class discussion. I have found that these guides can pave the way to meaningful discussions.

Depending on the size of the class, I sometimes divide my students into four or five small groups and assign an area to each group. The students then give reports or lead discussion on their areas, knowing that others in the class, armed with my study guide, will have had a chance to think about some of the questions ahead of time. Ideally, the five discussion areas not only stimulate thought about the specific topics but also lead students to their own ideas for related topics. When I teach Erdrich to graduate students, I encourage them to spring away from my five topic areas and find their own. When they do, they almost invariably lead the seminar in interesting directions and sometimes come up with ideas that they can develop into conference papers or articles.

I give the novels in the order of publication, starting with *Love Medicine*. *Love Medicine* is a special case, however, because Erdrich issued it twice. The shorter, first version appeared in 1984. Then in 1993 she published an expanded version, with four new chapters and several smaller changes.

Love Medicine, 1984 (rev. and exp., 1993)

Summary

Several Ojibwe and Cree families (with some Anglo blood mixed in) struggle with love, survival, and their own personalities in modern North Dakota. There are at least three generations and at least ten important characters. First generation: Nector, Marie, Lulu; second generation: Gerry, Gordie, June, Henry, Jr.; third generation: Albertine, Lipsha, King. Because this novel was constructed of a number of short stories, it is almost impossible to give a meaningful plot summary of the whole.

Discussion Areas

Love The theme of love is important in this novel, from the title to the last line, where June is brought home. How is that love shown? How does it differ from the love shown in non-Indian families? Are there any antilove characters? And, oh yes, what is "love medicine"?

Religion What are we to make of the Catholic presence in the novel? Is Catholicism a positive, a negative, or a neutral presence? Is it poison or medicine to the people? In what ways does it intersect or conflict with a more Native or "natural" religion? How would you describe the Native alternative to Catholicism?

Family Assuming that the Kashpaw and the Lulu-Lamartine families are typical, how would you characterize Erdrich's depiction of the typical family structure, dependency patterns, communication styles, and authority relationships among modern Indians? Does the family seem to be, according to Erdrich, a positive or a negative force in Indian culture?

Time and unity Is this a novel or merely a collection of short stories? Why does Erdrich tell the story in what appears to be such a confused or disjointed way? Would it have been better if she had arranged all the chapters in chronological order?

Theme What is the large point or main idea of the novel? Do you leave the novel feeling encouraged or discouraged about these Indians and their way of life? Is it an antiwhite novel? an anti-Indian novel? Does it have a political point to make? an emotional point to make? Is Erdrich trying to show us the way? What way, and for whom? What alternative medicines are there to the love medicine of the title? Are they effective?

The Beet Queen, 1986

Summary

Most of the central characters in this loosely structured novel are Anglo men and women who live in and around Argus, North Dakota. The narrative begins when the three children of Mr. Ober and Adelaide Adare are separated from their father, who dies, and their mother, who abandons them. Karl, Mary, and Jude are then separated from one another and spend the rest of the novel not quite getting back together again. A parallel plot involves the birth of Wallacette to Celestine James. Wallacette, who goes by the name of Dot, becomes the Beet Queen at the end of the novel. Another important character is Sita Kozka, whose various misadventures end in her death.

Discussion Areas

Abandonment The novel begins in abandonment, when Mr. Ober commits suicide and leaves his illegitimate family with no home or means of support. Does Erdrich seem to suggest that the abandonment of children is necessarily a bad thing? Are the children better off without such parents?

Parenting On one level *The Beet Queen* is about varieties of parenting, particularly mothering. To what extent does the novel seem to suggest that birth mothers are irresponsible and that adoptive mothers do a better job? What about fathers? Do they seem to have any role at all in raising a child?

Gender issues Karl and Wallace are both gay. How does the novel depict their sexual orientation? Does the novel depict heterosexual relationships as in any way better or more positive?

Saint(?) Mary Mary is revered as a miracle-producing saint, but at times she seems more like a witch with hands that glow in the dark. What are we to make of her? Is there a functional contrast between her and Fleur or between her and Sister Leopolda, other possible witch-saints?

Sita as comic character Is Sita a serious or a comic character? What is her purpose in a novel that seems to try to make genuine commentary about parenting and disrupted families? Are we to laugh at Sita's failed businesses and marriages and even at her strange career as a corpse? If so, how does that laughter function?

Tracks, 1988

Summary

The events in *Tracks* take place before most of those in *Love Medicine*, but several of the characters will seem familiar: Lulu, Eli, and Nector, for example, appear, as do some other familiar names, like Pillager, Lazarre, and Morrissey. The more central characters are Nanapush and Pauline, who in alternate chapters tell the story of Fleur, Lulu's mother.

Discussion Areas

Where the tracks lead Note carefully all references to tracks, footprints, shoes, paws, walking, and so on, and try to trace the pattern or trail that will help make sense of the title of this novel. Do the tracks all lead to death? Is this a novel, finally, about death and dying and the trails that lead there? Are Pauline and Fleur murderers?

Religion What role does religion—organized, Catholic, Native—play in *Tracks*? What about Father Damien? What about Pauline? What about the lake man in Machimanito? What about Nanapush? Are we supposed to come away from this novel hating Christians and loving a more Native or natural religion or spirituality?

Those two narrators Why did Erdrich select two narrators for this novel? Is Nanapush "right" about things and Pauline "wrong," or is that too simple an explanation of what is gained by alternating narrators? Do we get a better picture of Fleur this way or just a more confusing one? Is Fleur the main character or really only a minor one?

Sexuality and birth Take note of the sex and birth scenes in *Tracks*. How are they similar? How are they different? How are sex and power related in this novel? How are birth and death related? How do Pauline and Nanapush differ in their view of sex? How do Pauline and Fleur differ in their view of birth?

Water and trees Water, ice, rain, sweat, steam, mist, lakes, drowning, bathing: What is the significance of the water imagery in *Tracks*? Do you see any patterns? Is that significance the same for all the characters? Trees speak, groan, crack, whine, and slam against the earth. Do the trees somehow stand for Indians? What about the final big scene, where Fleur cuts a mess of them down before the Turcot Company takes the rest?

The Bingo Palace, 1994

Summary

The novel starts with Gerry Nanapush escaping from jail again and Lulu sending a copy of his WANTED picture to Lipsha, who returns to the reservation. Lipsha falls in love with Shawnee Ray Toose. Lyman Lamartine, who also loves Shawnee Ray, sets plans in motion to transform the land near Matchimanito Lake into a casino. The novel ends with Lipsha stranded in a car in a terrible blizzard—reminiscent of the snowfall that opens *Love Medicine*. Will he, like his mother June, freeze to death?

Discussion Areas

The supernatural This novel continues the use of what are sometimes called supernatural features—visions, strange voices, ghosts, spirits, lake monsters, unexplained ways of knowing. What are we to make of such features? Do they lend an air of Ojibwe authenticity to the novel? Do they strain our ability to take the novel seriously? Do they make the novel a fairy tale of some sort?

Lipsha's growth Lipsha seems to grow in the course of this novel—from a derelict at the start to a baby-saving hero at the end. What are the apparent stages in that growth? What makes him change? Does the change appear to be permanent or just a quick flash of growth? Do you think he will get the girl in the end, or is he essentially a dead man walking?

Burning love What about Zelda's tale of Xavier's love for her? Does that tale have echoes elsewhere in the novel? Does the burning love enlighten? heat? destroy? burn? thaw? cook?

Motherhood There seem to be a lot of mother-child relationships in the novel: Zelda-Albertine, June-Lipsha, Shawnee Ray-Redford, Lulu-Gerry. What about that baby at the end? Does Erdrich seem to have a good-mother / bad-mother dichotomy in mind? If so, who is which and why? Is motherhood more prominent than fatherhood?

Humor What do we make of the humor in the novel? What seems funny to you? Does the humor merely make us laugh, or is there a serious spike to it? The most prominent comic scene is the vision-quest skunk; is there a serious side to the comedy? What about the ending? Is there any humor in the more serious events of the novel? Is the novel, finally, tragic or comic?

Tales of Burning Love, 1996

Summary

Jack Mauser turns out to be the real name of Andy, the mud engineer who tries to seduce June at the start of *Love Medicine*. After his encounter with June, Jack has a string of lovers and four wives: Eleanor Schlick, a professor; Candice Pantamounty, a dentist; Marlis Cook, an entertainer; and Dot Adare Nanapush, wife of the convict Gerry Nanapush. Plagued by debts and woman troubles, Jack half-stages his own death when his house burns down, though he secretly escapes. Meanwhile, his four surviving widows attend his funeral. After the funeral, they are caught in a car in a blizzard. To keep one another awake, they tell true tales, mostly about their relationships with Jack Mauser.

Discussion Areas

Jack Mauser's growth The focal character, Jack, seems through most of the novel to be hopelessly boyish and immature and is even accused by one of his future wives of being a "sexual Neanderthal." Does Jack grow up in the course of the novel? If so, in what ways? Does his story have a happy ending?

Eleanor's sexuality Eleanor is herself something of a sexual predator, even seducing one of her undergraduate students. Describe her on-again, off-again relationship with Jack, starting from the time she grinds his hand into broken glass. What is the long-term prognosis for her relationship with Jack?

Burning love Consider the various kinds of burning in the novel and the varieties of "burning love." How does Jack's having been a fireman figure in? June's death by freezing? Jack's house burning? the quality of his love for his various wives? What light does Lawrence Schlick's death shed on burning love?

Authorship If you did not know the sex of the author of this novel, what evidence would you find that the author was a woman? Consider particularly the portrayal of Jack Mauser. Would a man write about him in the same way? Is this a feminist novel?

The return of June and Leopolda Why does Erdrich seem to need to resurrect June and Sister Leopolda in this novel? Is Erdrich just having fictional fun with familiar characters, or do they serve serious narrative purposes? Do they somehow frame Jack's life or loves?

The Antelope Wife, 1998

Summary

When Scranton Roy's regiment attacks a quiet Indian village in Minnesota, he murders several Indians and then deserts with an Indian baby whom he raises—until she runs off and finally joins a deer herd. The descendants of that soldier and that baby meet many generations later in modern-day Minneapolis. Cally Roy interacts with her mother, Rozin, and her twin grandmothers, Zosie and Mary, who had much earlier shared sexual relations with the grandson of Scranton Roy. Rozin's marriage with Richard Whiteheart Beads ends unhappily, but Rozin eventually finds a more enduring bond with Frank Shawano, who has spent much of his life trying to perfect the recipe for a wonderful cake called a *blitzkuchen*. The novel ends with a metaphor of beads as life—elements capable of different designs and configurations.

Discussion Areas

Cally Roy To what extent is Cally the central consciousness of the novel? To what extent is the novel structured on her development, her altered understanding of the past, and her place in several intersecting families? Does she grow or change? Do we care about her? Does it matter that she is a surviving twin?

Animal people Why does Erdrich give us so many animal-connected people: the Antelope Wife of the title (presumably Sweetheart Calico), talking dogs, woman-suckling puppies, porcupine men? Is there some sort of we-are-all-one-species message here?

Gender issues Why does Erdrich have Scranton Roy nurse two babies? Are there other, more subtle forms of gender crossing? What about Frank and the German prisoner of war? Do they occupy feminine roles as cooks? Are there masculine women in the novel?

The men This novel seems clearly to be about women. Is it true, as some reviewers have suggested, that the men are pasteboard characters, almost caricatures, who never reveal themselves to us in any depth? Is Frank an exception? What about Richard Whiteheart Beads? What about Scranton Roy?

Beads Is Erdrich's closing image of beads as people or as life strands a useful one in this novel? Why does Erdrich seem to need to explain the beads and beading at the very end of the novel? Does the novel reveal who the "beader" is?

The Last Report on the Miracles at Little No Horse, 2001

Summary

In 1996, Father Damien Modeste, after almost a century with the Ojibwe, writes to the pope to confess that he has been a fraudulent priest. Intertwined with the life of this she-he priest are the lives of familiar characters like Lulu, Marie, Margaret, Fleur, Nanapush, Nector, and Napoleon, as well as some new characters like Father Wekkle and Mary Kashpaw. We learn how a young woman named Agnes DeWitt becomes a nun who has a sexual obsession with playing the piano, then a farmer's common-law wife, then a bank robber's hostage, and finally a priest at a reservation called Little No Horse. At about the same time that Father Damien is writing to the pope, Father Jude Miller comes to Little No Horse on a mission from the Vatican to investigate the miraculous life of the recently deceased Sister Leopolda.

Discussion Areas

Father Damien Do you find Father Damien to be an attractive character? If so, why? Does it bother you that he is an impostor, a thief, a liar? He easily forgives others their sins; can we forgive his affair with another priest and his spending stolen money on a Steinway?

Conversion Father Damien goes to Little No Horse to convert the Ojibwe to Catholicism. By the end, has he nearly become converted to the traditional Ojibwe practices he set out to replace? If so, is that a good thing? Is this an anti-Catholic novel?

The black dog What do you make of the black dog that hounds Father Damien? Is he the devil? Does he really speak? Is he evidence that Father Damien is insane? Does he explode all pretense to realism in the novel? Is this dog different from other talking animals we have seen in Erdrich's fiction?

Gender In this novel a passionate woman spends most of her life impersonating an unpassionate man. Is there a message in Agnes–Father Damien's life about male-female roles and attitudes? Do the alternating gender pronouns annoy or confuse you? Is there a connection between gender and the various kinds of passion referred to in the novel?

Nanapush Do you find Nanapush as attractive a character as Father Damien does? Is he, like his namesake Nanabozho, a trickster figure of mythological proportions, or is he just a funny, oversexed, foolish, and wise old man? If you find him attractive, does your liking of him decrease your liking of the Anglo people in the novel?

The Master Butchers Singing Club, 2003

Summary

The novel begins just after World War I with the arrival in the United States of a young German sniper named Fidelis Waldvogel, who becomes a butcher in Argus. He is soon joined by his wife, Eva, and her son, Franz, and Fidelis and Eva proceed to have three more sons—Markus, Erich, and Emil. All four sons eventually become soldiers in World War II, but on different sides. Other Argus characters are involved in an intersecting plot. Delphine, the daughter of the town drunk Roy Watzka, has a long-term relationship with Cyprian Lazarre, who turns out to be gay. Other Argus characters are an undertaker named Clarisse, who seems to be involved with the deaths of a family in Roy Watzka's cellar, and a repulsive sheriff who loves her but whom she disembowels. The novel ends with surprising revelations about who the mother of Delphine really is.

Discussion Areas

Songs and singing Why and how is singing important in this novel? Does singing merely provide comfort and comradeship and a way to reconnect with times past, or is it more than that? Are some songs more important than others? Is singing ever wrong?

Varieties of love Love takes many forms in this novel. A gay gymnast loves a straight woman, or does he? A sheriff loves an undertaker, or does he? A drunkard loves a ragpicker, or does he? A butcher loves his best friend's widow and then the woman who nurses her, or does he? What implied statement about love does Erdrich make?

Children and parenting A baby is delivered into an outhouse; a boy almost suffocates in a womb hand dug in an earth mound; a butcher has no time for his sons; Indian babies are murdered by soldiers at Wounded Knee. Is Erdrich making a statement here about the responsibilities that adults have to children? How do Delphine and Step-and-a-Half, who have no biological children, contribute to the theme of parenting?

God Delphine makes several statements about God's failures. Do you agree with her that God is a drunken lout?

Antiwar sentiments Does Erdrich use Delphine's voice to make an antiwar statement through the various references to fighting and wounding and killing? Think particularly about the opposition between Fidelis and Cyprian, the way the Waldvogel boys wind up on opposite sides in World War II, and the outcomes of their enlistments. Is it important that Fidelis is a butcher? Is war one big butcher shop?

NOTES ON CONTRIBUTORS

Debra K. S. Barker (Rosebud Lakota) is associate professor of English at the University of Wisconsin, Eau Claire, where she has served as chair of the American Indian Studies Committee and codirector of the American Indian Studies Program. Her publications include articles on the history of the boarding school system and how it affected American Indians, on American Indian biographies, on American Indian grave desecration, and on the commodification of American Indian art.

Gay Barton is on the faculty at Abilene Christian University, where she has served as James W. Culp Distinguished Professor of English. Among her teaching interests are the works of twentieth-century women writers and Native American novelists. She is coauthor with Peter G. Beidler of *A Reader's Guide to the Novels of Louise Erdrich* (1999) and is currently working on a book analyzing Erdrich's narrative technique.

Peter G. Beidler is Lucy G. Moses Professor of English at Lehigh University. A Chaucerian by training, he is a self-taught specialist in Native American fictions, which he has taught for thirty years. Among his recent works in Native American studies are *A Reader's Guide to the Novels of Louise Erdrich* with Gay Barton (1999) and *The Native American in the Saturday Evening Post* with Marion F. Egge (2000).

Alanna Kathleen Brown is professor of English at Montana State University. She received the Phi Kappa Phi Western Region Distinguished Scholar Award, 1998–2001, and in 2004 an NEH Research Fellowship, for her work on the early Native American writers Mourning Dove and D'Arcy McNickle. She served on the Executive Council of the Western Literature Association, 1996–98 and was elected to the Executive Committee of the Division of American Indian Literatures, MLA, 1996–2000.

Nancy L. Chick is associate professor of English at the University of Wisconsin–Barron County. Her publications include articles on Toni Morrison's "Recitatif," Judith Ortiz Cofer's *Silent Dancing*, Jamaica Kincaid's *Lucy*, Louis Owens, and Marita Bonner. Her interests include multicultural literature, feminist pedagogy, and interdisciplinary studies.

G. Thomas Couser is professor of English at Hofstra University. In addition to numerous articles, he has written *American Autobiography: The Prophetic Mode* (1979), *Altered Egos: Authority in American Autobiography* (1989), *Recovering Bodies: Illness, Disability,* and *Life Writing* (1997), and *Vunerable Subjects: Ethics and Life Writing* (2003).

Vanessa Holford Diana is assistant professor of English and director of the Women's Studies Program at Westfield State College, where she teaches courses in multicultural American literature. She has published essays on Paula Gunn Allen, Gloria Naylor, Leslie Marmon Silko, Sui Sin Far, and Zitkala-Sa. She is currently working on a comparative study of fiction and autobiographical writings by Sophia Alice Callahan, Frances Harper, Pauline Hopkins, Mourning Dove, Sui Sin Far, and Zitkala-Sa.

James R. Giles is professor of English at Northern Illinois University, DeKalb. He is the author of *Violence in the Contemporary American Novel: An End of Innocence* (2000); *The Naturalistic Inner-City Novel in America: Encounters with the Fat Man* (1995); *Understanding Hubert Selby, Jr.* (1998); *Confronting the Horror: The Novels of Nelson Algren* (1989); and *Irwin Shaw: A Study of the Short Fiction* (1983). He is also the author of the Twayne Authors series volumes on Claude McKay, James Jones, and Irwin Shaw.

Gwen Griffin (Sisseton-Wahpeton Dakota, Oklahoma Cherokee) is professor of English at Minnesota State University, Mankato, where she teaches Native literature, American literature, and technical writing. A previous Newberry Fellow and participant in "Indian Voices in the Academy," she currently serves on the editorial board of *Studies in American Indian Literatures* and as director of the Native American Literature Symposium.

P. Jane Hafen (Taos Pueblo) is associate professor of English at the University of Nevada, Las Vegas. Griffin and Hafen have served on the Executive Board of the Western Literature Association and were Fellows at the D'Arcy McNickle Center for the History of the American Indian at the Newberry Library. They are currently co-editing a volume of essays on Native American literary strategies. Hafen is author of *Reading Louise Erdrich's* Love Medicine (2003).

Sharon Hoover, professor emerita of English at Alfred University, occupied the Gertz Chair in Writing. After a career in educational publishing, she became active in Willa Cather studies. She also writes on Native American studies. Her most recent book is *Willa Cather Remembered* (2002).

Dee Horne is associate professor of English at the University of Northern British Columbia. She is the author of *Contemporary American Indian Writing: Unsettling Literature* (1999). She has also published articles in professional journals and poems in literary journals.

Patrick E. Houlihan studied creative writing with the Creek poet Joy Harjo and Native American literature with Louis Owens at the University of New Mexico, Albuquerque. He currently teaches composition, creative writing, Native American literature, and journalism at Albuquerque TVI Community College.

Connie A. Jacobs teaches composition, American and southwest literature, and cultural studies at San Juan College, where she is associate professor. Her publications include articles on Louise Erdrich and Esther Belin and a book, *The Novels of Louise Erdrich: Stories of Her People* (2001). She is currently working on a collaborative project that examines images of Native Americans in children's literature.

Amelia V. Katanski is assistant professor of English at Kalamazoo College, where she teaches courses on American Indian literature, ethnic literatures, and autobiography. She is currently completing a manuscript on representations of the boarding school experience in American Indian literature.

Paul Lumsden is an English instructor at Grant MacEwan College, Edmonton. His teaching interests are thematic and cross-cultural readings that focus on how different narrative traditions and cultures intersect and interact.

Tom Matchie is professor of English at North Dakota State University, Fargo. He has published numerous articles on midwestern and multicultural authors, including Louise Erdrich and Michael Dorris as well as Tom McGrath, Louis Hudson, Jon Hassler, Mary Crow Dog, Elizabeth Cook-Lynn, Ella Deloria, Sharon Butala, Sandra Cisneros, Thomas King, and Sherman Alexie.

David T. McNab is a Métis historian who has worked for more than two decades on aboriginal land and treaty rights in Canada. He is assistant professor of Native studies in the School of Arts and Letters at Atkinson College, York University, and has been a claims adviser for Nin.Da.Waab.Jig., Walpole Island Heritage Centre, Bkejwanog First Nations, since 1992. His publications include *Earth, Water, Air and Fire: Studies in Canadian Ethnohistory* (1998) and *Circles of Time: Aboriginal Land Rights and Resistance in Ontario* (1999).

John McWilliams is professor at Middlebury College. His books include *Political Justice in a Republic: James Fenimore Cooper's America* (1972); *Hawthorne, Melville, and the American Character* (1984); *The American Epic: Transforming a Genre* (1989); *The Last of the Mohicans: Civil Savagery and Savage Civility* (1994); and *New England's Crises and Cultural Memory* (2004).

Dean Rader is assistant professor at the University of San Francisco, where he teaches in the English department and serves as associate dean for arts and humanities. He has published essays, reviews, poems, and translations in books and journals and is on the editorial board of *Studies in American Indian Literatures*. He is coauthor with Jonathan Silverman of *The World Is a Text* (2002), and co-editor with Janice Gould of *Speak to Me Words: Essays on Contemporary American Indian Poetry* (2003).

James Ruppert holds a joint appointment in English and Alaska Native studies at the University of Alaska, Fairbanks. He is a past president of the Association for the Study of American Indian Literatures and has written many articles on Native American literature and the complex interface between Native American literature and mainstream American literature. His publications include *Mediation in Contemporary Native American Fiction* (1995), and he co-edited, with John Purdy, an anthology of Native American literature, *Nothing but the Truth* (2000).

Greg Sarris is author of an award-winning collection of short stories, *Grand Avenue* (1994), which he adapted and acted as co-executive producer with Robert Redford for the HBO miniseries of the same name. He currently is the Fletcher Jones Professor of Writing and Literature at Loyola Marymount University and is serving his sixth elected term as chairman of his tribe, the Federated Indians of the Graton Rancheria.

Susan Scarberry-García is the author of *Landmarks of Healing: A Study of House Made of Dawn* (1990) and *Dancing Spirits: Jose Rey Toledo, Towa Artist* (1994), as well as numerous articles on Native art, music, and literature. She is past president of the Association for the Study of American Literatures and past chair of the Executive Committee of the Division of American Indian Literatures of the MLA. She writes comparatively about Native North American and Native Siberian arts and literature. She is currently Hulbert Endowed Chair of Southwest Studies at Colorado College.

Karah Stokes is associate professor of English at Kentucky State University, Frankfort. She has published articles on Louise Erdrich, Charles Chestnutt, and Gloria Naylor. Her essay in this volume is part of a larger study in progress on the strategies American women writers use to combat and heal the effects of physical and textual violence.

Kari J. Winter, associate professor of American studies at the State University of New York, Buffalo, is the author of *Subjects of Slavery, Agents of Change: Women and Power in Gothic Novels and Slave Narratives, 1790–1865* (1992), the editor of *The Blind African Slave; or, Memoirs of Boyrereau Brinch, Nicknamed Jeffrey Brace* (2004), and the author of numerous articles on African American, American Indian, and feminist literature. Her essays on Erdrich have been published in *Studies in American Indian Literatures, Inquiry,* and *Northwest Review*.

SURVEY PARTICIPANTS

We wish to acknowledge and to thank the following scholars who, along with the volume's contributors, shared their classroom experiences, materials, and suggestions on how best to teach Louise Erdrich.

Chadwick Allen, *Ohio State University, Columbus*
Scott Andrews, *University of California, Riverside*
Lori L. Burlingame, *Eastern Michigan University*
Rhonda Cawthom, *University of South Carolina, Columbia*
Mary Chapman, *University of Alberta*
Janina P. Ciezadlo, *Columbia College, Chicago*
Dennis Cutchins, *Brigham Young University, Provo*
Patsy J. Daniels, *Lane College*
Carl Dietrich, *Owens Community College*
Kathleen Donovan, *South Dakota State*
Robin Riley Fast, *Emerson College*
Louise Flavin, *University of Cincinnati, Raymond Walters College*
Denis Fournier, *University of Mary*
Larry Hartsfield, *Fort Lewis College*
Helen Jaskoski, *California State University, Fullerton*
Rosemary King, *Arizona State University, Tempe*
Linda J. Krumholz, *Denison University*
Danielle Mahlum, *University of Minnesota*
Janet Mauney, *University of Alabama, Tuscaloosa*
Lara Merlin, *Rutgers University, New Brunswick*
Robert Reid, *University of Guam*
Gretchen Ronnow, *Wayne State University*
Richard Sax, *Madonna University*
Lisa Spaulding, *University of Nebraska, Lincoln*
Ernest Stromberg, *University of Oregon*
Cynthia Taylor, *University of Southern Colorado*
Paola Trimarco, *Korea University*
Karen Wallace, *University of Wisconsin, Oshkosh*
Kathryn Walterscheid, *University of Missouri, Saint Louis*
Sharon Wilson, *University of Northern Colorado*
Pauline Woodward, *Endicott College*
Bernice B. Zamora, *University of Southern Colorado*

WORKS CITED

Books and Articles

Agee Horr, David, ed. *Chippewa Indians VII: Commission Findings on the Chippewa Indians*. New York: Garland, 1974.

Alexie, Sherman. *The First Indian on the Moon*. Brooklyn: Hanging Loose, 1993.

———. *Indian Killer*. New York: Atlantic Monthly, 1996.

Allen, Paula Gunn. *Grandmothers of the Light*. Boston: Beacon, 1991.

———. Introduction. *Spider Woman's Granddaughters*. Boston: Beacon, 1989. 1–25.

———, ed. "The Sacred Hoop: A Contemporary Perspective." Allen, *Studies* 3–22.

———. *The Sacred Hoop: Recovering the Feminine in American Indian Traditions*. Boston: Beacon, 1986.

———, ed. *Studies in American Indian Literature: Critical Essays and Course Designs*. New York: MLA, 1983.

———. "Who Is Your Mother? Red Roots of White Feminism." Allen, *Sacred Hoop* 209–21.

Andelin, Helen. *Fascinating Womanhood*. New York: Bantam, 1992.

Anzaldúa, Gloria, and Cherríe Moraga, eds. Fwd. Toni Cade Bambara. *This Bridge Called My Back: Writings by Radical Women of Color*. New York: Kitchen Table, 1983.

Babcock, Barbara. "A Tolerated Margin of Mess: The Trickster and His Tales Reconsidered." *Critical Essays on Native American Literature*. Ed. Andrew Wiget. Boston: Hall, 1985. 15–85.

Bainbridge, Andrew. "The Rise of the Loving Son [Sun]." *Co-existence? Studies in Ontario–First Nation Relations*. Peterborough, ON: Frost Centre for Canadian Heritage and Development Studies, Trent U, 1992. 6–10.

Bakhtin, Mikhail. *The Dialogic Imagination*. Ed. Michael Holquist. Trans. Caryl Emerson and Holquist. Austin: U of Texas P, 1981.

Baraga, Frederic. *A Dictionary of the Ojibway Language*. 1878. Saint Paul: Minnesota Historical Soc., 1992.

Barnouw, Victor. *Wisconsin Chippewa Myths and Tales and Their Relation to Chippewa Life*. Madison: U of Wisconsin P, 1977.

Baker, Brian, and Rick Eckert. "Anishinabe in Wisconsin." Davis 402–04.

Barry, Nora, and Mary Prescott. "The Triumph of the Brave: *Love Medicine*'s Holistic Vision." *Critique* 30.2 (1989): 123–37.

Baym, Nina. "The Feminist Teacher of Literature: Feminist or Teacher?" *Papers on Language and Literature: A Journal for Scholars and Critics of Language and Literature* 24.3 (1988): 245–64.

Beidler, Peter G. "Louise Erdrich." *Native American Writers of the United States.* Ed. Kenneth M. Roemer. Vol. 175 of *Dictionary of Literary Biography.* Detroit: Gale, 1997. 84–100.

Beidler, Peter G., and Gay Barton. *A Reader's Guide to the Novels of Louise Erdrich.* Columbia: U of Missouri P, 1999.

Benton-Banai, Edward. *The Mishomis Book.* Minneapolis: Red School House, 1988.

Berkley, Miriam. "Louise Erdrich." Rev. of *Love Medicine,* by Louise Erdrich. *Publishers Weekly* 15 Aug. 1986: 58–59.

Bevis, William. "Native American Novels: Homing In." Swann and Krupat, *Recovering* 580–620.

Bhabha, Homi K. *The Location of Culture.* London: Routledge, 1994.

Bird, Gloria. "Searching for Evidence of Colonialism at Work: A Reading of Louise Erdrich's *Tracks.*" *Wicazo Sa Review* 8 (1992): 40–47.

Bleeker, Sonia. *The Chippewa Indians: Rice Gatherers of the Great Lakes.* New York: Morrow, 1955.

Bourgeois, Arthur P., ed. "Nanabozho." *Ojibwa Narratives of Charles and Charlotte Kawbawgam and Jacques LePique, 1893–1895.* Detroit: Wayne State UP, 1994. 25–29.

Brehm, Victoria. "The Metamorphosis of an Ojibway Manido." *American Literature* 68 (1996): 675–706.

Bressler, Charles E., ed. *Literary Criticism: An Introduction to Theory and Practice.* 2nd ed. New York: Simon, 1999.

Bright, William. *A Coyote Reader.* Berkeley: U of California P, 1993.

Brogan, Kathleen. "Haunted by History: Louise Erdrich's *Tracks.*" *Prospects* 21 (1996): 169–72.

Broker, Ignatia. *Night Flying Woman: An Ojibway Narrative.* Saint Paul: Minnesota Historical Soc., 1983.

Brown, Dee. *Bury My Heart at Wounded Knee: An Indian History of the American West.* New York: Holt, 1971.

Brown, Joseph Epes. *The Spiritual Legacy of the American Indian.* New York: Crossroads, 1982.

Bruce, Doreen. Telephone interview. 31 Jan. 2000.

Bruchac, Joseph. "Four Directions: Some Thoughts on Teaching Native American Literature." *Studies in American Indian Literatures* 3.2 (1991): 2–7.

——. *Survival This Way: Interviews with American Indian Poets.* Tucson: U of Arizona P, 1987.

——. "Whatever Is Really Yours: An Interview with Louise Erdrich." Bruchac, *Survival* 73–86. Rpt. in Chavkin and Chavkin 94–104.

Caldwell, Gail. "Writers and Partners." *Boston Globe* 26 Sept. 1986: 15. Rpt. in Chavkin and Chavkin 64–69.

Camp, Gregory. "Chippewa in North Dakota." Davis 401–02.

——. "Working Out Their Salvation: The Allotment of Land in Severalty and the Turtle Mountain Chippewa Band, 1897–1920." *American Indian Culture and Research Journal* 14.2 (1990): 19–38.

Carter, Angela. "Louise Erdrich: *The Beet Queen.*" *Expletives Deleted: Selected Writings.* London: Vintage, 1992. 151–54.

Castillo, Susan Perez. "The Construction of Gender and Ethnicity in the Texts of Leslie Silko and Louise Erdrich." *Yearbook of English Studies* 24 (1994): 228–36.

———. "Postmodernism, Native American Literature, and the Real: The Silko-Erdrich Controversy." *Massachusetts Review* 32 (1991): 285–94.

Champagne, Duane. "American Indian Studies Is for Everyone." *Natives and Academics: Researching and Writing about American Indians.* Ed. Devon A. Mihesuah. Lincoln: U of Nebraska P, 1998. 181–89.

Chavkin, Allan, ed. *The Chippewa Landscape of Louise Erdrich.* Tuscaloosa: U of Alabama P, 1999.

———. Introduction. Chavkin, *Chippewa Landscape* 1–7.

Chavkin, Allan, and Nancy Feyl Chavkin, eds. *Conversations with Louise Erdrich and Michael Dorris.* Jackson: UP of Mississippi, 1994.

Clark, Joni. "Why Bears Are Good to Think and Theory Doesn't Have to Be Murder: Transformation and Oral Tradition in Louise Erdrich's *Tracks.*" *Studies in American Indian Literatures* 4.1 (1992): 28–48.

Coleman, Bernard, Ellen Frogner, and Estelle Eich. *Ojibwa Myths and Legends.* Minneapolis: Ross, 1961.

Coltelli, Laura. "Louise Erdrich and Michael Dorris." Coltelli, *Winged Words* 41–52. Rpt. in Chavkin and Chavkin 19–29.

———, ed. *Winged Words: American Indian Writers Speak.* Lincoln: U of Nebraska P, 1990. 135–53.

The Columbia Dictionary of Modern Literary and Cultural Criticism. Ed. Joseph Childers and Gary Hentzi. New York: Columbia UP, 1995.

Cook-Lynn, Elizabeth. *Anti-Indianism in Modern America: A Voice from Tatekeya's Earth.* Urbana: U of Illinois P, 2001.

———. *"Why I Can't Read Wallace Stegner" and Other Essays: A Tribal Voice.* Madison: U of Wisconsin P, 1996.

Cooper, James Fenimore. *The Last of the Mohicans.* Ed. John McWilliams. Oxford: Oxford UP, 1994.

———. *The Pioneers.* Ed. Donald A. Ringe. New York: Penguin, 1988.

Copway, George (Kahgegagahbowh). *The Traditional History and Characteristic Sketches of the Ojibway Nation.* Boston: Sanborn, 1850.

Covert, Colin. "The Anguished Life of Michael Dorris." *Minneapolis Star Tribune* 3 Aug. 1997: A1+.

Crèvecoeur, Hector St. Jean de. *The Divided Loyalist: Selected Letters and Sketches.* Ed. Marcus Cunliffe. London: Folio Soc., 1978.

Croft, Georgia. "Something Ventured." *Valley News* (White River Valley, VT) 28 Apr. 1987: 1–2. Rpt. in Chavkin and Chavkin 89–93.

Cryer, Dan. "A Novel Arrangement." *Newsday* 30 Nov. 1986: 19–23. Rpt. in Chavkin and Chavkin 80–85.

Davis, Mary B., ed. *Native America in the Twentieth Century: An Encyclopedia*. New York: Garland, 1994.

Deloria, Vine, Jr. "If You Think about It, You Will See That It Is True." *Spirits and Reason: The Vine Deloria, Jr. Reader*. Ed. Barbara Deloria, Dristen Foehner, and Sam Scinta. Golden: Fulcrum, 1999. 110–20.

Delorme, David P. "History of the Turtle Mountain Band of Chippewa Indians." *North Dakota History* 12 (1955): 121–34.

Densmore, Frances. *Chippewa Customs*. Smithsonian Inst. Bureau of Amer. Ethnology. Bull. 86. Washington: GPO, 1929. Saint Paul: Minnesota Historical Soc., 1979.

———. *Chippewa Music I*. Smithsonian Inst. Bureau of Amer. Ethnology. Bull. 45. Washington: GPO, 1910.

———. *Chippewa Music II*. Smithsonian Inst. Bureau of Amer. Ethnology. Bull. 53. Washington: GPO, 1913.

Dewdney, Selwyn. *The Sacred Scrolls of the Southern Ojibway*. Toronto: U of Toronto P, 1975.

Dobyns, Henry. "Native Demography before 1700." *The Native North American Almanac: A Reference Work on Native North Americans in the United States and Canada*. Ed. Duane Champagne. Detroit: Gale, 1994. 189–98.

Dorris, Michael. *The Broken Cord*. New York: HarperCollins, 1989.

———. *Cloud Chamber*. New York: Scribner, 1997.

———. *Rooms in the House of Stone*. Minneapolis: Milkweed, 1993.

———. *Working Men*. New York: Holt, 1993.

———. *A Yellow Raft in Blue Water*. New York: Warner, 1987.

Drinnon, Richard. "The Metaphysics of Dancing Tribes." *The American Indian and the Problem of History*. Ed. Calvin Martin. New York: Oxford UP, 1987. 106–13.

Erdoes, Richard, and Alfonso Ortiz, eds. *American Indian Myths and Legends*. Pantheon Fairytale and Folklore Library. New York: Pantheon, 1984.

Erdrich, Heid Ellen. *Fishing for Myth: Poems by Heid E. Erdrich*. Minneapolis: New Rivers, 1997.

Erdrich, Louise. *The Antelope Wife*. New York: HarperCollins, 1999.

———. *Baptism of Desire*. New York: Harper, 1989.

———. *The Beet Queen*. New York: Henry Holt, 1986.

———. *The Bingo Palace*. New York: HarperCollins, 1994.

———. *The Birchbark House*. New York: Hyperion, 1999.

———. *The Blue Jay's Dance: A Birth Year*. New York: HarperCollins, 1995.

———. *Books and Islands in Ojibwe Country*. Washington: Natl. Geographic Soc., 2003.

———. "Conversions." *Day In, Day Out: Women's Lives in North Dakota*. Ed. Bjorn Benson, Elizabeth Hampsten, and Kathryn Sweney. Grand Forks: U of North Dakota P, 1988. 22–27.

———. *Four Souls*. New York: HarperCollins, 2004.

———. *Grandmother's Pigeon*. Illus. Jim LaMarche. New York: Hyperion, 1999.

———. Interview with Allan Chavkin and Nancy Feyl Chavkin. Chavkin and Chavkin 220–53.

———. Interview with Jan George. *North Dakota Quarterly* 53 (1985): 240–46.

———. *Jacklight*. New York: Henry Holt, 1984.

———. *The Last Report on the Miracles at Little No Horse*. New York: HarperCollins, 2001.

———. *Love Medicine*. 1984. Expanded ed. New York: Holt, Rinehart, 1993.

———. *The Master Butchers Singing Club*. New York: HarperCollins, 2003.

———. *Original Fire: Selected and New Poems*. New York: HarperCollins, 2003.

———. *The Range Eternal*. New York: Hyperion, 2002.

———. "Skunk Dreams." *Georgia Review* 47 (1993): 85–94. Rpt. in *The Best American Essays, 1994*. Ed. Tracy Kidder. New York: Houghton, 1994. 110–20.

———. *Tales of Burning Love*. New York: HarperCollins, 1996.

———. "A Time for Human Rights on Native Ground." *New York Times* 29 Dec. 2000: A, op-ed.

———. *Tracks*. New York: Henry Holt. 1988.

———. "Where I Ought to Be: A Writer's Sense of Place." *New York Times Book Review* 28 July 1988: 1+.

Erdrich, Louise, and Michael Dorris. *The Crown of Columbus*. New York: Harper-Collins, 1991.

———. Interview with Bill Moyers. *A World of Ideas with Bill Moyers*. New York: Doubleday, 1989. 460–69. Rpt. in Chavkin and Chavkin 138–50.

———. Interview with Hertha D. Wong. *North Dakota Quarterly* 5.1 (1987): 196–218. Rpt. in Chavkin and Chavkin 30–53.

———. *Route 2*. Northridge: Lord John, 1991.

Fast, Robin Riley. *The Heart Is a Drum: Continuance and Resistance in American Indian Poetry*. Ann Arbor: U of Michigan P, 1999.

Faulkner, William. *Go Down, Moses*. New York: Random, 1942.

Fine, Michelle, et al., eds. *Off White: Readings on Race, Power, and Society*. New York: Routledge, 1997.

Flavin, James. "The Novel as Performance: Communication in Louise Erdrich's *Tracks*." *Studies in American Indian Literatures* 3.4 (1991): 1–12.

Flavin, Louise. "Gender Construction amid Family Dissolution in Louise Erdrich's *The Beet Queen*." *Studies in American Indian Literatures* 7.2 (1995): 17–24.

———. "Louise Erdrich's *Love Medicine*: Loving over Time and Distance." *Critique: Studies in Contemporary Fiction* 31.1 (1989): 55–64.

Forbes, Jack. "Colonialism and Native American Literature: Analysis." *Wicazo Sa Review* 3.3 (1987): 17–23.

Foster, Douglas. "Double Vision: An Interview with the Authors." *Mother Jones* May–June 1991: 26+. Rpt. in Chavkin and Chavkin 168–72.

Freeman, Judith. "Taking a Chance." *Washington Post* 6 Feb. 1994: WBK5.

Frenkiel, Nora. "Louise Erdrich." *Baltimore Sun* 17 Nov. 1986: B1+. Rpt. in Chavkin and Chavkin 75–79.

Friedman, Susan Stanford. "Identity Politics, Syncretism, Catholicism, and Anishinabe Religion in Louise Erdrich's *Tracks*." *Religion and Literature* 26.1 (1994): 107–33.

Gish, Robert R. "Life unto Death, Death into Life." Chavkin, *Chippewa Landscape* 67–83.

Gleason, William. " 'Her Laugh an Ace': The Function of Humor in Louise Erdrich's *Love Medicine*." Wong, *Casebook* 115–35.

Gourneau, Patrick. *History of the Turtle Mountain Band of Chippewa Indians*. 9th ed. N.p.: n.p., 1993.

Graff, Gerald. *Beyond the Culture Wars: How Teaching the Conflicts Can Revitalize American Education*. New York: Norton, 1992.

Grantham, Shelby. "Intimate Collaborations, or 'A Novel Partnership.' " *Dartmouth Alumni Magazine* Mar. 1985: 43–47.

Hafen, P. Jane. "Let Me Take You Home in My One-Eyed Ford: Popular Imagery in Contemporary Native American Fiction." *Multicultural Review* 6.2 (1997): 38–45. Rpt. in *Annual Edition: Multicultural Education, 1998–1999*. 5th ed. Ed. Fred Schulz. New York: Dushkin, 1998. 153–59.

———. "Sacramental Language: Ritual in the Poetry of Louise Erdrich." *Great Plains Quarterly* 16 (1996): 147–55.

Hagen, William T. *American Indians*. Rev. ed. Chicago: U of Chicago P, 1979.

Hallowell, A. Irving. "Ojibwa Culture and World View." *Contributions to Anthropology: Selected Papers of A. Irving Hallowell*. Chicago: U of Chicago P, 1976. 353–474.

Hansen, Elaine Tuttle. "What If Your Mother Never Meant To? The Novels of Louise Erdrich and Michael Dorris." *Mother without Child*. Berkeley: U of California P, 1997. 115–57.

Hausman, Gerald. *Turtle Island Alphabet: A Lexicon of Native American Symbols and Culture*. New York: St. Martin's, 1992.

Hirshfield, Jane. *Nine Gates: Entering the Mind of Poetry*. New York: HarperCollins, 1997.

Holman, C. Hugh, and William Harmon. *A Handbook to Literature*. 5th ed. New York: Macmillan, 1986.

Holy Bible. King James Version. New York: Amer. Bible Soc., 1999.

hooks, bell. "Toward a Revolutionary Feminist Pedagogy." *Falling into Theory: Conflicting Views on Reading Literature*. Ed. David H. Richter. New York: St. Martin's, 2000. 79–84.

Horne, Dee. *Contemporary American Indian Writing: Unsettling Literature*. Amer. Indian Studies 6. New York: Lang, 1999.

Howard, James. *The Plains-Ojibwa or Bungi, Hunters and Warriors of the Northern Prairies with Special Reference to the Turtle Mountain Band*. Lincoln: J and L Reprint, 1977.

Huey, Michael. "Two Native American Voices." Chavkin and Chavkin 122–27.

Jacobs, Connie A. *The Novels of Louise Erdrich: Stories of Her People*. New York: Lang, 2001.

Jaskowski, Helen. "From Time Immemorial: Native American Traditions in Contemporary Short Fiction." *Since Flannery O'Connor: Essays on the American Short Story*. Ed. Loren Logsden and Charles W. Mayer. Macomb: Western Illinois UP, 1987. 54–71. Rpt. in Wong, *Casebook* 27–34.

Johnston, Basil. *The Manitous: The Spiritual World of the Ojibway*. New York: HarperCollins, 1995.

———. *Ojibway Ceremonies*. Toronto: McClelland 1978.

———. *Ojibway Heritage*. New York: Columbia UP, 1976.

———. *Ojibway Tales*. Lincoln: U of Nebraska P, 1976.

Jones, Malcolm. "Life, Art Are One for Prize Novelists." Interview with Louise Erdrich. *St. Petersburg Times* 10 Feb. 1985: 1D1+. Rpt. in Chavkin and Chavkin 3–9.

Kakutani, Michiko. "Columbus' Diary and Queen Isabella's Jewels." *New York Times* 19 Apr. 1991: C25.

Krupat, Arnold. *The Voice in the Margin: Native American Literatures and the Canon*. Berkeley: U of California P, 1989.

Landes, Ruth. *Ojibwa Religion and the Midéwinin*. Madison: U of Wisconsin P, 1968.

———. *The Ojibwa Woman*. New York: Norton, 1971.

Larson, Sidner. "The Fragmentation of a Tribal People in Louise Erdrich's *Tracks*." *American Indian Culture and Research Journal* 17.2 (1993): 1–13.

Lawrence, D. H. *Studies in Classic American Literature*. New York: Penguin, 1981.

Libbey, O. G., ed. *Collections of the North Dakota State Historical Society*. Vol. 5. Grand Forks: Normanden, 1923.

Lincoln, Kenneth. *Indi'n Humor: Bicultural Play in Native America*. New York: Oxford UP, 1993.

———. *Native American Renaissance*. Berkeley: U of California P, 1983.

Lindquist, Mark A., and Martin Zanger, eds. *Buried Roots and Indestructible Seeds: The Survival of American Indian Life in Story, History, and Spirit*. Madison: U of Wisconsin P, 1993.

Locke, John. *Second Treatise on Civil Government*. *Locke on Politics, Religion, and Education*. Ed. Maurice Cranston. New York: Macmillan, 1965. 18–103.

Loomba, Ania. *Colonialism/Postcolonialism*. London: Routledge, 1998.

Lyford, Carrie A. *The Crafts of the Ojibwa*. US Office of Indian Affairs. Educ. Div. Phoenix: Phoenix Indian School, 1943.

Manguel, Alberto. *A History of Reading*. Toronto: Knopf, 1996.

Maristuen-Rodakowski, Julie. "The Turtle Mountain Reservation in North Dakota: Its History as Depicted in Louise Erdrich's *Love Medicine* and *The Beet Queen*." *American Indian Culture and Research Journal* 12.3 (1988): 33–48.

McNab, David T. *Circles of Time: Aboriginal Land Rights and Resistance in Ontario*. Waterloo, On.: Wilfred Laurier UP, 1999.

———. " 'Gathering Gum from the Silver Pine': A Cree Woman's Dream and the

Battle of Belly River Crossing (1869–70)." *Saskatchewan History* 52.2 (2000): 15–27.

———. "Of Beads and a Crystal Vase: Michael Dorris's *Cloud Chamber*, an Exploration of Language into Darkness." *Philological Papers* 46 (2000): 109–19.

———. "The Perfect Disguise: Mi'kmaq Oral Testimony and Frank Speck's Pilgrimage to Ktaqamkuk—the Place of Fog—in 1914." *American Review of Canadian Studies* 30.4 (2000): 85–104.

McNab, David, Bruce Hodgins, and S. Dale Standen. " 'Black with Canoes': Aboriginal Resistance and the Canoe: Diplomacy, Trade, and Warfare in the Meeting Grounds of Northeastern North America, 1600–1800." *Technology, Disease, and Colonial Conquests, Sixteenth to Eighteenth Centuries: Essays Reappraising the Gun and Germ Theories*. Ed. George Raudzens. Amsterdam: Brill, 2001. 237–92.

McNickle, D'Arcy. *The Surrounded*. Albuquerque: U of New Mexico P, 1992.

McQuade, Donald, et al., eds. *The Harper American Literature*. 2nd ed. Vol. 1. New York: HarperCollins, 1994.

Meisenhelder, Susan. "Race and Gender in Louise Erdrich's *The Beet Queen*." *Ariel* 25.1 (1994): 45–57.

Mendelsohn, Daniel. "Smoked Signals." Rev. of *The Last Report on the Miracles at Little No Horse*, by Louise Erdrich. *New York Magazine* 1 Apr. 2001: 110.

Meyer, Melissa L. E-mail to Amelia V. Katanski 8 Oct. 1989.

———. " 'We Can Not Get a Living as We Used To': Dispossession and the White Earth Anishinaabeg, 1889–1920." *American Historical Review* 96.2 (1991): 368–94.

———. *The White Earth Tragedy: Ethnicity and Dispossession at a Minnesota Anishinaabe Reservation, 1889–1920*. Lincoln: U of Nebraska P, 1994.

Middlebrook, Diane Wood. *Suits Me: The Double Life of Billy Tipton*. Boston: Houghton, 1998.

Minh-ha, Trinh. *Woman, Native, Other: Writing Postcoloniality and Feminism*. Bloomington: Indiana UP, 1989.

Mitchell, David. "A Bridge to the Past: Cultural Hegemony and the Native American Past in Louise Erdrich's *Love Medicine*." *Entering the Nineties: The North American Experience*. Ed. Thomas E. Shirer. Sault Sainte Marie: Lake Superior State UP, 1991. 62–70.

Mohatt, Gerald, and Joseph Eagle Elk. *The Price of a Gift: A Lakota Healer's Story*. Lincoln: U of Nebraska P, 2000.

Molin, Paulette Fairbanks. "Ojibway in Minnesota." Davis 398–99.

Momaday, N. Scott. *House Made of Dawn*. New York: Harper, 1968. New York: HarperPerennial. 1999.

———. *In the Presence of the Sun: Stories and Poems*. New York: St. Martin's, 1992.

———. "The Man Made of Words." *Literature of the American Indian: Views and Interpretations*. Ed. Abraham Chapman. New York: NAL, 1975. 96–110.

———. *The Way to Rainy Mountain*. Albuquerque: U of New Mexico P, 1969.

Morrison, Toni. *Beloved*. New York: Knopf, 1987.

Morson, Gary Saul. *Narrative and Freedom*. New Haven: Yale UP, 1994.

Mosher, Howard Frank. *Where the Rivers Flow North*. New York: Penguin, 1978.

Moyers, Bill. "Louise Erdrich and Michael Dorris." *A World of Ideas*. New York: Doubleday, 1989. 460–69. Rpt. in Chavkin and Chavkin 138–50.

Murfin, Ross, and Supryia M. Ray. *The Bedford Glossary of Critical and Literary Terms*. Boston: Bedford, 1997.

Murray, Stanley N. "The Turtle Mountain Chippewa, 1882–1905." *North Dakota History* 51.1 (1984): 14–37.

Nabokov, Peter, ed. *Native American Testimony: A Chronicle of Indian-White Relations from Prophecy to Present, 1492–1992*. New York: Penguin, 1978.

Naipaul, V. S. *The Mimic Men*. New York: Penguin, 1967.

Neihardt, John G. *Black Elk Speaks*. 1932. New York: Simon, 1972.

Northrup, Jim. *Walking the Rez Road*. Stillwater: Voyageur, 1993.

Nowick, Nan. "*Belles Lettres* Interview: Louise Erdrich." *Belles Lettres* 2.2 (1986): 9. Rpt. in Chavkin and Chavkin 70–74.

Ong, J. Walter. *Orality and Literacy: The Technology of the Word*. New York: Routledge, 1991.

Opie, Iona, and Peter Opie. *The Classic Fairy Tales*. 1974. New York: Oxford UP, 1980.

Overholt, Thomas W., and J. Baird Callicott, eds. *"Clothed-in-Fur" and Other Tales: An Introduction to an Objiwa World View*. Washington: UP of America, 1982.

Owens, Louis. *Other Destinies: Understanding the American Indian Novel*. Norman: U of Oklahoma P, 1992.

Passaro, Vince. "Tales from a Literary Marriage." *New York Times Magazine* 21 Apr. 1991: 34+. Rpt. in Chavkin and Chavkin 157–67.

Peirce, Charles S. *The Philosophy of Peirce: Selected Writings*. Ed. Justus Buchler. London: Kegan Paul, 1978.

Peterson, Nancy J. "History, Postmodernism, and Louise Erdrich's *Tracks*." *PMLA* 109 (1994): 982–94.

———. "Indi'n Humor and Trickster Justice in *The Bingo Palace*." Chavkin, *Chippewa Landscape* 144–60.

Pittman, Barbara L. "Cross-Cultural Reading and Generic Transformation: The Chronotope of the Road in Erdrich's *Love Medicine*." *American Literature* 67 (1995): 777–92.

Prucha, Francis Paul. *American Indian Policy in Crisis*. Norman: U of Oklahoma P, 1976.

———. *Americanizing the American Indians: Writings by the "Friends of the Indian," 1880–1900*. Cambridge: Harvard UP, 1973.

Purdy, John. "Against All Odds." Chavkin, *Chippewa Landscape* 8–35.

Purdy, John, and James Ruppert, eds. *Nothing but the Truth: An Anthology of Native American Literature*. Upper Saddle River: Prentice, 2000.

Rader, Dean. "Word as Weapon: Visual Culture and Contemporary American Indian Poetry." *MELUS* 27.3 (2002): 147–68.

Radin, Paul. *The Trickster: A Study in American Indian Mythology.* New York: Green-wood, 1956.

Rainwater, Catherine. "Ethnic Signs in Erdrich's *Tracks* and *The Bingo Palace.*" Chavkin, *Chippewa Landscape* 144–60.

———. "Reading between Worlds: Narrativity in the Fiction of Louise Erdrich." *American Literature* 62 (1990): 405–22.

Rapoport, Robin. Unpublished essay, Univ. of Vermont, 1999.

Revard, Carter. "Herbs of Healing: American Values in American Indian Literature." *Family Matters and Tribal Affairs.* Tucson: U of Arizona P, 1999. 161–83.

Riley, Patricia, ed. *Growing Up Native American: An Anthology.* New York: Morrow, 1993.

Rothenberg, Paula S., ed. *White Privilege: Essential Readings on the Other Side of Racism.* New York: Worth, 2001.

Ruffo, Armand. "Inside Looking Out: Reading *Tracks* from a Native Perspective." *Looking at the Words of Our People: First Nations Analysis of Literature.* Ed. Jeannette Armstrong. Penticton, BC: Theytus, 1993. 162–76.

Ruoff, A. LaVonne Brown. Afterword. Chavkin, *Chippewa Landscape* 182–88.

———. *American Indian Literatures: An Introduction, Bibliographic Review, and Selected Bibliography.* New York: MLA, 1990.

Ruoff, A. LaVonne Brown, and Donald B. Smith, eds. *Life, Letters, and Speeches: George Copway (Kahgegagahbowh).* Lincoln: U of Nebraska P, 1997.

Ruppert, James. "Celebrating Culture: *Love Medicine.*" Wong, *Casebook* 67–84.

———. *Mediation in Contemporary Native American Fiction.* Norman: U of Oklahoma P, 1995.

Said, Edward. *The World, the Text, and the Critic.* Cambridge: Harvard UP, 1984.

Saint Ann's Centennial: One Hundred Years of Faith, 1885–1985. Belcourt: n.p., 1985.

Sands, Kathleen M. "*Love Medicine:* Voices and Margins." Wong, *Casebook* 35–42.

Sarris, Greg. "Encountering the Native Dialogue: Critical Theory and American Indian Oral Literatures." *College Literature* 18.3 (1991): 126–31.

———. *Keeping Slug Woman Alive: A Holistic Approach to American Indian Texts.* Berkeley: U of California P, 1993.

———. "Reading Louise Erdrich: *Love Medicine* as Home Medicine." Sarris, *Keeping* 115–45.

Sarve-Gorham, Kristan. "Games of Chance: Gambling and Land Tenure in *Tracks, Love Medicine,* and *The Bingo Palace.*" *Western American Literature* 34.3 (1999): 277–300.

———. "Power Lines: The Motif of Twins and the Medicine Women of *Tracks* and *Love Medicine.*" *Having Our Way: Women Rewriting Tradition in Twentieth-Century America.* Ed. Harriet Pollack. Lewisburg: Bucknell UP, 1995. 167–90.

Scarberry-García, Susan. *Landmarks of Healing: A Study of* House Made of Dawn. Albuquerque: U of New Mexico P, 1990.

Schneider, Lissa. "*Love Medicine:* A Metaphor for Forgiveness." *Studies in American Indian Literatures* 4.1 (1992): 1–13.

Schneider, Mary Jane. *North Dakota's Indian Heritage.* Grand Forks: U of North Dakota P, 1990.

Schultz, Lydia A. "Fragments and Ojibwe Stories: Narrative Strategies in Louise Erdrich's *Love Medicine.*" *College Literature* 18.3 (1991): 80–95.

Schumacher, Michael. "Louise Erdrich and Michael Dorris: A Marriage of Minds." *Writer's Digest* June 1991: 28+. Rpt. in Chavkin and Chavkin 173–83.

Sergi, Jennifer Leigh. "Storytelling: Tradition and Preservation in Louise Erdrich's *Tracks.*" *World Literature Today* 66 (1992): 279–82.

Shohat, Ella, and Robert Stam. *Unthinking Eurocentricism: Multiculturalism and the Media.* London: Routledge, 1994.

Siegel, Lee. "De Sade's Daughters." *Atlantic Monthly* Feb. 1997: 97+.

Silko, Leslie Marmon. *Ceremony.* New York: Penguin, 1986.

———. "Here's an Odd Artifact for the Fairy-Tale Shelf." Rev. of *The Beet Queen*, by Louise Erdrich. *Impact/Albuquerque Journal Magazine,* 7 Oct. 1986: 10–11. Rpt. in *Studies in American Indian Literatures* 10.4 (1986): 177–84.

———. "Language and Literature from a Pueblo Perspective." *English Literature: Opening Up the Canon.* Ed. Leslie A. Fiedler and Houston A. Baker, Jr. Baltimore: Johns Hopkins UP, 1981. 54–72.

———. *Yellow Woman and a Beauty of the Spirit: Essays on Native American Life Today.* New York: Simon, 1996.

Smith, Jeanne Rosier. "Transpersonal Selfhood: The Boundaries of Identity in Louise Erdrich's *Love Medicine.*" *Studies in American Indian Literatures* 3.4 (1991): 27–36.

———. *Writing Tricksters: Mythic Gambols in American Ethnic Literature.* Berkeley: U of California P, 1997.

Smith, Theresa S. *Island of Anishinaabeg: Thunderers and Water Monsters in the Traditional Ojibwe Life-World.* Moscow: U of Idaho P, 1995.

Spinks, C. W. *Semiosis, Marginal Signs and Trickster: A Dagger of the Mind.* London: Macmillan 1991.

Stokes, Geoffrey. "Behind Every Woman . . . ? Louise Erdrich's True-Life Adventures." *Voice Literary Supplement* 48 (1986): 7–9. Rpt. in Chavkin and Chavkin 54–63.

Stokes, Karah. "What about the Sweetheart? The 'Different Shape' of Anishinabe Two Sisters in Louise Erdrich's *Love Medicine* and *Tales of Burning Love.*" *MELUS* 24.2 (1999): 89–105.

Stripes, James D. "The Problem(s) of (Anishinaabe) History in the Fiction of Louise Erdrich: Voices and Context." *Wicazo Sa Review* 7.2 (1991): 26–33.

Swann, Brian, and Arnold Krupat, comps. *I Tell You Now: Autobiographical Essays by Native American Writers.* Lincoln: U of Nebraska P, 1987.

———, eds. *Recovering the Word: Essays on Native American Literature.* Berkeley: U of California P, 1987.

"Tallow." *The New Shorter Oxford English Dictionary on Historical Principles.* 1993.

Tanner, John. *The Falcon: A Narrative of the Captivity and Adventures of John Tanner during Thirty Years' Residence among Indians in the Interior of North America.* 1830. New York: Penguin, 1994.

Toelken, Barre. "Poetic Retranslation and the 'Pretty Languages' of Yellowman." *Traditional American Indian Literatures: Texts and Interpretations.* Ed. Karl Kroeber. Lincoln: U of Nebraska P, 1981. 65–116.

Towery, Margie. "Continuity and Connection: Characters in Louise Erdrich's *Love Medicine.*" *American Indian Culture and Research Journal* 16.4 (1992): 99–122.

Treaties and Agreements of the Chippewa Indians. Washington: Inst. for the Development of Indian Law, 1974.

Treuer, David. *The Hiawatha.* New York: Picador USA, 1999.

———. *Little.* New York: Picador USA, 1995.

Trueheart, Charles. "Marriage for Better or Words." *Washington Post* 19 Oct. 1988: B1+. Rpt. in Chavkin and Chavkin 115–21.

Turner, Frederick W., III, ed. *The Portable North American Indian Reader.* New York: Penguin, 1973.

Van Dyke, Annette. "Of Vision Quests and Spirit Guardians." Chavkin, *Chippewa Landscape* 130–43.

———. "Questions of the Spirit: Bloodlines in Louise Erdrich's Chippewa Landscape." *Studies in American Indian Literatures* 4.1 (1992): 13–26.

Van Kirk, Sylvia. *Many Tender Ties: Women in Fur-Trade Society, 1670–1870.* Norman: U of Oklahoma P, 1980.

Vecsey, Christopher. *Imagine Ourselves Richly: Mythic Narratives of the North American Indians.* New York: Crossroad, 1988.

———. *Traditional Ojibwa Religion and Its Historical Changes.* Philadelphia: Amer. Philosophical Soc., 1983.

Velie, Alan R., ed. *American Indian Literature.* Rev. ed. Norman: U of Oklahoma P, 1991.

Vizenor, Gerald. *Anishinabe Nagamon: Songs of the People.* Minneapolis: Nodin, 1965.

———. "Casino Coups." *Wicazo Sa Review* 9.2 (1993): 80–84.

———. *The Everlasting Sky: New Voices from the People Named the Chippewa.* New York: Crowell-Collier, 1972.

———. "Harold of Orange: A Screenplay." *Studies in American Indian Literatures* 5.3 (1993): 53–88.

———. *Manifest Manners: Narratives on Postindian Warriors of Survivance.* Lincoln: U of Nebraska P, 1994.

———. "Naanabozho and the Gambler." *Native American Literature: An Anthology.* Ed. Lawana Trout. Chicago: NTC/Contemporary, 1999. 162–65.

———, ed. *Narrative Chance: Postmodern Discourse on Native American Indian Literatures.* Albuquerque: U of New Mexico P, 1989. Norman: U of Oklahoma P, 1993.

———. *The People Named the Chippewa: Narrative Histories*. Minneapolis: U of Minnesota P, 1984.

———, ed. *Touchwood: A Collection of Ojibway Prose*. Saint Paul: New Rivers, 1987.

Warren, William. *History of the Ojibway Nation*. 1885. Minneapolis: Ross, 1974. Rpt. in Vizenor, *Touchwood* 10–45.

Warrior, Robert Allen. *Tribal Secrets: Recovering American Indian Intellectual Traditions*. Minneapolis: U of Minnesota P, 1995.

Weatherford, Jack. *Native Roots: How the Indians Enriched America*. New York: Fawcett, 1991.

Weil, Richard H. "Destroying a Homeland: White Earth, Minnesota." *American Indian Culture and Research Journal* 13.2 (1989): 69–95.

Welker, Glenn. "Chippewa/Ojibway/Anishinabe Literature." 1–8. 9 Feb. 2003. <http://www.indians.org/welker/chippewa.htm>.

White, Richard. *The Middle Ground: Indians, Empires, and Republics in the Great Lakes Region, 1650–1815*. Cambridge: Cambridge UP, 1991.

Wiedemann, Thomas. *Greek and Roman Slavery*. Baltimore: Johns Hopkins UP, 1981.

Wiget, Andrew, ed. *Handbook of Native American Literature*. New York: Garland, 1996.

Williams, Paul. "Oral Traditions on Trial." *Gin Das Winan: Documenting Aboriginal History in Ontario*. Ed. David McNab and S. Dale Standen. Toronto: Champlain Soc., 1996. 29–34.

Womack, Craig S. *Red on Red: Native American Literary Separatism*. Minneapolis: U of Minnesota P, 1999.

Wong, Hertha D. Sweet. "Adoptive Mothers and Thrown-Away Children in the Novels of Louise Erdrich." *Narrating Mothers: Theorizing Maternal Subjectivities*. Ed. Brenda O. Daly and Maureen T. Reddy. Knoxville: U of Tennessee P, 1991. 174–92.

———, ed. *Louise Erdrich's* Love Medicine: *A Casebook*. New York: Oxford UP, 2000.

Wood, Dave. "Authors' Love Story Reflected in Columbus." *Minneapolis Star Tribune* 2 May 1991: E1+.

Audiovisuals

Densmore, Frances. *Healing Songs of the American Indian*. Record. Ethnic Folkways Lib. FE 4251.

Erdrich, Louise. Interview. *New Letters on the Air: Contemporary Writers on Radio*. Audiotape. Kansas City: U of Missouri, 1988.

Erdrich, Louise, and Michael Dorris. Interview with Paul Bailey. *Writers Talk Ideas of Our Time*. Videocassette. Northbrook: Roland Collection, 1987.

———. Interview with Bill Moyers. *A World of Ideas with Bill Moyers*. Videocassette. PBS, WNET, New York, 1990.

Robertson, Robbie. "Twisted Hair." Robertson and the Red Road Ensemble. *Music for the Native Americans*. CD. Village Recorder, 1994.

Sainte-Marie, Buffy. "Starwalker." *Up Where We Belong*. CD. Manta Eastern Sound, 1996.

Silko, Leslie Marmon. Interview. *Native American Novelists*. Videocassette. Films for the Humanities ser., 1995.

INDEX

Alexie, Sherman, 101n1, 113n3, 113n6
Algren, Nelson, 148
Allen, Paula Gunn, 17, 18, 57n7, 98, 100, 115, 169n10, 179
Andelin, Helen, 185
Anzaldúa, Gloria, 175
Aristotle, 190n2
Arthur, Chester, 29, 225, 227

Babcock, Barbara, 64n6
Bailey, Paul, 20
Bainbridge, Andrew, 33
Bakhtin, Mikhail, 7, 18, 201, 202, 203, 204, 208n3, 209n7
Balzac, Honoré de, 168n1
Banks, Dennis, 229
Baraga, Frederic, 52
Baker, Brian, 31n2
Barnouw, Victor, 20, 52, 53, 54, 55, 56, 57n6, 60
Barry, Nora, 17
Barton, Gay, 18, 81n1, 125
Baym, Nina, 175
Beauvoir, Simone de, 189n2
Beede, Cyrus, 29
Beidler, Peter G., 18, 19, 46, 81n1, 125
Belcourt, Father Anthony, 227
Bellecourt, Clyde, 229
Benton-Banai, Edward, 34, 37
Berkley, Miriam, 150
Bevis, William, 17, 115
Bhabha, Homi K., 192, 198, 200n7
Bible, 105
Bird, Gloria, 200n2
Black Elk, 96, 101n1, 159
Bleeker, Sonia, 26
Boccaccio, Giovanni, 145
Bourgeois, Arthur P., 60
Brehm, Victoria, 20, 64n7, 168n6
Bressler, Charles E., 178
Bright, William, 64n3
Brogan, Kathleen, 19, 64n9
Broker, Ignatia, 98
Brown, Dee, 17, 159
Brown, Joseph Epes, 114
Browning, Robert, 107
Bruce, Doreen, 30
Bruchac, Joseph, 18, 23, 114, 149, 156
Bryant, William Cullen, 168n7
Butler, Judith, 185

Caldwell, Gail, 51, 151
Callicott, J. Baird, 43
Camp, Gregory, 20, 30, 68, 69, 75n6
Carter, Angela, 189
Cashpaw, 203
Castillo, Susan Perez, 19, 107, 190n4
Champagne, Duane, 97
Chaucer, Geoffrey, 145
Chavin, Allan, 5, 18, 35, 51, 56, 72, 75n1, 125, 151, 152, 153, 158, 205
Chavkin, Nancy Feyl, 5, 18, 35, 51, 56, 72, 75n1, 151, 152, 158, 205
Chopin, Frédèric, 146
Clapp, Moses E., 84
Clark, Joni, 19
Coleman, Bernard, 26
Coltelli, Laura, 18, 155, 158
Columbus, Christopher, 16, 24, 152
Conrad, Joseph, 114
Cook-Lynn, Elizabeth, 18, 148, 153
Cooper, James Fenimore, 100, 101n4, 158, 159, 160, 162, 163, 164, 165, 166
Copway, George (Kahgegagahbowh), 32, 43
Covert, Colin, 149, 154, 156, 157
Crèvecoeur, St. Jean de, 115
Croft, Georgia, 151
Curtis, Edward, 159, 168n2
Cryer, Dan, 147, 149, 151

Dawes, Henry, 68, 75n3
Deloria, Vine, Jr., 135–36
Delorme, David P., 27, 28–29, 30
Densmore, Frances, 43, 44, 45, 57n2, 64n7, 66, 70, 71–72, 73, 74, 75n2, 76n10
Dewdney, Selwyn, 31n3
Dobyns, Henry, 23
Dorris, Michael, 5, 7, 16, 18, 20, 41n8, 65n12, 75n1, 98, 147–57, 170
Dorris, Persia, 36
Drinnon, Richard, 60

Eagle Elk, Joseph, 125
Eckert, Rick, 31n2
Eich, Estelle, 26
Erdoes, Richard, 57n5, 64n3
Erdrich, Heid, 40n3
Erdrich, Lisa, 36
Erdrich, Ludwig, 13
Erdrich, Rita Gourneau, 36

Fast, Robin Riley, 108
Faulkner, William, 2, 63n1, 114, 150, 158,
    160–61, 162, 163, 164, 165, 166, 167,
    168, 168n1, 202
Fine, Michelle, 128
Flavin, James, 65n11
Flavin, Louise, 17, 53, 176, 178–79, 181, 184
Forbes, Jack, 126
Foster, Douglas, 156
Freeman, Judith, 101n2
Frenkiel, Nora, 157
Friedman, Susan Stanford, 59, 61, 64n8
Frogner, Ellen, 26

George, Jan, 104
Gish, Robert, 46, 154
Gleason, William, 151
Gourneau, Patrick, 28, 31n4
Graff, Gerald, 189
Grantham, Shelby, 148, 149, 157
Gray, Thomas, 113n2

Hafen, P. Jane, 17, 100, 110
Hagen, William T., 169n9
Hallowell, A. Irving, 43
Hansen, Elaine Tuttle, 190n3
Harjo, Suzann, 149
Harmon, William, 107
Hausman, Gerald, 33
Hawthorne, Nathaniel, 114
Hirshfield, Jane, 51, 57
Hodgins, Bruce, 33
Holman, C. Hugh, 107
Holquist, Michael, 208n3, 209n7
hooks, bell, 175, 176, 180, 182
Horne, Dee, 200n13
Horr, David A., 203, 208n4, 235
Howard, James, 28
Huey, Michael, 150

Jacobs, Connie A., 18, 81n2, 125
Jaskowski, Helen, 57n1, 149
Jesus, 110, 167
Johnston, Basil, 20, 25, 26, 32, 43, 44, 50,
    120, 200n1
Jones, Malcolm, 51, 65n12, 147
Joseph, Chief, 159
Joseph Eagle Elk, 125–26

Kakenowash, 227
Kakutani, Michiko, 152
Kingston, Maxine Hong, 64n3
Kittson, Norman, 225
Krupat, Arnold, 18–19

LaFarge, Oliver, 100
Landes, Ruth, 20, 25, 31n3, 43, 57n2

Larson, Sidner, 19, 62
Lawrence, D. H., 160, 168n3
Leigh, Vivien, 185
Leopold II, 195
Libbey, O. G., 203, 208n4
Lincoln, Kenneth, 1, 19
Linquist, Mark A., 125
Little Shell (Es-ssence), 29, 224, 227, 228
Locke, John, 162
Loomba, Ania, 191
Lyford, Carrie A., 45

Macpherson, James, 161
Malo, John, 227
Manguel, Alberto, 32
Manido'gicĭgo'kwe (Spirit Day Woman), 66,
    67, 68, 69, 70, 71, 72, 73, 74–75, 75n1,
    75n2
Maristeun-Rodakowski, Julie, 64n1
McNab, David T., 33, 34, 41n12, 148
McNickle, D'Arcy, 158
McQuade, Donald, 168n7
Meisenhelder, Susan, 175, 176, 177, 179,
    180, 182, 184
Mendelsohn, Daniel, 143
Meyer, Melissa, 67–68, 69–70, 75n4, 75n7,
    84
Middlebrook, Diane Wood, 142
Millett, Kate, 180
Milton, John, 107
Minh-ha, Trinh, 18
Mitchell, David, 128
Mohatt, Gerald, 125–26
Molin, Paulette Fairbanks, 31n2
Momaday, N. Scott, 1, 5, 17, 46, 49, 168n5
Moraga, Cherríe, 175
Morrison, Toni, 64n3, 200n9
Morson, Gary Saul, 209n9
Mosher, Howard Frank, 158, 160, 161, 162,
    163, 164–65, 166–67
Moyers, Bill, 20, 150, 162, 170
Murfin, Ross, 106
Murray, Stanley, 24, 28, 29, 30, 69, 75n5,
    75n6

Nabokov, Peter, 19
Naipaul, V. S., 200n6
Neihardt, John G., 95–96, 101n1, 159, 162
Northrup, Jim, 98
Nowick, Nan, 118

Oberholzer, Ernest, 16
Omakayas, 37–39, 40
Ong, J. Walter, 116
Opie, Iona, 53
Opie, Peter, 53
Orozco, José Clemente, 110, 113n7

Ortiz, Alfonso, 57n5, 64n3
Overholt, Thomas W., 43
Owens, Louis, 17, 97, 155, 204, 209n4, 209n6, 209n8

Passaro, Vince, 151, 157
Paul, Saint, 200n6
Peirce, C. S., 170
Peltier, Leonard, 34, 41n7
Peterson, Nancy J., 17, 64–65, 65n10
Pillager band (Pilleurs), 69–70, 203
Pittman, Barbara L., 51
Prescott, Mary, 17
Prucha, Francis Paul, 68, 75n3
Purdy, John, 19, 46

Rader, Dean, 113n4
Radin, Paul, 17
Rainwater, Catherine, 17, 51, 59, 96, 115, 134, 200
Rapoport, Robin, 185
Ray, Supryia M., 106
Reagan, Ronald, 229
Red Bird, David, 57n5
Remington, Frederick, 159, 168n2
Revard, Carter, 112n1
Rice, Julian, 101n1
Riley, Patricia, 19
Robertson, Robbie, 40n1
Rolo, Mark Anthony, 156
Rothenberg, Paula S., 128
Rowlandson, Mary, 107–08, 109, 110, 113n5, 113n6
Ruffo, Armand, 196, 200n1, 200n10
Ruoff, A. LaVonne Brown, 18, 19, 150
Ruppert, James, 19, 46, 51, 116, 148

Said, Edward, 18
Sainte-Marie, Buffy, 41n12
Sands, Kathleen M., 121
Sarris, Greg, 19, 46, 128, 200n11, 202
Sarve-Gorham, Kristan, 19, 57n1, 81n2
Scarberry-García, Susan, 46
Schneider, Lissa, 114
Schneider, Mary Jane, 20, 30
Schultz, Lydia A., 19, 117
Schumacher, Michael, 51, 147, 150, 152
Scott, Sir Walter, 161
Seattle, Chief, 159
Sells, Cato, 65n10
Senachwine, 159
Sergi, Jennifer Leigh, 19
Shakespeare, William, 107, 114
Shohat, Ella, 191

Siegel, Lee, 154
Silko, Leslie Marmon, 1, 5, 11–12, 17, 19, 168n5, 179, 189, 190n4
Smith, Jean Rosier, 19, 58, 64n3, 154, 168n4
Smith, Theresa S., 60, 64n7, 75n8, 76n10, 76n11
Spinks, C. W., 204
Stam, Robert, 191
Standen, S. Dale, 33
Stokes, Geoffrey, 151
Stokes, Karah, 57n3, 129n1
Stripes, James D., 19
Swann, Brian, 19

Tanner, John, 57n2
Toelken, Barre, 170
Thoreau, Henry David, 161
Tipton, Dorothy/Billy, 142–43
Towery, Margie, 81n2
Treuer, David, 98
Trueheart, Charles, 149, 151, 156
Turner, Frederick Jackson, 159
Turner, Frederick W., III, 159

Van Dyke, Annette, 46, 81n2, 154, 169n10
Van Kirk, Sylvia, 86
Vecsey, Christopher, 20, 25, 26, 31n3, 43, 44, 60, 64n7, 76n10
Velie, Alan R., 19, 61, 62
Vizenor, Gerald, 5, 7, 19, 20, 27, 43, 44–45, 61, 64n3, 96, 98, 120, 125, 198, 199n1, 201, 209n5, 209n6

Warren, William, 43, 45
Warrior, Robert Allen, 19, 96
Waters, Frank, 100
Wayne, John, 105–07, 109, 111, 113n3
Weatherford, Jack, 19, 114
Weil, Richard H., 84, 85–86
Welch, James, 5
Welker, Glenn, 7
White, Richard, 86
Wiedemann, Thomas, 190
Wiget, Andrew, 19
Williams, Paul, 33
Womack, Craig S., 19, 96, 100
Wong, Hertha D. Sweet, 18, 51, 64n1, 81n2, 86, 125, 149, 151, 185
Wordsworth, William, 161
Wood, Dave, 152
Wright, James, 113n2

Zanger, Martin, 125

Modern Language Association of America
Approaches to Teaching World Literature
Joseph Gibaldi, series editor

Achebe's Things Fall Apart. Ed. Bernth Lindfors. 1991.
Arthurian Tradition. Ed. Maureen Fries and Jeanie Watson. 1992.
Atwood's The Handmaid's Tale *and Other Works*. Ed. Sharon R. Wilson,
    Thomas B. Friedman, and Shannon Hengen. 1996.
Austen's Emma. Ed. Marcia McClintock Folsom. 2004.
Austen's Pride and Prejudice. Ed. Marcia McClintock Folsom. 1993.
Balzac's Old Goriot. Ed. Michal Peled Ginsburg. 2000.
Baudelaire's Flowers of Evil. Ed. Laurence M. Porter. 2000.
Beckett's Waiting for Godot. Ed. June Schlueter and Enoch Brater. 1991.
Beowulf. Ed. Jess B. Bessinger, Jr., and Robert F. Yeager. 1984.
Blake's Songs of Innocence and of Experience. Ed. Robert F. Gleckner and
    Mark L. Greenberg. 1989.
Boccaccio's Decameron. Ed. James H. McGregor. 2000.
British Women Poets of the Romantic Period. Ed. Stephen C. Behrendt and
    Harriet Kramer Linkin. 1997.
Brontë's Jane Eyre. Ed. Diane Long Hoeveler and Beth Lau. 1993.
Byron's Poetry. Ed. Frederick W. Shilstone. 1991.
Camus's The Plague. Ed. Steven G. Kellman. 1985.
Cather's My Ántonia. Ed. Susan J. Rosowski. 1989.
Cervantes' Don Quixote. Ed. Richard Bjornson. 1984.
Chaucer's Canterbury Tales. Ed. Joseph Gibaldi. 1980.
Chopin's The Awakening. Ed. Bernard Koloski. 1988.
Coleridge's Poetry and Prose. Ed. Richard E. Matlak. 1991.
Conrad's "Heart of Darkness" and "The Secret Sharer." Ed. Hunt Hawkins and
    Brian W. Shaffer. 2002.
Dante's Divine Comedy. Ed. Carole Slade. 1982.
Dickens' David Copperfield. Ed. Richard J. Dunn. 1984.
Dickinson's Poetry. Ed. Robin Riley Fast and Christine Mack Gordon. 1989.
Narrative of the Life of Frederick Douglass. Ed. James C. Hall. 1999.
Eliot's Middlemarch. Ed. Kathleen Blake. 1990.
Eliot's Poetry and Plays. Ed. Jewel Spears Brooker. 1988.
Shorter Elizabethan Poetry. Ed. Patrick Cheney and Anne Lake Prescott. 2000.
Ellison's Invisible Man. Ed. Susan Resneck Parr and Pancho Savery. 1989.
English Renaissance Drama. Ed. Karen Bamford and Alexander Leggatt. 2002.
Works of Louise Erdrich. Ed. Gregg Sarris, Connie A. Jacobs, and
    James R. Giles. 2004.
Dramas of Euripides. Ed. Robin Mitchell-Boyask. 2002.
Faulkner's The Sound and the Fury. Ed. Stephen Hahn and Arthur F. Kinney. 1996.

Flaubert's Madame Bovary. Ed. Laurence M. Porter and Eugene F. Gray. 1995.

García Márquez's One Hundred Years of Solitude. Ed. María Elena de Valdés and Mario J. Valdés. 1990.

Gilman's "The Yellow Wall-Paper" and Herland. Ed. Denise D. Knight and Cynthia J. Davis.

Goethe's Faust. Ed. Douglas J. McMillan. 1987.

Gothic Fiction: The British and American Traditions. Ed. Diane Long Hoeveler and Tamar Heller. 2003.

Hebrew Bible as Literature in Translation. Ed. Barry N. Olshen and Yael S. Feldman. 1989.

Homer's Iliad *and* Odyssey. Ed. Kostas Myrsiades. 1987.

Ibsen's A Doll House. Ed. Yvonne Shafer. 1985.

Works of Samuel Johnson. Ed. David R. Anderson and Gwin J. Kolb. 1993.

Joyce's Ulysses. Ed. Kathleen McCormick and Erwin R. Steinberg. 1993.

Kafka's Short Fiction. Ed. Richard T. Gray. 1995.

Keats's Poetry. Ed. Walter H. Evert and Jack W. Rhodes. 1991.

Kingston's The Woman Warrior. Ed. Shirley Geok-lin Lim. 1991.

Lafayette's The Princess of Clèves. Ed. Faith E. Beasley and Katharine Ann Jensen. 1998.

Works of D. H. Lawrence. Ed. M. Elizabeth Sargent and Garry Watson. 2001.

Lessing's The Golden Notebook. Ed. Carey Kaplan and Ellen Cronan Rose. 1989.

Mann's Death in Venice *and Other Short Fiction.* Ed. Jeffrey B. Berlin. 1992.

Medieval English Drama. Ed. Richard K. Emmerson. 1990.

Melville's Moby-Dick. Ed. Martin Bickman. 1985.

Metaphysical Poets. Ed. Sidney Gottlieb. 1990.

Miller's Death of a Salesman. Ed. Matthew C. Roudané. 1995.

Milton's Paradise Lost. Ed. Galbraith M. Crump. 1986.

Molière's Tartuffe *and Other Plays.* Ed. James F. Gaines and Michael S. Koppisch. 1995.

Momaday's The Way to Rainy Mountain. Ed. Kenneth M. Roemer. 1988.

Montaigne's Essays. Ed. Patrick Henry. 1994.

Novels of Toni Morrison. Ed. Nellie Y. McKay and Kathryn Earle. 1997.

Murasaki Shikibu's The Tale of Genji. Ed. Edward Kamens. 1993.

Pope's Poetry. Ed. Wallace Jackson and R. Paul Yoder. 1993.

Proust's Fiction and Criticism. Ed. Elyane Dezon-Jones and Inge Crosman Wimmers. 2003.

Rousseau's Confessions *and* Reveries of the Solitary Walker. Ed. John C. O'Neal and Ourida Mostefai. 2003.

Shakespeare's Hamlet. Ed. Bernice W. Kliman. 2001.

Shakespeare's King Lear. Ed. Robert H. Ray. 1986.

Shakespeare's Romeo and Juliet. Ed. Maurice Hunt. 2000.

Shakespeare's The Tempest *and Other Late Romances.* Ed. Maurice Hunt. 1992.

Shelley's Frankenstein. Ed. Stephen C. Behrendt. 1990.

Shelley's Poetry. Ed. Spencer Hall. 1990.

Sir Gawain and the Green Knight. Ed. Miriam Youngerman Miller and
    Jane Chance. 1986.

Spenser's Faerie Queene. Ed. David Lee Miller and Alexander Dunlop. 1994.

Stendhal's The Red and the Black. Ed. Dean de la Motte and Stirling Haig. 1999.

Sterne's Tristram Shandy. Ed. Melvyn New. 1989.

Stowe's Uncle Tom's Cabin. Ed. Elizabeth Ammons and Susan Belasco. 2000.

Swift's Gulliver's Travels. Ed. Edward J. Rielly. 1988.

Thoreau's Walden *and Other Works*. Ed. Richard J. Schneider. 1996.

Tolstoy's Anna Karenina. Ed. Liza Knapp and Amy Mandelker. 2003.

Vergil's Aeneid. Ed. William S. Anderson and Lorina N. Quartarone. 2002.

Voltaire's Candide. Ed. Renée Waldinger. 1987.

Whitman's Leaves of Grass. Ed. Donald D. Kummings. 1990.

Woolf's To the Lighthouse. Ed. Beth Rigel Daugherty and Mary Beth Pringle. 2001.

Wordsworth's Poetry. Ed. Spencer Hall, with Jonathan Ramsey. 1986.

Wright's Native Son. Ed. James A. Miller. 1997.